Working at the Interface of Cultures

Social scientists study people and society yet, too often, the view is put forward that there is some kind of culture-free, objective reality that can be observed. This collection of essays, by leading cross-cultural researchers, puts the personal experience of the observer back at centre stage.

Each contributor relates his or her own personal experience of working with different cultures and examines the influence this encounter has had on his or her way of thinking, way of working and way of perceiving the world. The contributors have all been stimulated and inspired to reflect on and rediscover their culture of origin by attempting to understand and write about the cultures they lived in, and each essay describes the process of this intellectual growth and development.

Working at the Interface of Cultures lifts the objective mask of science to reveal the subjective encounter with difference that shapes scholarly understanding. These autobiographies offer encouragement to younger social scientists embarking on the cross-cultural journey by showing how personal and academic transformation can occur. Each also offers a unique introduction to the work of a well-known cross-culturalist. A fascinating collection to read for fun, these essays are also an important contribution to the discussion of reflexivity within the social sciences.

Michael Harris Bond has taught social psychology for the last two decades at the Chinese University of Hong Kong, where he is Professor of Psychology. His previous publications include the *Handbook of Chinese Psychology* (1996) and *Social Psychology across Cultures* (1993), with P.B. Smith.

Working at the Interface of Cultures

Eighteen lives in social science

Edited by Michael Harris Bond

London and New York

GN
345.7
.W67
1997

First published 1997
by Routledge
11 New Fetter Lane, London EC4P 4EE

Simultaneously published in the USA and Canada
by Routledge
29 West 35th Street, New York, NY 10001

Typeset in Times by
Ponting–Green Publishing Services,
Chesham, Buckinghamshire
Printed and bound in Great Britain by
MPG Books Ltd, Bodmin, Cornwall

British Library Cataloguing in Publication Data
A catalogue record for this book is available from the
British Library

Library of Congress Cataloguing in Publication Data
Working at the interface of cultures: eighteen lives in social science
    / edited by Michael Harris Bond
        p.   cm.
    Includes bibliographical references and index.
    1. Cross-cultural studies.   2. Cross-cultural orientation.
3. Intercultural communications.   4. Ethnopsychology.
I. Bond, Michael Harris, 1944–
GN345.7.W67   1997
303.48'1–dc21   97–15834

ISBN 0–415–15846–X

The initial mystery that attends any journey is: how did the traveller reach his starting point in the first place? How did I reach the window, the walls, the fireplace, the room itself; how do I happen to be beneath this ceiling and above this floor? Oh, that is a matter of conjecture, for argument pro and con, for research, supposition, dialectic! I can hardly remember how. Unlike Livingstone, on the verge of darkest Africa, I have no maps to hand, no globe of the terrestrial or the celestial spheres, no chart of mountains, lakes, no sextant, no artificial horizon. If ever I possessed a compass, it has long since disappeared. There must be, however, some reasonable explanation for my presence here. Some step started me toward this point, as opposed to all other points on the habitable globe. I must consider; I must discover it.

Louis Bogan, *Journey Around My Room*

Contents

Contributors

J. W. Berry, Department of Psychology, Queen's University, Kingston, Ontario, Canada

Ernest E. Boesch, Saarbrücken, Germany

Michael Harris Bond, Department of Psychology, The Chinese University of Hong Kong, Shatin, N. T., Hong Kong

Kenneth J. Gergen, Department of Psychology, Swarthmore College, Pennsylvania, USA

Mary M. Gergen, Department of Psychology and Women's Studies, Pennsylvania State University, USA

George M. Guthrie, Pennsylvania State University, USA

Geert Hofstede, Velp, The Netherlands

Gustav Jahoda, Department of Psychology, University of Strathclyde, Glasgow, Scotland

Çiğdem Kağitçibaşi, Department of Psychology, KOC University, Istanbul, Turkey

Fathali M. Moghaddam, Psychology Department, Georgetown University, Washington, DC, USA

Edward E. Sampson, California State University, Northridge, California, USA

Jai B. P. Sinha, ASSERT, Patna, India

Stella Ting-Toomey, Department of Speech Communication, California State University–Fullerton, USA

Harry C. Triandis, Department of Psychology, University of Illinois, Champaign-Urbana, Illinois, USA

Joseph E. Trimble, Department of Psychology, Western Washington University, Bellingham, Washington, USA

Peter Weinreich, Department of Psychology, University of Ulster at Jordanstown, Newtownabbey, Northern Ireland

Anna Wierzbicka, Department of Linguistics, Australian National University, Canberra, Australia

Kuo-shu Yang, Department of Psychology, National Taiwan University, Taipei, Taiwan

Preface
The psychology of working at the interface of cultures

Michael Harris Bond

> The point here is that experience, because it mobilizes all of man's resources –
> intellectual, inarticulate, implicit, physical, social, and even his will to change
> matters – enables him to transcend the obvious. And that is something that is
> very hard to do when you stick to the psychology of the known. . .
>
> George Kelly, *The psychology of the unknown*

This book is a collection of reflections on transformation, reflections by prominent behavioural scientists on how they spun the daily stuff of their cross-cultural experience into the tapestry of their scientific work on culture. Its intent is to illuminate one part of the creative process for social scientists working with culture.

The study of the creative process has been relatively neglected in the behavioural sciences despite its manifest importance in the scientific process (Sternberg and Lubart, 1996). As graduate students, we are carefully inducted into the mysteries of experimental design, behavioural measurement, and statistical analysis. These procedural guidelines then enable us to evaluate the hypotheses we wish to scrutinise scientifically. But, as a recently minted PhD, I waited expectantly, wondering when and where would these hypotheses present themselves. This was no idle speculation, as I had tenure to earn. Clearing this hurdle required publications based upon the careful assessment of scientific ideas. But where was I to find this precious commodity now that I had been cut loose from my inspired graduate advisers and was working in a country where I could barely speak the language?

I now realise that I had been well trained for the 'context of evaluation' in psychological research but untrained for the 'context of discovery', to use Reichenbach's (1938) terms. Mine seems not an unusual outcome of most graduate training where little, if any, attention is paid to understanding and enhancing the creative process upon which growth of the discipline depends (Sternberg and Lubart, 1996). A few advisers, e.g., Bavelas (1987), regard such training as part of their mandate, and fortunate indeed are the students exposed to such exceptional teachers. The rest of us must mobilise our own resources to 'steal thunder from the gods' in the form of ground-breaking hypotheses. I am convinced that many, daunted by this awesome prospect, give up the quest and retreat to do technique-driven or paradigm-elaborating research (Kuhn, 1962). Others flounder about seeking whatever stimulation they can. I now realise that for me such stimulation was everywhere I turned in Japan and then in Hong Kong. However, it took some time to realise that my muse was so close at hand.

INTERFACING CULTURALLY

Culture as the prison of the known

Travel can be one of the most rewarding forms of introspection.

Lawrence Durrell, *Bitter lemons*

People routinely ask me if I plan to return to Canada after Hong Kong reverts to Chinese sovereignty on 1 July 1997. I occasionally respond by saying that I would fear losing my source of inspiration for scientific ideas should I return from a foreign culture to a familiar culture. Every time I return to Canada I feel myself being slowly enveloped by my mother tongue, by Canadian terms of social discourse, by Anglo-Saxon etiquette, and individualistic political logic. My world falls into place and fits again. My shadow, cast by my foreignness in Hong Kong society, slowly disappears; the sunlight of difference is clouded over with sameness, and I lose sight of my cultural reference points.

It is in this sense that I can understand Kelly's (1977) earlier comment about 'the psychology of the known'. He is referring to the repository of taken-for-granted constructs and propositions that constitute the cultural legacy of anyone born into any culture at any time in history. This legacy is so routinely and so repeatedly reinforced in our daily lives that it assumes the mantle of facticity. As Kelly (ibid., p. 5) proposes:

What we tend to do is accept familiar constructs as downright objective observations of what is really there. . . . We continue to refer to [familiar constructs] as objective observations, as the 'givens' in the theorems of daily existence.

By living and working in unknown Hong Kong instead of known Canada, the surprise of cultural difference is always at hand; I am forced into cultural mindfulness (Gudykunst, 1991) on a regular basis, since I can rarely relax into a world of familiar faces, forms, and formulas. Some would experience such a change as disturbing, taxing, and stressful. Indeed, the response to foreign living is often labelled culture *shock* (Furnham and Bochner, 1986) for good, painful reason. But foreign living also offers its share of delights. . .

The scientific yield

Here I have written simply as a human being and the truth I have tried to tell concerns the sea-change in oneself that comes from immersion in another and savage culture.

Laura Bohannon, *Return to laughter*

Many observers have commented on the power of travel to challenge people psychologically by exposing them 'to alternative ways of thinking and living' (Watson and Lippitt, 1958). This challenge takes the form of questioning their taken-for-granted assumptions about how to be human. Dressing, childrearing, schooling, socialising, doing business, relaxing – all seem so differently done elsewhere. How is it that they live their lives so differently from us, one wonders?

Of course reaching such questions requires that one travels in atypical ways; one must first expose oneself to the unfamiliar. One must escape from the well-worn tourist places and pathways which are often designed precisely to minimise such exposure. And one must spend enough time observing to allow difference to blossom and show itself.

But, as Kelly (1977) has argued, mere exposure is insufficient to generate change; engagement is necessary:

> But if he engages himself he will be caught up in the realities of human existence in ways that would never have occurred to him. He will breast the onrush of events. He will see, he will feel, he will be frightened, he will be exhilarated, and he will find himself feared, hated, and loved. Every resource at his disposal, not merely his cognitive and professional talents, will be challenged. So involved will he be that, in order to survive, he will have to cope with his circumstances inarticulately as well as verbally, primitively as well as intelligently, and he will have to pull himself together physically, socially, biologically, and spiritually.

The net result of this engagement is action, a testing of one's being-in-the-world. One bargains, tries to make a date, boards a crowded train, books a ticket in a foreign language, grades a test based on students' understanding of one's lectures, pushes one's application forward for a promotion, etc., etc. Now one is fully interfacing with the foreign culture; one is really living overseas, not merely travelling there!

The personal consequence of this action is the reconstruction process it stimulates:

> and action produces something unexpected for men [*sic*] to contemplate and experience, and, finally, the newest experience throws the recollections of prior experiences into fresh perspective, thus reducing them to the level of mere chronicler's facts, facts whose historical meaning takes its shape from present rather than past interpretations.
>
> (Kelly, 1977, p. 8)

So, what was initially experienced as public indifference from one's host nationals later may become construed as withdrawal from social overload; their inscrutability may become understood as restraint; their family cliquishness may become appreciated as focused nurturance in a world without social welfare, their tolerance of injustice may become conceptualised as fear of retaliation from powerful others, and so forth. These are a few of the reconstructions I can identify in my own thinking about Chinese social life (Bond, 1994).

As social scientists engaged at the interface of cultures, our construction systems are also subject to change in exactly the same ways. The topics of our intellectual inquiry resonate in our daily life. Like Kukla's (1988, p. 151) ethnophenomenologists, '[we immerse ourselves] in that culture's worldview in order to observe in [ourselves] the effect of such an immersion'. We are positioned so that we can develop ideas, hypotheses, and theories about the different cultural dynamics of the people with whom we are living by construing the actions of our interaction partners (and ourselves!) in new ways (see, e.g., Bond, 1994). The stimulus for such reconstruction is the daily, as well as scientific, need to anticipate events correctly. Our art and our life may come to imitate one another in this reconstruction process by which each is enriched.

New culture as a resource

Every wall is a door.
Ralph Waldo Emerson

It is perhaps through this forced reconstruction process that we can understand Greenfield's (1995, p. 5) assertion that 'An out-group member can see, and therefore study, aspects of the dominant culture that insiders have taken for granted or even repressed.' This 'seeing' is in fact a discovery, as Greenfield illustrates in her revelations about interviewing Zinacanteco Maya girls and their mothers about weaving. She quickly came to realise that 'The procedure used to collect information in such a society must permit the cooperative construction of knowledge' (p. 8). This methodological re-alignment was one component of a wider cultural worldview which Greenfield was prodded to appreciate more fully through this action-derived discovery. This example makes an earlier observation by Scheuch (1967, p. 15) seem prescient, indeed:

> to warn that 'the research tools do not fit' is a reflection of the fact that a researcher from a foreign culture is usually unaware of the existential basis of his own thinking even in the social sciences. Thus the 'pains' involved in doing cross-cultural research are reflections of the very corrective . . . that cross-cultural research is supposed to provide for a social science developing within a particular social system.

This position dovetails neatly with that of many cross-culturalists (e.g., Hofstede, 1996) who assert that our cultural heritage makes us 'aspect seeing' and 'aspect blind' (Wittgenstein, 1968). That is, our culture of origin provides an 'education of attention' (Gibson, 1979) of our sensibilities to culture-relevant aspects of social reality. The scientific consequence of this 'socialised resonance' is put in practical terms by Triandis (1996, pp. 24–5):

> Such results suggest that to some extent researchers with particular cultural orientations do a good job when developing scales that reflect that orientation, but do not do as good a job in developing scales that reflect other orientations.

This point may be fundamental in understanding how culture shapes scientific psychology and is worth pursuing in more detail.

So, each of us brings his or her cultural sensibilities and lacunae to the cross-cultural banquet. Through the process of thoughtful sharing, one another's cultural inputs become apparent.

Coping with fragmentation

> For is and is-not come together;
> Hard and easy are complementary;
> Long and short are relative;
> High and low are comparative;
> Pitch and sound make harmony;
> Before and after are a sequence.
> Lao Tzu, *The way of virtue*

In his fragmentation corollary, Kelly (1963, p. 83) asserts that 'A person may successfully employ a variety of construction subsystems which are inferentially incompatible with one another.' In the cross-cultural context, this separation takes the form of developing a construing system for dealing with members of a new culture that differs from the construing system for anticipating interpersonal events in one's culture of origin. So, for example, I anticipate different outcomes when a Canadian and when a Japanese say or signal the equivalent forms of 'yes'. In Canada, a 'yes' is a commitment to act accordingly; in Japan, it is a signal of positive social intentions, but not necessarily a commitment to comply. Similarly, I respond differently if that affirmation is subsequently negated by the actions of the person who initially agreed. I have developed different operating procedures in these two cultures and construe events differently when interacting with their culture representatives. Given the cueing from distinctive contexts, this separation is easy to maintain.

But I have a passion for order. And, as a behavioural scientist, I want to discover a system whereby these cultural incompatibilities may be harmonised within a higher level of generality. So, for example, people of all cultural groups strive to maintain the social order within which they must function. This is the universal process. However, the more individualistic Canadians do so by insisting that a person's word is his or her contract, the collectivist Japanese by insisting that a person's word maintains the harmony of his or her relationships. It is precisely this kind of specific difference within general uniformity that I wish to formulate and then articulate as a behavioural scientist. I am struggling to realise Kelly's (1963, p. 56) organisation corollary:

> Every person characteristically evolves, for his convenience in anticipating events, a construction system embracing ordinal relationships between constructs.

In this last example, the higher order construct is 'maintaining the social order';

the subordinate constructs become collectivist or individualistic cultural systems and their attendant processes.

I share with Kelly (1977) the belief that such an integration is promoted by active, reflective exchanges across cultural lines. These stimulate conceptual reorganisation. Such a presumption underlies Greenfield's (1995, p. 6) exhortation for a 'conscious use of perspective' in cross-cultural research. In constructing measurement tools, for example, she writes:

> If, however, one wants to elucidate cultural differences in an unbiased fashion, then it is best to have a bicultural (or multicultural) team and to collaboratively develop a single instrument for all the cultures *before* the study begins. Objectivity in the sense of *no* perspective is impossible. The only questions are *what* perspective informs a particular piece of research, to what extent the researchers are aware of their perspectives, and whether the perspectives illuminate or obfuscate the subject at hand.

Others (e.g., Triandis, 1976) have described this research – focused interaction across cultural lines – as 'cultural de-centering'. I believe it stimulates a process of 'cross-cultural re-centering' by pushing us all to evince higher-order principles by which the cultural diversity may be integrated, by which we may come to understand the ways in which all men are the same.

I believe that in each of the essays in this volume, the discerning reader may discover this synthesising impulse at work, this grasping for higher-order, transcendent principles by which apparent fragmentation may be harmonised.

WHO WORKS AT THE INTERFACE?

> That is at bottom the only courage that is demanded of us: to have courage for the most strange, the most singular and the most inexplicable that we may encounter. That mankind has in this sense been cowardly has done life endless harm. . .
>
> Rainer Maria Rilke

The cross-cultural encounter is not to everyone's taste. Berger (1987), for example, has written thoughtfully about the cognitive struggle called 'uncertainty reduction processes' that are attendant upon dealing with the 'stranger' (Simmel, 1950). It is an encounter freighted with disruption of daily routines, surprises, miscommunication, physical unpleasantness, cognitive overload – in short, all the hassles of culture shock (Oberg, 1960).

A troubling side to this encounter is the continuous existential challenge that another coherent world view provokes for one's own world view. After many months living with a Nigerian tribe, the anthropologist Bowen (1964, p. xv) writes, 'I'd grown fearful of the constant temptation to question my own values that these people and this world afforded me.' This is the deep psychological territory probed by terror management theory (Solomon, Greenberg and Pyszezynski, 1991), itself derived from Becker's (1973) earlier work on the sustaining function of our cultural scripts. These are put at risk by the encounter with difference, and many recoil from such an assault on their 'ontological security' (Laing, 1962).

One might then well ask, 'Who would willingly put themselves into such a crucible?' Or perhaps, 'Who would choose to stay in such a crucible?' Or perhaps for the purposes of this collection, 'Who survives this crucible and then chooses to write about their experiences?' Much has been researched about intercultural effectiveness (e.g., Ward, 1996), but not with a particular focus on who does noteworthy behavioural research on cross-cultural behaviour. The answer to this question is of immediate relevance to you, the reader of this collection, because you are in the intellectual hands of just such persons.

They are the authors of the constructions that follow. Not only have they produced significant research out of the cross-cultural encounter, they have accepted my challenging proposal to reflect on how that encounter has shaped their research. Some prominent cross-culturalists declined to make this self-exploration; of those who accepted, many reported how difficult this unfamiliar task became. This testing selection process may lead you to qualify how you construe their reflections.

As I make sense of their lives in social science, our contributors are articulate scholars with the necessary high levels of openness to experience (McCrae and Costa, 1985) required to tolerate their encounters with the difference, the surprise, the novelty, and the frustration ushered in by going across cultures. In addition they were able to orchestrate the resources, material, personal, social, and spiritual, necessary to sustain themselves in a foreign land.

This stamp of survival is an important consideration. In his sociality corollary, Kelly (1963, p. 95) wrote: 'To the extent that one person construes the construction processes of another, he may play a role in a social process involving the other person.'

All of the scholars represented in this collection have succeeded, in some sense, at working effectively across cultural lives to produce their cross-cultural work. They may have raised a family in a foreign setting, worked overseas for discrete periods with host nationals, collaborated by mail with co-authors from different language and cultural traditions, or merely talked thoughtfully in their own country with people who are different. Such successful negotiation of another cultural system indicates their command of 'tacit knowledge' (Wagner and Sternberg, 1986), viz., practical know-how regarding the cultures in which they function. Such 'understanding-in-action' does not, of course, always translate into the articulated understanding that is written up as social science discourse. But, in the minds of prepared and thoughtful social scientists, it may. How this 'magical synthesis' occurs, how this transformation is achieved, I do not know (see Davidson and Sternberg, 1994, on insight). I suggest, however, that working successfully across cultural lives facilitates that process by attuning us socially.

Finally, I believe that they possess an unusual form of faith, which Kelly (1977, p. 16) described well. It is 'a faith that, given a new vantage point through experience, we can formulate better versions of what is going on in the mind of man'. Such I believe are some of the distinguishing features of your travel guides; I commit you to their care.

When you reach an advanced age and look back over your lifetime, it can seem to have had a consistent order and plan, as though composed by some novelist. Events that when they occurred had seemed accidental and of little moment turn out to have been indispensable factors in the composition of a consistent plot. So who composed that plot? . . . Just as your dreams are composed by an aspect of yourself of which your consciousness is unaware, so, too, your whole life is composed by the will within you. And just as people whom you will have met apparently by mere chance become leading agents in the structuring of your life, so, too, will you have served unknowingly as an agent, giving meaning to the lives of others. . .

It is even as though there were a single intention behind it all, which always makes some kind of sense, though none of us knows what the sense might be, or has lived the life that he quite intended.

Joseph Campbell, Epilogue

REFERENCES

Bavelas, J. B. (1987). Permitting creativity in science. In D. N. Jackson and P. Rushton (eds), *Scientific excellence* (pp. 307–327). Newbury Park, CA: Sage.

Becker, E. (1973). *The denial of death.* New York: Free Press.

Berger, C. R. (1987). Communicating under uncertainty. In M. E. Roloff and G. R. Miller (eds), *Interpersonal processes* (pp. 39–62). Newbury Park, CA: Sage.

Bond, M. H. (1994). Continuing encounters with Hong Kong. In W. J. Lonner and R. S. Malpass (eds), *Psychology and culture* (pp. 41–46). Needham Heights, MA: Allyn & Bacon.

Bowen, E. S. (1964). *Return to laughter: An anthropological novel.* New York: Anchor.

Davidson, J. E., and Sternberg, R. J. (1984). The role of insight in intellectual giftedness. *Gifted Child Quarterly, 28,* 58–64.

Furnham, A., and Bochner, S. (1986). *Culture shock: Psychological reactions to unfamiliar environments.* London: Methuen.

Gibson, J. J. (1979). *The ecological approach to visual perception.* Boston, MA: Houghton Mifflin.

Greenfield, P. M. (1995). *Research methods: Culture as process.* Paper presented at the sixth European Congress of Psychology, Athens, Greece, July.

Gudykunst, W. B. (1991). *Bridging differences: Effective intergroup communication.* Newbury Park, CA: Sage.

Hofstede, G. (1996). An American in Paris: The influence of nationality on organization theories. *Organization Studies, 17,* 525–537.

Kelly, G. A. (1963). *A theory of personality: The psychology of personal constructs.* New York: W. W. Norton.

Kelly, G. A. (1977). The psychology of the unknown. In D. Bannister (ed.), *New perspectives in personal construct theory* (pp. 1–19). London: Academic Press.

Kuhn, T. S. (1962). *The structure of scientific revolutions.* Chicago: University of Chicago Press.

Kukla, A. (1988). Cross-cultural psychology in a post-empiricist era. In M. H. Bond (ed.), *The cross-cultural challenge to social psychology* (pp. 141–152). Newbury Park, CA: Sage.

Laing, R. D. (1962). Ontological insecurity. In H. M. Ruitenbeek, *Psychoanalysis and existential philosophy* (pp. 41–69). New York: E. P. Dutton.

McCrae, R. R., and Costa, P. T. Jr (1985). Openness to experience. In R. Hogan and W. H. Jones (eds), *Perspectives in personality* (Vol. 1, pp. 145–172). Greenwich, CT: JAI Press.

Oberg, K. (1960). Cultural shock: Adjustment to a new cultural environment. *Practical Anthropology, 7,* 177–182.

Reichenbach, H. (1938). *Experience and prediction.* Chicago, IL: University of Chicago Press.

Scheuch, E. (1967). Society as a context in cross-national comparisons. *Social Science Information, 6,* 7–23.

Simmel, G. (1950). The stranger. In K. Wolff (ed. and trans.), *The sociology of George Simmel.* New York: Free Press.

Solomon, S., Greenberg, J., and Pyszezynski, T. (1991). Terror management theory of self-esteem. In C. R. Snyder and D. Forsyth (eds), *Handbook of social and clinical psychology* (pp. 21–40). New York: Pergamon.

Sternberg, R. J., and Lubart, T. I. (1996). Investing in creativity. *American Psychologist, 51,* 677–688.

Triandis, H. C. (1976). On the value of cross-cultural research in social psychology: Reactions to Faucheux's paper. *European Journal of Social Psychology, 6,* 331–341.

Triandis, H. C. (1996). 'Converging measurement of horizontal and vertical individualism and collectivism.' Unpublished manuscript, University of Illinois.

Wagner, R. K., and Sternberg, R. J. (1986). Tacit knowledge and intelligence in the everyday world. In R. J. Sternberg, and R. K. Wagner (eds), *Practical intelligence: Nature and origins of competence in the everyday world* (pp. 51–83). New York: Cambridge University Press.

Ward, C. (1996). Acculturation. In D. Landis and R.S. Bhagat (eds), *Handbook of intercultural training,* 2nd edn (pp. 124–147). Thousand Oaks, CA: Sage.

Watson, J., and Lippitt, R. (1958). Cross-cultural experience as a source of attitude change. *Journal of Conflict Resolution, 2,* 61–66.

Wittgenstein, L. (1968). *Philosophische Untersuchungen.* Oxford: Basil Blackwell.

1 What kind of game in a far-away forest?

Ernest E. Boesch

THE QUESTION

Every science has its subjective side. Our motivations do not stem from mere rational considerations; a study of the subjective roots of scientific zeal would in fact be very promising. Yet, although scientists do not object to the analysis of the more private sides of geniuses like Einstein or Freud, they not only tend to resist strongly any attempt at looking behind their own professed objectivity, but also to look askance at those who more candidly confess to their more subjective motivations and reactions. Objectivity, too, exacts a price, although different: it consists in creating a make-belief-reality of abstract concepts and, all too often, unrealistic data. Thus, the task we face is to find the balance between an honest assessment of one's own role, a gathering of culturally valid data, and the critical evaluation of both.

Yet, to which purpose this 'honest assessment of one's role'? After all, we want to produce findings useful to others, be they researchers or practitioners – soul-searching appears irrelevant: if Cole and Scribner (1974) discover that the development of Piagetian concept constancies is influenced by schooling, this finding is practically useful without any recourse to the subjectivity of its authors. If a doctor cures a patient, we are not interested in knowing whether he did it for money, by professional duty or by human compassion; yet, if the doctor happens to fail systematically certain cures, his personal motives might become relevant. But there are more general reasons for self-reflection: should we try to be aware of our subjective goals, should we stop confounding personal motives with objective necessities, would not our life become richer, and academic life more relaxed?

Self-scrutiny might be even more fitting in our somewhat strange endeavour to carry our psychological research into alien lands. Research on other peoples demands much modesty and detachment, while unfamiliar surroundings generate reactions of insecurity, often complex, defensive or compensatory. Self-awareness might then, for instance, prevent us from speaking of 'natives', 'subjects', 'cases' and 'samples'; it would contribute to a less pretentious language and to a more humble conception of our role as 'researchers'.

Thus, I see many uses for this kind of self-scrutiny, but does it have to be published? Public 'confessions' are always suspect; they are never entirely candid, revealing either too much or too little. But striving to draw an honest picture, one may hope to encourage others to look more closely at their own 'reasons which the reason ignores' – and thus, by being subjective, to make science more objective. Yet, in order to prevent the 'self-disclosure' in these pages being misunderstood as a lack of scientific objectivity, let me stress that it describes the subjective side of a research process the 'rational' side of which has been documented in various other publications (for a bibliography see Boesch, 1991, 1992). Of course, our scientific work did proceed along the usual routines of hypothesis formation, data gathering and analysis, but let us keep in mind that without subjective motivations it would have been done differently – or rather, not at all.

What then were my reasons for working in Thailand? I am sorry not to be able to tell that already at an early age I felt attracted by the enigmas of that or any other culture. It is true that as a young boy I was an avid reader of American Indian stories but I cannot recall that they stimulated any more general cultural curiosity. When, in 1955, the United Nations Economic, Social, and Cultural Organization (UNESCO) unexpectedly offered me the directorship of the International Institute for Child Study in Bangkok, I ignored both the location of Bangkok and the country to which it belonged (Thailand was then not yet a tourist destination), and had developed neither a particular interest in alien cultures nor any culture-escape nostalgia of which I would have been conscious. Yet, why then did I accept UNESCO's offer?

GETTING ON MY WAY

I had left my own country, Switzerland, only four years ago for Saarbrücken, to join what it was hoped would become the European University. Until that time I had worked as a school psychologist, and thus, when accepting the chair of psychology, I had no other university experience than that of my own student days. When UNESCO's offer reached me, I had just about become reasonably familiar with my work and the internal academic routines. It was therefore very hesitantly that I went to see our then French Rector about it. His reaction was simple: 'Monsieur Boesch,' he said, 'the offer honours you and it honours our university. If you accept, you will learn something, and the university will profit from it. So you accept.' I must confess that later I found such generous common sense to be rather rare in university life.

If the Rector's reaction cleared the way, it does not explain my personal acceptance. This, I surmise, relates to a number of factors, both old and recent, more or less personal ones. I had grown up in a divorced family, had received a strict, narrow-minded religious education; between the two world wars, we suffered severely from the economic recession, soon even to be darkened by the shadow of the growing German Nazism up to, finally, the four-year-long threat of a Nazi invasion of Switzerland. It was a sombre world of limited opportunities, and under such conditions, a youngster will tend to develop escape strategies. Mine was to become a poet, but with this plan in mind – I decided to study medicine. A writer, I thought, should live close to real life and not just in the world of books.

For financial reasons, I soon changed from medicine to psychology, and it so happened that to realise this plan I was in the best possible place at that time. I had chosen to study in Geneva, the university farthest away from my home town during the war – another escape gesture – and there was the Institut Jean Jacques Rousseau with professors as renowned as Claparède and Piaget. However, my studies and my subsequent work as a school psychologist having, as far as I can see, no particular bearing on the problem discussed here, I shall not consider them any further.

Yet, to accept in 1951 the call to the University of the Saar was perhaps an escape, too, although I did not realise it as such: an escape from what I felt to be the narrowness of my home town and its connections with my childhood, but also an escape from the limitations my school psychological work was subjected to. Did university life really turn out to be more rewarding? As mentioned, I was not prepared to be a university professor, and thus, although probably discharging my duties honourably and genuinely interested in my work, I was bound to a heavy routine of 'catching up' and of groping my way. I did not consciously suffer from it, but it confined me in an intellectuality rather adverse to my former artistic leanings. Adding to this situation a seriously disturbed marriage, the Bangkok offer could indeed have appeared to open the door toward a new kind of life, full of uncertainties, but also of promises.

I had never seriously dreamed of going to exotic places. Yet the frustrations and denials we suffer in our lives will induce images of alternative forms of existence, which tend to trace a 'wish-course' for the future we anticipate or hope for; I called these images 'fantasms' – a term I have explained and justified elsewhere (Boesch, 1976, 1983a, 1991). These future projections, however, often remain vague, somehow waiting for specific situations in order to become concrete. It is like being in love with love: we may yearn for a lover, unable though to conjure up his or her image, but suddenly, in a perhaps unexpected encounter, we 'recognise' the hoped-for one. Although often remaining largely unconscious, such fantasmic anticipations tend to direct powerfully our actions, evaluations and choices. Thus, the opportunity to go to Thailand did not correspond to any conscious planning or even daydreaming – yet, once on the table, it was like an unexpected and nevertheless fitting promise.

ON THE TRAIL

I did not, of course, accept it as such, but in all conscious honesty as a limited professional task, certainly exciting, but not viewed in any way as an escape. The time perspective was three years, and I planned to fill them with serious work useful to the Thais as well as, on my return, to my university. I did, indeed, work seriously and hard, but not in the way I had anticipated; goals, particularly as unspecified ones as the one given to me in Thailand, may develop in unexpected ways according to situation – and to underlying subjective tendencies.

At that time, I was less astonished to be selected for the mission than I am today. It is true that, by some advisory activity in the Pestalozzi village (for war orphans) in Switzerland and during international meetings of UNESCO, I had caught some glimpses of alien cultures, yet I did not possess any of the required knowledge, neither in anthropology, nor in cultural psychology, not even in geography. I naively accepted the offer by UNESCO as a token of my qualification as a child psychologist (which was reasonably justified), and as naively thought that qualification would be of use also in Thailand (which it was not). The task given to me was to prepare local staff in psychological techniques and theory in order to do research on the role of culture in child rearing and its impact on child development. I knew thus that I would enter the field of cultural psychology, but I was unaware that I was also going to start on a long track of discovering the cultural limitations of Western psychology.

UNESCO was not much help. The obligatory, so-called 'briefing' consisted of much useless advice from people who from all appearances had stayed in Thailand not more than a couple of weeks or in the sheltered confines of some embassy; I was even warned that, 'Nothing there would be the same as here, not even the leaves of grass.' I got the cholera–typhus–paratyphus inoculations with their terrifying fever reactions, and I bought myself a pistol before embarking, which was idiotic (in spite of some military training) because useless against really dangerous beasts (which, besides snakes, I would never meet) and not at hand if needed anyhow. But the prospect of an alien land is always unsettling in some ways, and we therefore tend to cling to symbols of our action potential.

And unsettling it was, indeed. Not because of wild animals, although my first night in a kind of wooden hut over a pond was filled with unknown and somehow disquieting noises (Boesch, 1994); otherwise, although I met many curious and interesting things, nothing seemed to be unsettling. I was well received by the staff of the Institute, was promised every help by the Ministry of Education, received friendly help, too, from Robert Textor at the Cornell Center (under Professor Lauriston Sharp), was well lodged in a modest, but comfortable house with a friendly and efficient servant, bought myself a car and enjoyed the support of the local UNESCO mission: all was well arranged for embarking me on a career as another of those foreign 'experts' who brought their wisdom to underdeveloped Thailand. What, then, could have unsettled me?

When first meeting the staff of the Institute, they asked me whether I wanted to learn Thai. My answer was affirmative, although there was no apparent need – all the people I had to deal with spoke English, I could teach in English and would scarcely be expected to engage in psychological work with Thai children myself. And friends familiar with the country warned me that Thai was a language too difficult to learn during my relatively short stay. That, however, challenged me – I would show them! Yet, more deeply, self–other fantasms may have been at work: I had always been forced, against many odds, to prove myself – accepting defeat threatened my self-image; not understanding the language would exclude me from much social contact, but I wanted to be 'one of them'.

LANGUAGE AND IDENTIFICATION

This can be a strong but dangerous wish. 'Wanting to belong' may induce one to overestimate closeness, and to form wishful images of the target group. Yet, it was, I surmise, essentially this wanting to be 'one of them' which put me on the way to becoming a cultural psychologist. Thus, before and after my work at the Institute, I spent long hours learning Thai, spoken as well as written, and found this challenge extremely stimulating. The staff at the Institute helped me, but of greatest help was Luang Kee from the Ministry of Education. He had written four primers for teaching reading and writing to Thai children, at that time among the best ones I knew in any language; they contained easy short descriptions from everyday Thai life, and thereby not only helped me to learn the language, but also familiarised me with aspects of Thai life which my daily Bangkok experience could not show me. I made quick progress and in about six months was able to sustain a simple conversation in Thai – although not without occasional hilarious tone mistakes (as when, wanting to buy a shirt with short sleeves, I asked for 'a tiger with shaking arms'; or when much later, lecturing to an audience of doctors and nurses, I transformed a 'tendency towards' into an 'an oblique breast' – to the obvious amusement of the giggling nurses). Yet, such small challenges only added to the general fascination and satisfaction the Thai language held for me.

The language, of course, opened doors. Not only the door to chatting and conversing, but to more 'serious' activities. An early one was translation. I had until then never worked in other than European languages which, after all, are rather like dialects of a common idiom, while with Thai I met a really different language. Soon, the translation of questionnaires or of test items raised unsuspected problems; I realised that the rituals of translation–back-translation did not suffice to guarantee linguistic equivalence. In the beginning, I wrote out questionnaires in English, and then the whole staff convened to translate them; we sat in a circle of about ten people, but once each had suggested a version he or she deemed correct, they often agreed on a formulation mainly due to fatigue or boredom or in deference to the proposal by the highest ranking among them. I started to understand that a translation could be correct and wrong at the same time: in each language one and the same word may mean several things, and only some meanings in these denotational clusters would correspond; furthermore, even among apparently similar denotations, connotations might strongly differ, and connotations being partly individual and often unconceptualised components of meanings, agreements were indeed difficult to reach.

A second aspect of language new to me was its hierarchical anchoring: not only did the terms used with persons of different standing – by age, by sex, by social status – partly differ, but one did also say things differently, or not at all. This nicety raised, of course, awkward problems for the methodology of interviewing. Seeing pupils kneel when speaking to their teacher, I could not help wondering what they would dare to express and what not. Language, I began to realise, was more than simply a medium for communication: to speak was a social action. By its form and content, language was to shape social relationships, and therefore, to understand speech, understanding the words was not enough: one had also to understand its context. This all the more, since language also helps to create fictitious realities, not only by lies or confabulations, but by the less obvious, subtle art of make-believe, combining the tone and the form of language with smiles or other signs. This richness exists, of course, in all languages, but how much familiarity does it take to understand, leave alone to master, it in an alien culture?

My progress in learning the language was highly rewarding; yet, it not only opened doors towards otherwise inaccessible areas of Thai culture, but closed others. Indeed, the more I understood the subtleties of language and social interaction, the more I began to doubt the possibility of transferring psychological methods, and particularly questionnaires, from one culture to another. This doubt, however, was more than technical; it had to do with my identification, with my wanting to be 'one of them'.

So let me go back to this motif. Wanting to be one of them is, of course, not automatic; it depends upon the nature of 'them'. What was it that 'hooked' me in Thailand? In some ways, Thailand was the complete opposite of my past: hot and sunny in contrast to cold St Gall and grey Saarland, friendly smiling and relaxed people in contrast to the purposefully serious Europeans, a compassionate, tolerant religion in warmly coloured temples instead of culpabilising Christianism in gloomy churches; a teeming, animated nature, contrasting with the secretive one in Europe, which captivated my interest (in my house and garden I encountered – besides termites, stinging black and burning red ants – turtles, six different kinds of snakes, tukaes, house geckos, bats, all kinds of birds, toads and frogs); I found food to my taste, acquired new habits of socialising, of clothing, of body care, learned even more spontaneity, curiosity and fresh awareness – it would have been interesting to examine in which respects I changed, in which ones I remained constant; although, more likely, I both changed and remained constant in every respect, albeit to varying degrees.

Thus, wanting to be 'one of them' soon became more than simply wanting to share social togetherness: it turned into a wish to identify. One does not apply questionnaires and tests to people one identifies with; they cease to be 'subjects'. Instead of observing and measuring detachedly, one would rather tend towards some kind of 'empathic understanding'. To dispel any suspicion of having gone uncritically native, we did, in fact, not only use questionnaires and other methods presumed to be 'culture-free', but even attempted, for some time, to apply them in cross-cultural comparison (e.g., Boesch, 1960, 1975). But my belief in our methods was progressively waning (see Boesch, 1971), and over the years I tried to convince myself that free interviewing should be the *voie royale* – with, as I will have to confess, much disappointment, the reasons for which I shall explain later.

RELATING TO THE PREY

While I learned the language, we pursued of course the training and planning activities at the Institute, where my local colleagues became as much my teachers in Thai culture as I was theirs in psychology. Needless to say, I also spent much time filling my gaps in anthropological knowledge and in Thai research. We carried out a kind of pilot research project in Bangkok schools which, however, served more to train the staff in psychological techniques than to investigate a specific problem (Boesch, 1960).

In fact, we tested children and interviewed parents with the hope of finding the thread by which the 'real' research could start. This was, indeed, a major preoccupation: the assignment I had been given was to study the impact of culture on child rearing and development – a broad and very unspecific topic! How to 'operationalise' culture, to concentrate it into an 'independent variable'? I felt somehow 'flooded' by culture without knowing how to specify it. The anthropological classifications known to me at that time did not offer much help – I found them to lack psychological relevance; neither to my mind did the then much-used classification of educational styles into permissive and authoritarian – Thai parents were both, to different degrees according to age, sex, or situation, and in ways often too subtle to be easily categorised. Furthermore, parents were not the only, and often not even the main, educators: elder siblings, grandparents, aunts and uncles, neighbours, and of course teachers, could all take part in the educational action. And anyhow, language again! There was little chance of obtaining valid information on such complex processes by the usual interviewing.

The impact of culture on child rearing and development: this broad formulation of my task prevented me from choosing the most obvious approach, viz., to select some reasonably significant single variables for study. Piaget had urged me to study the conceptual development – conservation problems – of Thai children, certainly an important topic; a German UNESCO research fellow chose to factor-analyse semantic differentials – interesting, too. Yet, I felt such topics to be too arbitrary *a priori* choices. For a time we pondered concentrating on the punishment–reward system, but for reasons stated above, I doubted that we could obtain valid data by interviews, and felt even more that these variables would fail to tap the 'really significant' aspects of culture.

These doubts, I venture to suggest in retrospect, stemmed from my personal way of experiencing culture. The situations and events which made up my everyday life were each easy to describe but difficult to explain; they all seemed to form an intricate web, connected by threads which one could sense but not isolate and name. In other words, the culture of my experience was not a cluster of definable variables whose connections could be elucidated by analysis of variance; it rather appeared like a symphony with multiple interwoven sonorities, harmonies, dissonances and counterpoints. That was not, of course, how I would have expressed it at the time; I simply felt somehow drawn into this global picture, unable to differentiate any strand which would have made sense without the rest.

Thus, although I justified it by good rational arguments, my difficulty in operationalising was related to the subjective meaning that 'culture' had for me. An anthropologist, before going into the field, has been 'inoculated' against this kind of 'immersion' by his theoretical studies; he has his 'cadres of adjustment', while I walked in uncharted territory. However, while Thai culture was indeed a new way of life for me, I did not want simply to experience it, but also at least as much to understand it. Or, understanding it, meant to find its core, the essential elements which would allow one to explain its different aspects. This is more than a longing for the magic formula which would solve the mysteries of the world, but corresponds to a common psychological tendency.

Indeed, how many Europeans and Americans did I not meet in Bangkok who all had their petty theories about 'why the Thais are how they are' – mostly consisting of some 'general factor' which appeared to satisfy the speaker: 'It's Buddhism which makes them unaggressive'; 'Their authoritarian upbringing has deprived them of initiative'; 'It's because of the climate that they are lazy' – and so on. Such easy formulae explained what seemed baffling; by reducing the unknown to the familiar, they also reduced threat and freed the speaker from the need to examine his host-world – and perhaps also himself – more closely.

No doubt, experiencing a new culture may satisfy and enrich, but it also unsettles. It disturbs habits of living acquired and practised since childhood, shakes convictions and patterns of thinking, requires emotional reorientations and – perhaps most important – questions the validity of future anticipations on which, consciously or unconsciously, we base our lives. In other words, the new culture demands not only a restructuring of our private fantasms, but also a reevaluation of our own cultural roots. 'Experts' are not confronted with such disturbances; they come as competent and cool observers, spend their contractual time, fulfil their obligations, and leave again not much different from how they had come. This situation was not mine; emotionally involved, I faced all the demands of restructuring which, as it turned out, would take years. However that was, restructuring my 'I–world relationship' called for more than the study of isolated variables. What I was looking for was perhaps some 'general factor', in the idiom of the statistician, although I was not ready to trust factor analysis to find it.

I finally found my way of approach in the third year of my stay in Thailand. Let me quote my own description of the event:

> While driving on the main road to the airport, a 'samlor' (a tricycle riksha) turned unconcernedly, without the driver's looking around, from a side lane directly into the path of our car, and it was only by a rapid braking that we avoided an accident. Pondering this incident, I was suddenly struck by the thought that for this riksha driver side lane and highway formed a different structure than for me: For me, at the junction between the two lay an invisible frontier, forcing me to slow down and to ascertain the safety of proceeding further. Space, over and beyond its physical outlay, was mentally structured, containing limitations for our actions which, I presumed, varied by culture and, probably, also by individual.

> (Boesch, 1991, p. 9; see also 1994)

Although an apparently simple insight, it had important consequences: action theory, which I had professed at my university since 1951, became cultural-ecological; our world, as we live it, is both structured by action and structures our action – an uninterrupted feed-back system which after all in 1957, before cybernetic thinking entered psychology, was not that obvious a thought.

This insight did of course not provide me with a 'general factor', a formula explaining Thai culture, but it had an advantage over other definitions of culture: it handed me so-to-say my proper key to unravelling the cultural texture, but it consisted of more than just rational understanding. Karl Bühler would have called it an 'Aha-Erlebnis', a 'that's-it experience', and such an experience possesses a high subjective valence. It marks our mental 'action potential', the one to master a complex problem, to end a situation of perplexity and doubt. Being able to find what I have just called a key increased my confidence in being able to unravel the maze of cultural intricacies, to arrive at an intelligible structure. That, of course, was only a hope, but it gave me a direction.

This insight into the culture-specific structuring of space (already suggested by Lewin – but at that time I ignored it – and later confirmed by Hall and others) might have given rise to concrete research designs. We could have studied, for instance, the houses, compounds, fields, and the actions and customs relating to them. What better start for a cultural psychology than the home area? We could also – as I did later – have extended this approach to time and social space; but at that moment we could do none of this. My 'enlightenment' occurred towards the end of my UNESCO assignment, and I had to hasten back to pick up teaching at my university. 'Hasten' is the right word in this context: I could not enjoy any break between the work for UNESCO and that at my university, as also later, for many years, the double directorship at the Department of Psychology and the Research Institute, soon to be established, would require all my time, including so-called holidays.

SPLIT IDENTITY AND RESEARCH

I did not of course return to my university as I had left it. From child psychology I had turned to cultural psychology, and this was more than just a change of label. At that time, behaviourism dominated our science, yet, while I never had been a behaviourist, my new approach, 'emic' rather than 'etic', hermeneutic more than nomothetic, put me more squarely outside the respectable circles. But I also carried back the prestige of one 'who has been there', at that time not too numerous in Germany and therefore appreciated by developmental agencies. Before all, however, I was able to introduce new perspectives in my teaching although it was probably useful to my students intellectually more than professionally. But that is another story I have already told elsewhere (e.g., Boesch, 1992).

In 1962, my university established a Socio-psychological Research Center for Development Planning and named me its director. This appointment opened up opportunities for further research in Thailand. But, as the name indicates, our research had to be useful to the planning of assistance to developing countries. This made social change our main topic, more particularly 'exogenous' change (Boesch, 1966). Our reasoning was simple: in contrast to 'endogenous' change due to various processes inside the culture, exogenous change was thought to be stimulated by the import of goods, knowledge and ideas from the outside, brought in through various channels and carriers, the main ones being, on the one hand, merchants who imported goods, and on the other hand, intellectuals who imported knowledge and ideas, assimilated and thereby transformed them, and, by being 'role models' or teachers, transmitted them to larger parts of the population.

I carried out a first kind of pilot study with administrative elites in 1966 (Boesch, 1970) and then, on the basis of that experience, decided to look more carefully at the interaction between doctors and patients, assuming that they presented us with a paradigmatic model of elites communicating new knowledge to their 'target groups'. This is not intended to be a research report, so I shall not detail the results here (see Boesch, 1977); but some scrutiny of the personal meanings of this doctor–patient study is relevant here.

I had been trained as a child psychologist and a psychotherapist, so my picking out doctors and patients rather than teachers and students or merchants and clients looked understandable; particularly so on methodological grounds: in the medical interaction, the transmission of information could be more easily controlled than in the other instances. In addition, because the highly trained modern doctors interacted with traditional, barely educated patients, the 'modern–traditional dichotomy' promised to become particularly interesting. It was, no doubt, a neat, rational research plan.

We may also notice that the structural view induced by the 'samlor' incident became here enlarged by a dynamism of interaction between unequal partners, one able to heal, the other needing to be healed. This did not replace the structural view: we were going to study a social space with its own distances and barriers and techniques of approach; but within this structural system we conceived of a dynamism of take and give, of mutual influences and dependencies (because, in subtle ways, the doctor was dependent on his patient, too). Culture as a field of action was considered here in both its structural and dynamic dimension. Finally, the doctor–patient interaction, although focused around an illness, constituted an intersection of two different goal systems, self-conceptions, beliefs and social loyalties; thus, the denotational contents of the interaction differed as to con-notations, or meanings: the specific action, by its cultural imbeddedness, became also symbolic (Boesch, 1991). The project was as rich in content as it was promising.

Yet, what was my own involvement? Thai culture and its people, during my first three years, gave me the impression that I was becoming more and more 'one of them'; within it, I developed or unfolded new attitudes toward reality. I left it not only with nostalgia, but also profoundly disoriented. I felt a stranger in Europe, or, one might say, I suffered from 'split identity'. Thus, was it not that I had become a patient myself and Thai culture my desired healer? But was I not also a doctor bringing, by our work, development and hoped-for improvement to Thailand? Because Thai culture, too, was split: the gap between the elites and the uneducated was deep, as was also, in some ways, the one between the sexes. Such hindsight cannot be more than a guess, yet it hints at a not unlikely hidden involvement in this project. There was yet another aspect: doctor–patient interactions concern very personal relationships; to extend our investigation that far promised to make me 'one of them' much more intimately – gaining insight into situations and areas normally hidden to an outsider should deepen my identification no less than my cultural understanding. Of course, the project did give us valuable additional insights into Thai culture, but as certainly it did not heal my identification split. One is a stranger and remains one, however much one may strive to become 'one of them'. Anyone intimately exposed to an alien culture will learn that fact of cross-cultural life.

The processes of social change could produce identity splits in various areas of life. For our doctor–patient research team we were able to rent a house at a strikingly favourable rate, although it was beautiful, new, and had even not yet been inhabited. Its owner, as an air force pilot, belonged to the educated elite. Yet, we soon discovered that he and his family did not dare to live in the house because its main post was losing resin – or 'oil': in Thai tradition that is commonly believed to be a bad omen; when, one day, the caretaker of the house was found dead inside, its calamitous meaning was confirmed beyond any doubt. Since the evil spirit residing in the post was believed to have no power over foreigners, the house was let to our group (though, when they learned about the reason, not all were pleased). Thai doctors, I soon found out, were not immune either to traditional superstitions – some I met practised simultaneously modern medicine and spiritual healing. More serious were, in my mind, the splits lived by the peasant patients. Torn between their traditional healers and modern hospital medicine, they finally trusted neither the one nor the other, and the modern doctors, very bad communicators on the average, gave them little incentive to transfer their loyalties. The farmers, too, were living between two worlds, not really at home any more in the one, and not yet in the other.

Which made us, finally, carry out two studies on this being-between-two-worlds of the farmer. One was on the appeal which the big town, Bangkok, had for the villager (the village–town migration study; see Sripraphai and Sripraphai, 1981) and the second was on the anticipation of his future with regard to his present situation (the future anticipation study; Sripraphai and Sripraphai, 1988). As to the conceptual framework, the first study concentrated on the various innovations flowing from the town to the village and their impact on individual action; the second on the imagined future transformation of the present situation and its consequences for the actions of the individual. Subjectively, however, these projects related more closely to the doctor–patient study than appeared superficially. I will illustrate this relationship by an anecdote.

For the future study we rented a house, the owner of which, an old country woman, baked every morning a variety of small cakes which her daughter then carried on a two-wheeled cart to the near-by market. One day I asked her, 'If it happened that your customers came to like one of your cakes particularly and preferred it to the others, could you not then sell it at a higher price?' She looked at me with blank astonishment: 'Why, no,' she replied, 'I would betray the trust of my customers!' She would, of course, not survive long in our market philosophy, and I knew also enough other Thais who would not hesitate to profit from such a situation. But in my mind, and even against evidence from our village study, she epitomised the good, honest, traditional Thai culture against the one spoilt by modern change, and as I had emotionally sided with the patients in our previous study, I tended to identify with the Thai culture this cake peddler seemed to stand for. Our two new studies, also, somehow concealed, behind their rational conception, an idealising dichotomy: tradition against modernity and their interaction – coloured by my personal connotations. This did not, I have to emphasise, affect our rational work; but it certainly did affect the choice of our problems.

AND TO CONCLUDE?

But I have yet to fulfil my promise to tell about my disenchantment with free interviewing. I still believe it to be, besides participant observation, the supreme method for any kind of 'emic' research; but in my experience it simply was both too difficult and too demanding for the research assistants I could muster (Boesch, 1996). The free interview is not free at all: it requires familiarity with the culture, its language and its rules of interaction; conscientious, responsible data gathering; and a very close understanding of the theoretical framework to which the problem studied belongs. The model for it is the 'clinical method' designed by Piaget for his concept analyses, but the conceptual framework needed in cultural psychology is much more complex than in Piaget's relatively circumscribed problems. In practical terms, this consideration means that the project-training of the researchers should proceed intensively over at least one year and that they will then have to live close to their informants for lengthy periods – with all the financial consequences this requirement implies. There arise, of course, problems of consistency and validity, but I have considered them elsewhere (e.g., Boesch, 1971, 1991, 1996).

We have proceeded far enough to perhaps not find, but at least glimpse, an answer to our initial question: 'What kind of a game in a far-away forest?' The somewhat strange formulation of this question – comparing cultural research to staking game in an unknown forest – suggests that I wanted to deviate from the usual presentation of research results (see e.g., Boesch 1960, 1963, 1970, 1977, 1983b, 1991, 1992). We need, of course, to prove our scientific worth and to justify the expenses of research in foreign countries. We do so by our findings and by good and valid arguments which, however, are neither exhaustive nor sufficient explanations of our work. Sometimes they include critical evaluations, but these only too often remain methodological. More rare are questions of practical validity, and almost absent will be a scrutiny of the researcher's motivations. I explained at the beginning why I consider this issue to be important, too.

Research is an action, and the goals of actions are polyvalent, subjective no less than objective, motivated individually as well as collectively. In the course of this writing, I clarified for myself some private motivations I had not sufficiently considered before and will certainly have to go on considering. They are, of course, idiosyncratic, yet not without some general bearing. In an oppressive situation, we all develop images of alternative realities. In my case there were more than enough oppressive elements; yet, the 'otherness images' I formed did not include a particular interest in alien cultures; all I strove for, was to make an honourable living out of the opportunities given to me. Yet, when the far-away presented itself, I fell for it – it was like meeting unexpectedly a promised land, a fulfilment of secret aspirations. However, this apparent paradise was uncharted, a strange forest: intellectually, it became a problem; emotionally, a promise.

In a sense, fulfilment is never more than a promise; it is ephemeral, and its main value consists in its promise of return, that it may be reached again. The alien culture contained promises which should not be confounded with its everyday reality; striving to be 'one of them' did not mean to be like Kayoon or Sanoh or any other living Thai; it meant a group existing only in my fantasmic anticipations. Yet, this striving induced a search for 'the key' which would allow the unveiling of what provides fulfilment and thereby finding the path to becoming, none the less, 'one of them'. As a researcher, one will couch this process in rational terms and will, as we did, work hard at this rational task without being concerned about the underlying unconscious components of one's motivation. One may feel eager to achieve a respectable research report, while what one strives for in one's deepest self is what the alien culture symbolises.

Culture, of course, is no tangible reality; it is an image condensing multiple experiences, subjective projections and interpretations no less than objective facts. Thus, only too readily, culture becomes a symbol of hopes as well as fears: hopes of fulfilment, fears of frustration. As a symbol, it then tends to host our ego fantasms, the images of personal becoming. It is, indeed, a far-away forest, alien and unknown; we search it for that elusive game which is a self-fulfilment we long for yet never achieve.

But this search enriches our world-view and thereby our action potential, and while this outcome may not yet be fulfilment, it at least strengthens hope. This sounds egocentric, and it is. Had we not such deep personal stakes, we would never do significant research. But, by the same token, it is altruistic: by its promise of self-fulfilment, the alien culture also induces respect and a genuine concern for its otherness. Only cultures which concern us personally will evoke our interest and compassion; and only by confrontation with otherness will we truly develop our self.

REFERENCES

Boesch, E. E. (1960). The Thailand project, step one. *Vita Humana, 3*, 123–142.
Boesch, E. E. (1962). Autorität und Leistungsverhalten in Thailand. *Thailandstudien, 15*, 31–48.
Boesch, E. E. (1963). Raum und Zeit als Valenzsysteme. In H. Hiltmann and F. Vonessen (eds), *Dialektik und Dynamik der Person* (pp. 135–154). Cologne: Kiepenheuer & Witsch.
Boesch, E. E. (1966). Psychologische Theorie des sozialen Wandels. In H. Bester, and E. E. Boesch (eds), *Entwicklungspolitik: Handbuch und Lexikon* (pp. 335–416). Stuttgart/Mainz: Kreuz-Verlag/Mathias-Grünewald-Verlag.

Boesch, E. E. (1970). *Zwiespältige Eliten. Eine sozialpsychologische Untersuchung über administrative Eliten in Thailand*. Bern: Huber.

Boesch, E. E. (1971). *Zwischen zwei Wirklichkeiten. Prolegomena zu einer ökologischen Psychologie*. Bern: Huber.

Boesch, E. E. (1975). La détermination culturelle du soi. In: Association de psychologie scientifique de langue française (ed.), *Psychologie de la connaissance de soi* (pp. 99–119). Paris: Presses Universitaires de France.

Boesch, E. E. (1976). *Psychopathologie des Alltags. Zur Ökopsychologie des Handelns und seiner Störungen*. Bern: Huber.

Boesch, E. E. (1977). The medical interaction. A study in Thailand. *German Journal of Psychology, 1,* 27–43.

Boesch, E. E. (1980). *Kultur und Handlung. Einführung in die Kulturpsychologie*. Bern: Huber.

Boesch, E. E. (1983a). *Das Magische und das Schöne*. Stuttgart: Frommann-Holzboog.

Boesch, E. E. (1983b). Thailand research: problems of method and theory. In E. E. Boesch (ed.), *Thai culture: Report on the second Thai–European Research Seminar 1982* (pp. 3–23). Saarbrücken: Socio-psychological Research Centre on Development Planning.

Boesch, E. E. (1987). Cultural psychology in action theoretical perspective. In Ç. Kağitçibaşi (ed.), *Growth and progress in cross-cultural psychology* (pp. 41–52). Lisse: Swets & Zeitlinger.

Boesch, E. E. (1988). Handlungstheorie und Kulturpsychologie. *Psychologische Beiträge, 30,* 233–247.

Boesch, E. E. (1991). *Symbolic action theory and cultural psychology*. Berlin/New York: Springer.

Boesch, E. E. (1992). Ernst Boesch, 1916. In E. G. Wehner (ed.), *Psychologie in Selbstdarstellungen* (pp. 67–106). Bern: Huber.

Boesch, E. E. (1994). First experiences in Thailand. In W. J. Lonner and R. Malpass (eds), *Psychology and culture* (pp. 47–51). Boston: Allyn & Bacon.

Boesch, E. E. (1996). The seven flaws of cross-cultural psychology. The story of a conversion. *Mind, Culture and Activity, 3,* 2–10.

Cole, M., and Scribner, S. (1974). *Culture and thought*. New York: John Wiley.

Hall, E. T. (1969). *The hidden dimension*. New York: Doubleday Anchor.

Lewin, K. (1951). *Field theory in social science*. New York: Harper.

Sripraphai, P. and Sripraphai, K. (1981). *Social, eco-psychological determinants of migration tendencies in Thailand*. Saarbrücken: Socio-psychological Research Centre on Development Planning.

Sripraphai, P. and Sripraphai, K. (1988). *Future anticipations in a Thai village*. Saarbrücken/Fort Lauderdale: Breitenbach.

2 A natural experiment

Nature runs an untidy laboratory

George M. Guthrie

Recently I had a sense-of-history experience flying from Jakarta to Manila on a route that took me virtually the length of Borneo. From 30,000 feet, I peered through the white cumulus clouds of the tropics and imagined I could see McDougall and Hose at work with their pagan tribes. McDougall had deserted the Cambridge Expedition 'having learned nothing' to spend a couple of years with Hose, a district officer, in British Borneo. All that actually happened nearly a century ago. No present-day cross-cultural psychologist could arrange an experience of such intensity and duration. One would expect this same English psychologist, McDougall, famed for his instinct theory, author of *An introduction to social psychology* (1908) which went through over twenty editions, to have been profoundly influenced by two years in Borneo of 1900. A search of the index of his classic text reveals only one reference to his Borneo stint – one group of Dyaks had a high instinct of pugnacity. Cross-cultural experience does not necessarily change one's outlook. The impact of a new society on a sojourner has been called a natural experiment. As we will see, nature runs an untidy laboratory.

Had I been in London a century ago, I could have met Francis Galton, the founder of anthropometry, busy with his measurements of human growth and performance. Galton also had some intense experiences in other societies which he detailed in his *Art of travel* (1872) and other reports. In his account of an excursion in Namibia, he described 'shifts and contrivances in hot climates'. Galton looked upon the Namibians as primitive people who were quite below the English whom Galton used as a base. This patently racist outlook is rejected by modern social scientists, but in Galton's time it was taken for granted that preliterate people were inferior. None the less, I believe that Galton should be required reading for all cross-cultural psychologists. He was imaginative beyond anyone to be found today, developing finger-printing, the Galton whistle, composite photography, etc.

Among the earliest social scientists to venture into pre-industrial areas were the British, who explored the peoples of their possessions. Similarly, after they had acquired a colony or two in 1898, Americans began to explore one of their possessions, the Philippines. Among the first of that era to express the psychological theory of the time were two Americans, A. V. H. Hartendorp and H. Otley Beyer. Both gave aptitude tests to samples of Filipino teachers. Both stayed in the Philippines for the rest of their lives, Hartendorp as founder and editor of a Philippines literary magazine, and Beyer as Professor of Anthropology at the University of the Philippines. Both married Filipinas.

This chapter is based on my experiences in the Philippines sixty years later and fifteen years after that nation had become independent.

PSYCHOLOGICAL THEORY IN A CROSS-CULTURAL CONTEXT

In the years immediately following World War II, the years when psychology, especially the clinical brand, was coming of age, Freudian theory was the leading and the only orientation. Psychoanalysis offered an explanation of all forms of behaviour, foreign and domestic. The formative events, the crucial oral, anal and genital phases, determined the development of personality in all cultures. Freudians were rulers, all the rest were serfs. My escape to freedom was by way of the alternatives developed by Sullivan, Erikson and others distinguished as neo-Freudian. This orientation prompted me to look for differences in culture and behaviour of members of different socio-economic levels in our own society. Once I could see culture and personality in our neighbourhood, I was off and running. Differences in culture which are extensive should provide convincing opportunities to test the connections between childhood events and adult behaviour, both normal and abnormal.

To capitalise on such differences, I had to go to the natural laboratories created by other societies because it was not possible to manipulate crucial formative events within the usual confines of psychological laboratories. As we will learn, other societies do provide variations in antecedent conditions of personality formation but the independent variables are poorly controlled and effects are complex and usually contaminated. The natural laboratory is untidy.

It was this background of dissatisfaction with Freudian thinking that led me to my first venture in research on personality development in an alien culture. I had been at Penn State for eight years and was eligible for a sabbatical. I applied for a Fulbright appointment to a country where the citizens' culture and language were deeply rooted in a background that was not Indo-European but where English was widely understood. A former British colony such as those of east or west Africa would meet my needs. None of these countries had asked the Fulbright programme for a psychologist. Instead, I was offered and happily accepted the Philippines. Their cultural roots and language were Malayo-Polynesian, but, as a result of half a century of American rule, many spoke excellent English. I stress this matter of facility in English because psychologists have no tradition of and therefore do not allow time to learn exotic languages such as Swahili and Tagalog. Cross-cultural psychologists are realistic, to be sure, but cannot maintain the hard work of learning Urdu if none of their colleagues nor their department head reinforces it.

In my account I would like to suggest certain rules that one should follow in cross-cultural research. My affiliation in the Philippines was the Normal College in downtown Manila. The college was a training school for elementary school teachers. They had limited expectations of research that I might attempt. I had the good fortune to be assigned to work with two very able staff members, Pepita Jimenez, later Jimenez-Jacobs, and Amanda Tayag. In my year with them we produced two books and a non-verbal intelligence test.

Rule 1 Try to establish cooperative relationships with host country nationals. Their help can make a difference in innumerable ways. They can explain your activities and dispel suspicions about the strange activities of foreign researchers, e.g., he doesn't work for the CIA and all his files are not closed to his co-workers.

Rule 2 Treat your co-worker as your equal professionally. You may have more advanced degrees and more publications, but your co-worker has many assets such as an understanding of local society that would enrich your observations and protect you from making erroneous judgements of local traditions. Remember that the host nationals may resent or reject your ideas but hide their negative feelings.

Rule 3 Develop your instruments – questionnaires, tests and interviews – in the field. I felt it was important to assemble these efforts to leave something complete even though it was preliminary. The Normal College agreed and published these papers in a 142-page book, *The Filipino child in Philippine society* (Guthrie,1961).

Rule 4 Try to develop your research around topics of interest to your hosts.

A BOOK ON CHILDREARING

About the time of my appointment, a book was published in the United States, *Patterns of child rearing* by Sears, Maccoby and Levin (1957). Chapter by chapter the book examined the development of children in a New England town using a psychodynamic orientation. The authors used a standard interview which they reported in full in their book. We decided to use the same interview directed at the behaviour of children of the same age in towns served by the Normal College. My Philippine collaborator, Pepita Jimenez, a native speaker of Tagalog, the Manila area dialect, translated the interview from English to Tagalog. She arranged for seniors in their final practice teaching assignments to use the schedule with three mothers each and bring their responses to her for review. This trial run showed that the interviewers understood the task, they could obtain meaningful protocols, and they followed instructions carefully and with a delight in the task. But Jimenez found several problems with our interview: a Filipino baby is cared for by older siblings or by members of the child's extended family. Mothers were not the sole caretakers of the growing child and Filipino fathers were even less a significant model.

The problems Filipino parents faced were different from those of New England parents. Filipino children played with siblings and relatives and had little contact with unrelated peers. Filipino parents did not have problems of controlling TV watching! In short, the experiences of growing up were of a different order and not merely a matter of more or less. This was especially so in matters of the spirit world. Filipino kiddies had to cope with an unseen world of spirits, some benevolent, some dangerous and still others playful, but all invoked by adults to control the child and especially useful to keep the child from straying too far from home. The American reality of Sears *et al.* (1957) had no counterpart in the Philippines.

There was another dimension of control that was different for the two groups of children. There was a line of authority among the Filipino siblings. The oldest child had authority to control and punish all younger children, the second could demand obedience from three, four and five, and so on. This is a different family structure than Sears described.

We faced a choice between keeping an interview schedule that forced similarities between the two groups of children or modifying it to catch the unique experience of the Filipino child. We tried to do both by adding questions that were meaningful to Filipino mothers even though they were not as a rule part of the experience of the Sears mothers.

To collect our data we turned to the seniors on practice teaching again. Jimenez taught them interviewing and recording procedures. Thirty seniors each interviewed ten mothers. The answers were coded and a narrative developed, resulting in the book *Child rearing and personality development in the Philippines* (Guthrie and Jimenez-Jacobs, 1966). We had three purposes in the book:

1 to describe Filipino child rearing practices;
2 to contrast these with those described by Sears *et al.* (1957) in the United States;
3 to develop theoretical implications of the effects of different childrearing practices on adult personality patterns in the Philippines.

Thanks to Jimenez, we achieved the first purpose. We had some limited success with point 2, but were unable to apply psychodynamic theories to processes of personality development. The oral, anal and genital stages were too different due to differences in family structure and physical living arrangements. The data in this book were collected in 1960. Since then many alternative and modified theories of development have been formulated. But it still remains the case that most are fitted to modern industrial societies with small families and with children given only few household responsibilities.

ELEMENTARY SCHOOL EDUCATION

My Fulbright assignment was research rather than teaching. I attempted to carry out studies that would provide models for staff members at the Normal College and yield findings that would bear on the problems of elementary school education. The American invaders of the Philippines in 1898 had established schools throughout the islands and had imparted American philosophy and procedures to the newly created system. Filipino scholars and administrators had relied on American books and theories in spite of the fact that the children in their classrooms were different in ways that were not appreciated or understood. This seemed to be the situation for which *Parental Attitude Research Instrument* (PARI) was made to order. Published in 1958, the PARI (Schaefer and Bell, 1957) consisted of twenty-three five-item scales of maternal attitudes toward children and the tasks of childrearing. The respondent mother was asked to indicate strong or mild agreement or disagreement with statements such as:

1 Children should be allowed to disagree with their parents if they feel their own ideas are better.
2 Children should realise how much parents have to give up for them.

We did not translate the PARI into Tagalog. The set of 115 items was given to samples of Philippine mothers, to women students at the Normal College and to samples of American women college students.

There is a problem when one uses a set of statements and asks for agreement or disagreement. Philippine mothers are generally disposed to agree with most statements, a pattern of acquiescence that distorts the results when one compares responses from members of two groups. We dealt with this problem by simply ranking the items according to the percentage of respondents who indicated agreement. There are more sophisticated techniques for dealing with response bias but this is a technique that can be carried out without computers and does not entail complicated data processing which, at that time, was not readily available in the Philippines. The results clarified the strong loving-controlling relationships sought by Filipino mothers and many other facets of mother–child bonds among Filipino families (Guthrie, 1961, pp. 126–132).

We applied the same techniques in a study of conflicts in the outlook of Filipino teachers (Guthrie, 1961). Forty-three teachers were asked to write the three principles which they found most useful in dealing with school children. The teachers responded with such beliefs as 'Children are naturally good' and 'We teach children, not facts'. We took each statement and asked: 'What is the opposite of this point of view and what is the rationalisation for it?' By this method 119 statements were prepared. Following the strategy of the L scale on the MMPI, we developed an additional ten items that involved the admission of normal human shortcomings, e.g., 'As a teacher I get angry with a child once in a while' and 'I find it easy to like every child I meet'. The respondent was asked to respond with Agree, Disagree or Undecided.

Responses were grouped on the basis of similarity of content and interpretive statements were developed. For example, there appeared to be an area of conflict about a teacher criticising her pupils. Other areas included permissiveness and egalitarianism. One teacher responded with three principles: 'I teach children not facts', 'Right or wrong I respond to the child' and 'There is much good in every child'. She added: 'but I confess that when a child is lazy, I *peench*'. Peenching is a method of punishing that leaves no scar.

With other collaborators I developed chapters on children's beliefs in supernatural beings and their effect on children.

A NON-VERBAL INTELLIGENCE TEST

Very early in my stay in Manila, my Filipino colleagues said to me, 'We need a Filipino intelligence test. We cannot develop a test by translating a Wechsler or Binet.' We discussed the criteria a test should meet and developed a list somewhat as follows:

1 *Non-verbal* For use in a country with more than fifty dialects, a test cannot involve written or spoken instructions.
2 *Untimed* Filipino children are not responsive to instructions to work as quickly as possible.
3 *Familiar material in items* Western tests have unfamiliar Western content.
4 *Local norms* Norms are required for Filipino children with possibly different norms for urban and rural children.

Just before I left for Manila I had seen a non-verbal, untimed test, the *Columbia Mental Maturity Scale* (Burgmeister, Blum and Lorge 1954), a test developed for handicapped children in America. Items were non-verbal, untimed and of familiar material. The child was not asked to explain his or her choice. The subject was presented with a card with five figures on it and asked: 'Which one is different? Which one does not belong?' The test started with very easy items such as four squares and a circle. There were 100 cards or items arranged in order of difficulty from extremely easy to very difficult. The subject was required only to point to the one that did not belong with the others. For most six-year-olds, only one instruction '*Ano ang iba*?' was necessary. After that the child pointed to the one he/she thought did not belong with the others and the tester recorded the choice. We had found that we lost too much reliability if we asked the children to mark their own answer sheets. More difficult items might include four kittens and a puppy, or 5, 7, 9, 11, 13 (9 is the only non-prime number).

As one recognises immediately, we have a five-alternative, multiple-choice test. We had our testers record the subject's answers on answer sheets used in regular college classes. And we were able to use all of the software developed for college classes. Thus we were able to score the test, count the number of times each alternative was chosen, derive the correlation between each item and the total score of the subjects who chose each alternative and derive the difficulty level of each item.

The scoring programme also computed the KR20 estimate of reliability. With all of these analyses available it was possible to test hundreds of school children at each age level in elementary school. The testing time for each child was less than thirty minutes. The mean raw score, the number of correct answers, for a large city elementary school for Grade 1 was about 40 with an increase of five points for each succeeding grade. KR20 ranged from 0.80 to 0.95.

We were fortunate again in having a colleague, Felisa Librea, a talented artist, who did all the graphics. The final product was 100 cards, 8 cm by 33 cm, each with five line drawings of things familiar to Philippine children, *A Philippine Non-verbal Intelligence Test* (PNIT) (Guthrie, Tayag and Jimenez-Jacobs, 1977).

THE PEACE CORPS PROJECT

Two years later I had a different sort of experience, the direct result of my interest in selection and training and my Fulbright experience in the Philippines. I was asked to assume responsibility for several aspects of training the first four groups of Peace Corps volunteers assigned to the Philippines. The programme was at Penn State, beginning in the summer of 1961, just weeks after the Corps was announced. I had responsibility for two components: orientation to the Philippines and selection. There was virtually no material available dealing with the general problem of living in an alien society, although it was well known that as many as half of those who went on foreign assignments returned to the United States before their assignment was completed. Orientation programmes of the US State Department and Department of Defense were mostly concerned with their assignment and with their Philippine counterparts. They did not have time or materials to prepare Americans to work with the rank and file of Filipinos.

We did as academics do – we gathered papers written about the Philippines by social scientists and papers describing the emotional stresses experienced by sojourners. We invited to Penn State for four two-hour presentations a half a dozen American social scientists. We recorded their presentations and, with their editing, published a book, *Six perspectives on the Philippines* (Guthrie, 1968).

My analysis of the experience of living in a foreign environment evolved from a clinical descriptive approach to an analysis of the impact of change in terms of changes in reinforcement contingencies. The last paper in the series bore the unfortunate title 'What you need is continuity', which meant it was missed by literature searches and was not found by scholars in this area. This is unfortunate because I believe that changing reinforcement contingencies simulates many aspects of changing the society one is living in.

The selection process was the object of careful planning and data collection. We were influenced by the famous Office of Strategic Services (OSS) report *Assessment of men* (1948) on the selection and performance of personnel for the OSS during World War II. Candidates were given a battery of psychological tests and were observed in many contrived situations calculated to approximate circumstances which candidates might meet when dropped behind enemy lines. Data collection was systematic and information was pooled to generate predictions of performance. It was heady stuff for personality testing psychologists. But at this point the OSS project halted because follow-up performance data were not available. The agency did not know what became of many of their operatives after they were dropped into enemy country. Agents may have been captured, others deserted and many performed courageously and resourcefully. It was not possible to rate performance as a criterion against which to evaluate predicted performance.

We were more fortunate. We were able to get ratings of performance in the field at the end of the assignment of the volunteers we had trained. We pooled the ratings of Filipino and American supervisors to develop the performance ratings.

How well did we do? The correlation between our pooled predictions and our pooled ratings was 0.004, but at least it was positive. The Peace Corps, to its credit, gave up extensive selection efforts but never generated any evidence that later procedures such as self-selection were any better.

The correlation of 0.004 and anecdotal material from the field convinced me that moving to an alien society is a whole new ball game. The discontinuities from one society to another mean that one has to learn new ways of relating to others and change oneself so that one becomes a different person. For some, this is an exhilarating event; for others, a threat. And I don't know any way you can tell how anyone will react when a change of culture occurs. These findings also suggest that if one wishes to change personality one might move to a new place with new friends and new tasks. In collecting our follow-up data we were often impressed by a supervisor's remark, 'He's a different person in the Philippines.'

COUNSELLING AND CULTURE

As indicated earlier, the preeminent theory of personality in the Philippines has been that formulated by Freud. Psychologists in non-European settings adopted psychoanalysis because it was the only game in town. No one paused to ask whether a theory developed by a physician who was born and reared in Austria in the closing years of the nineteenth century, a theory based on the recollections of middle-class females, would be confirmed if the clients were from Delhi or Manila instead of Vienna. In my first speculation that different theories would have emerged from a Manila-based orientation in psychotherapy, I raised the possibility of testing the Western conceptual system with Filipino clients.

Such an opportunity arose when I met an American psychologist trained in the orientation of Rogers. Enter Father Henry Schumacher SVD, an American priest, a member of the Society of the Divine Word. He had spent fifteen years at San Carlos University in Cebu, Philippines serving as director of their counselling office. In this role he achieved some fascinating insights that offer some understanding of the differences between Filipino and American clients. Again, these were educated, middle-class patients working with a therapist of similar background. Father Shu, as he was known, had achieved some valuable insights into differences in Filipinos' response to counselling '*à la* Rogers'. A Western orientation emphasises inner determinants of both effective and troubled behaviour. Western therapists try to help their clients achieve insight into the causes of their tensions. By contrast Schumacher discovered that his clients emphasised the external determinants of current stresses and sought respite through change in their social situation.

These are contrasting outlooks, with one group emphasising dispositional causes, while the other emphasises situational forces. The Western client asks to change a disposition, the inner determinants of behaviour, while Schumacher's clients wanted changes in the way people were treating them. His observations suggested a new approach to psychotherapy. Instead of helping clients modify their reactions to their own problems, the therapist seeks to modify the way others are treating the client. In short, change your friends, get them to treat you better. As a social psychologist, I find this outlook potentially more helpful than one that emphasises undoing the residuals of childhood stresses. Work on the environment rather than the psyche; practice envirotherapy, not psychotherapy.

MODERNISATION IN THE PHILIPPINES

An official in the US Defense Department had become aware of the development of our training materials for the Peace Corps project and invited us to submit a related proposal to DoD (Department of Defense). We invited about ten psychologists and anthropologists to join us under the title, 'Impact of modernisation in the Philippines'. This was a highly productive project that led to half a dozen monographs and numerous papers.

The methods of research were largely descriptive. The results indicated that Filipinos, even those in barrios far removed from Manila, held modern outlooks and adapted to such modern intrusions as radio, television and improved methods of agriculture as readily as those immersed in the modern environment of Manila. We gained considerable insight into the world view of the urban poor, who were mostly immigrants from the crowded countryside.

FIELD EXPERIMENTS IN NUTRITION

The last and most satisfying application of psychological strategies was in a seven-year project concerned with improving the nutritional status of Filipino children using food available from the community. The Philippines has a serious problem with its babies, especially those in the age range of six to thirty-six months. Field studies indicate that birthweights are acceptable, especially since mothers tend to be small and gain little during pregnancy. The toddlers lag badly after four to six months of age, often weighing no more at eighteen months than they did at six months. Failure to thrive leads to high rates of illness and a high mortality rate of > 50/1000 live births in the first year and later to a curtailed response to learning opportunities in schools.

We undertook a series of longitudinal studies following mother and baby from birth for as much as a year to determine the factors that supported continuation or prompted termination of breastfeeding, the most desirable method of feeding a baby. We found that mothers were unanimous in their preference for nursing. Another pregnancy was the most common reason for termination after the baby had reached six months of age.

Mothers believed that breastfeeding was the most economical and most convenient method of feeding and was best for the baby. These findings were important because repetition of these reasons in attempts to lengthen the period of lactation was unnecessary. On the other hand, once we knew why mothers terminated we developed steps designed to reduce early weaning.

At the time of this research there was a good deal of criticism of infant formula companies for giving newly delivered mothers large samples of their product. It was asserted that the sample caused the mother to terminate breastfeeding, placing the newborn in mortal peril because the mother could not afford to continue to supply formula. We ran an experiment in a provincial hospital that distributed samples on the maternity ward. We arranged that sampling continue for two weeks and then samples were terminated for a similar interval, then samples, then no samples, until we had a sufficient number of mothers to give stable results. We followed up the mothers in home visits for six months. We found that the use of samples had no effect on subsequent breastfeeding (Guthrie, Guthrie, Fernandez and Estrera, 1985).

The Director of the Philippine Nutrition Center, reviewing the situation with me, raised the challenge, 'These families could produce enough food to maintain good growth. We show them how to do it. One hundred calories a day more would reduce the malnutrition which half our babies show. You're a psychologist, how can we get them to use more corn grits, coconut milk, dried fish and bananas, all foods readily available in the community?'

He had posed the problem of compliance, a problem for which I had a special resource. My wife is a nutritionist; our interests met. Rather than doing yet another survey, we undertook a series of field experiments in which we reinforced mothers in making changes necessary to reduce 'failure to thrive'.

We were able also to improve compliance in family planning practices. We found that we had to take cultural practices into account in our choice of reinforcements. Among the less acceptable were those that entailed a lottery. Mothers did not approve of a situation in which those who had poor compliance could still win larger prizes than those who had been fully compliant. At their suggestion we adopted a token system in which the tokens could be exchanged for T-shirts for children or Kodacolor prints of the target baby. Tokens reflected the level of compliance.

Earlier research had found that food supplement programmes had failed to produce improved growth in infants and toddlers. The failure was attributed to frequent illness caused, in turn, by impure water and poor sanitation. Barba, for her doctoral research in nutrition, asked the question: 'If we supplemented the diet of these children and made sure that they got the supplement each day, but did nothing about the environment, would they show improved growth?' (Barba, Guthrie and Guthrie, 1982). She selected two villages and twenty-four babies in each. Those in one village received a food supplement of locally available foods such as eggs, squash and bananas every day and medical care each week. Those in the control group received similar medical care but no supplement. Her supplemented group stayed in the same growth pattern as well-fed urban Filipino children while the other village's babies fell further and further behind, as did other children in rural families. Interestingly, in spite of improved growth, the better-fed children were sick just as many days as those who received no extra food, suggesting that their immune function had not responded to the improved diet.

After one year the experiment was terminated as planned. A follow-up one year later found that the growth curves of the two groups had converged so that the supplemented had declined to the level of the group that had received the toddlers' traditional diet. This finding suggests that mothers need continuing reinforcement to maintain improved feeding practices. Many questions in this area could be answered using small samples where high rates of compliance are elicited.

A BEHAVIOURISTIC APPROACH

There are an additional number of efforts in research by social psychologists that may lead to improved understanding of the processes of coping successfully or with difficulty to living in an alien society. Attribution theory as summarised by Jones (1976) has led to a series of experiments demonstrating that we habitually explain our own behaviour in terms of the demands of the situation while the actions of others are seen as expressions of their character. 'I did it because it was the thing to do. He did it because he's that kind of person.'

Zimbardo (1969) has reported a series of experiments in which subjects experienced varying degrees of anonymity. Living alone in a foreign setting can increase one's anonymity and generate a good deal of emotional turmoil.

Maintenance and modification of rates of responding in a task as simple as finger tapping provides a versatile model of behaviour in the larger community setting. Some of these experiments, summarised by Weiner (1963), have demonstrated that subjects find it extremely difficult to change their rates from slow to fast or fast to slow. Analogously, individuals find it difficult to change their activity level, i.e. their rates of responding, even though change would improve their frequency of reinforcement.

These three lines of social psychological research, namely attribution, de-individuation and changing reinforcement schedules, are examples of limited research designs that enable one to generate testable ideas about changing or stabilising behaviour in social situations without recourse to speculative processes that are thought to take place in the inaccessible realm of the unconscious.

CONCLUSION

This has been an account of some of my experiences in cross-cultural research. It is apparent that I have been responding to opportunities, many of which came on short notice. I was blessed with supportive or at least permissive department heads. I have also enjoyed the support and collaboration of a most helpful wife. Our three kids also enjoyed their stints abroad. Fortunately, none suffered from any condition that limited their travel.

For American academics interested in this kind of work there are three ports of entry: the Peace Corps, the Fulbright programme and sabbatical leaves. Other countries offer other sources of support to the neophyte. My experience is that the most frequent opportunities lie in the field of health, especially the health of mothers and infants. Of course it helps to have married a nutritionist! Another area that is widely supported is that of AIDS research. One might get one's foot in the door of this disease by volunteering at a local health department. In my opinion, not enough attention is paid to promoting safe sex. For example, consider major diseases: tuberculosis is airborne, cholera is waterborne, malaria is spread by mosquitoes; AIDS is spread almost solely by behaviour. Changes in behaviour would halt the spread of AIDS. Psychologists have a contribution to make by applying what they have learned in laboratory studies of risk taking. There is a huge field of health-related behaviour from conception to death. Social psychologists have concepts, research and action strategies that would reduce the spread of this lethal disease. This is an area where social psychologists might apply their experimental skills to designing field experiments of various magnitudes. There are much more challenging and rewarding activities awaiting than the descriptive and demographic efforts that currently clutter the field.

Finally cross-cultural work calls for a breadth of competence and interest that is not emphasised for those who stay at home. I had to learn much about cultural and physical anthropology, sociology, nutrition, physical growth and physical pathology. I learned much simply by going on field trips with rural doctors and rural unit nurses. On each project one must collaborate with members of disciplines one does not understand completely and with professionals who are inexperienced in work with psychologists and are initially sceptical about our contributions to the efforts of the team.

REFERENCES

Barba, C.V.C., Guthrie, H.A. and Guthrie, G.M. (1982). Dietary intervention and growth of infants and toddlers in a Philippine rural community. *Ecology of Food and Nutrition, 11*, 235–244.

Burgmeister, B.B., Blum, L.H., and Lorge, I. (1954). *Columbia Mental Maturity Scale*, Yonkers-on-Hudson, NY: World Books.

Galton, F. (1872). *Art of travel; or Shifts and contrivances available in wild countries*, (reissued 1971). Harrisburg, PA: Redwood Press, for Stackpole Books.

Guthrie, G.M. (1961). *The Filipino child in Philippine society*, Manila: Philippine Normal College Press.

Guthrie, G.M. (1968). *Six perspectives on the Philippines*, Manila: Bookmark.

Guthrie, G.M. and Jimenez-Jacobs, P. (1966) *Childrearing and personality development in the Philippines*, University Park, PA and London: Pennsylvania State University Press.

Guthrie, G.M., Tayag, and Jimenez-Jacobs, P. (1977). The Philippine non-verbal intelligence test. *Journal of Social Psychology, 102*, 3–11.

Guthrie, G.M., Guthrie, H.A., Fernandez, T.L. and Estrera, N.O. (1985). Infant formula samples and breastfeeding among Philippine urban poor. *Social Science Medicine,7*, 713–717.

Jones, E.E. (1976). How do people perceive the causes of behavior? *American Scientist, 64*, 300–305.

McDougall, W. (1908). *An introduction to social psychology*, London: Methuen.

Schaefer, E.S., and Bell, R.Q. (1957). Development of a parental attitude research instrument. *Child Development, 29*, 339–361.

OSS Assessment Staff (1948). *Assessment of men*. New York: Rinehart.

Sears, R.R., Maccoby, E.E. and Levin, H. (1957). *Patterns of child rearing*, Evanston, IL: Row Peterson.

Weiner, H. (1963). Conditioning history and maladaptive human behavior. *Psychological Reports, 17*, 934–942.

Zimbardo, P.G. (1969). The human choice. Individuation, reason and order versus deindividuation, impulse and chaos. In W.J. Arnold and D. Levine (eds), *Nebraska Symposium on Motivation*, Lincoln, NB: University of Nebraska Press.

3   Always something new out of Africa

Gustav Jahoda

IT ALL STARTED ON A WALK ...

Moritz Lazarus (1824–1903), the founder of the original version of *Völker-psychologie*, grew up in a town with a mixed German and Polish population, an ethnic mix which stimulated his interest in national differences. Without presuming to compare myself with him in other respects, we did have this kind of background in common: my father was of Czech, my mother of Hungarian origin; I was born in Vienna, and educated there and subsequently in Paris and London. This kind of multinational experience in terms of language, social norms, food habits, and so on, provided me with a relatively cosmopolitan perspective from an early age. At the time, of course, I never imagined that this early exposure would in any way be connected with my future career. It was only later that a serendipitous encounter led to a decisive turning point.

After serving in the British army I studied sociology and psychology at London University and subsequently obtained a post as a lecturer in social psychology at the University of Manchester. At the beginning of my third year there we had a visit from Ernest Beaglehole, a versatile social scientist who had published not only in social psychology, notably an important book on 'property' (Beaglehole, 1931), but also in anthropology (e.g., Beaglehole and Beaglehole, 1938). The staff member originally assigned as the host became ill, and the task fell to me. In the course of conversation during a walk around the city Beaglehole remarked that in his view a social psychologist, to do his work effectively, should get to know other cultures, preferably non-Western ones. This struck me as an illuminating idea, which I discussed with my wife of less than two years and obtained her enthusiastic endorsement. I asked to be allowed to attend the anthropology seminars conducted by Max Gluckman, found them inspiring, and decided to try for Africa. Accordingly, I applied for the first post advertised there, which was at the East African Institute of Social Research at Makerere, in Uganda, whose Director was the anthropologist Audrey Richards. I was duly called for an interview, and found myself being grilled by a galaxy of prominent anthropologists, several of whom I later came to know well.

I should explain that at the time most British anthropologists were highly critical of psychology, which they regarded, not without reason, as being unduly academic and remote from real life. At any rate, this negative view was reflected in the questions and comments of the panel. Initially I was rather meek, but decided after a while that I would not get the job, and thereafter embarked on as vigorous a defence as I was able to muster. After the interview I heard no more, dismissed the matter from my mind, and applied for a post at what was then the University College of the Gold Coast (now Ghana), and was duly appointed.

There is a postscript: many years later I was at a conference of social anthropology where Audrey Richards asked me why I had not replied to their job offer; the letter had apparently been lost in the post, and thus fate led me to West rather than East Africa. My colleagues in Manchester were rather puzzled by what appeared to them my highly eccentric decision to leave a tenured post for darkest Africa: in 1952 cross-cultural psychology was not yet on the map.

THE GOLD COAST – '*UN EMBARRAS DE RICHESSES*'

My post was in the Department of Sociology headed by the late Kofi Busia, a brilliant scholar who later became Prime Minister for a while, until toppled by yet another military coup. Although officially appointed to teach social psychology and research methods, I was soon asked to extend my teaching to statistics, criminology, and demography as well. Regarding the last two subjects, I just managed to keep a few pages ahead of the students! As soon as it became possible for me to keep my head a little above water, my thoughts turned to research.

As the only psychologist in a wonderfully exciting country, the opportunities were limitless. This was both an advantage and a problem, since it was hard to know where to start. The first year was spent getting to know the rich culture, and I started to learn the Akan language, *Twi*. It soon became apparent that this language choice would have restricted me to few of the many ethnic groups, and therefore I decided instead to acquire merely a few useful phrases in some of the other vernaculars, just enough to show good intentions. Incidentally, the other important step for gaining acceptance was a willingness, which few Europeans had at the time, to share people's meals; this required the kind of sturdy stomach I was fortunate then to possess.

On the frequent occasions when I was away 'on trek', my wife was left to boil and filter all the drinking water, struggle to light kerosene lamps, and so on. Moreover, she had to be constantly on the alert for scorpions and snakes which not infrequently invaded the bungalow and were a particular danger to our offspring; we arrived with one child, and another was born in Ghana. My wife was not content with staying at home. A trained social worker, she often went to neighbouring villages and helped the women with their problems. Moreover, the women often came to see her and our veranda became a favourite meeting place, to the dismay of some teaching staff hailing from South Africa. This active involvement by my better half became well known and greatly contributed to my being readily accepted when doing research.

Returning to the main theme, I cannot claim to have developed a coherent research plan. But as well as getting around the town, I went to visit villages as often as possible, getting a feel for the traditional ways of life; depending on degree of accessibility, this visiting was done in a Landrover, on a Harley-Davidson, or eventually often on foot, observing carefully and keeping a diary. There was only one topic I pursued consistently, and that concerned the Ghanaian images of Europeans, where some notable differences struck me early on. With highly educated Africans the relationship was an easy, egalitarian one; they saw Europeans just as ordinary people like themselves, with their virtues and faults. Accusations of 'evil imperialists' were confined to political discourse and did not affect face-to-face situations. Illiterate villagers, who had little if any direct contact with Europeans, conceived of them in terms of a limited number of roles, such as missionary, teacher or doctor. As such, Europeans were at or beyond the periphery of their social universe. In my encounters with them I found them courteous, dignified, and far from obsequious. By contrast, many of those with only a few years' schooling sometimes embarrassed me by their servility and a tendency to run down things African. On the surface it looked as though they regarded Europeans as superior beings, but the attitudes were more complex and evidence of aggressive feelings occasionally emerged. Intrigued by all this, I began a systematic study of the roots of these attitudes and behaviours, which in due course resulted in my first book (Jahoda, 1961a).

Although assiduously collecting data, I seldom found it possible to proceed immediately to analysis, let alone writing-up. Apart from my heavy teaching load, resources were meagre. Few people nowadays are likely to remember turning the handle of a calculating machine, as we had to do. During my third year we acquired a Swedish electromechanical one which for a while was a great boon, even though the generator supplying electricity to the campus was rather erratic. Then a keen physics technician wanted to know how it worked and – without permission – took it apart; unfortunately he was unable to put it together again, and that was that.

Otherwise, rather like an intellectual grasshopper, I was always on the look-out for either interesting problems or opportunities for testing Western theories. I have never been a respecter of disciplinary boundaries, pursuing whatever appeared interesting and employing whatever method was appropriate. Accordingly, I shall not attempt to impose *ex post* a set of categories upon my early work, but give 'sound-bite' examples of the exhilarating hodge-podge it was. My research began with students, but I was determined not to follow those who confined themselves to such an atypical section of the population – a practice which regrettably remains very widespread.

The Principal who set up the University College was a Cambridge man ('nothing but the best for Africa, and the best is Cambridge') and so it was modelled on Cambridge: for instance, in the refectory there was fine cutlery and china, with food being served by waiters. This suited the scions of the African urban elite, but was not easy for those coming from a traditional background. When I saw the families of students in remote villages eating with their hands from a common pot, it became clear to me that there were severe problems of adjustment in moving between two diferent cultural worlds, problems which the Principal had not sufficiently considered (Jahoda, 1955–6).

At that period experimental social psychology was a fresh and lively area, and I was infected by the enthusiasm. Hence I sought to replicate some of the experiments with my students. Alas, the attempts nearly all resulted in dismal failure, and from then onwards I became sceptical about the universality of social psychological 'laws' arrived at in this manner with Western student subjects. The actual experiments were never published, but I referred to this material much later in a critical article (Jahoda, 1979). More successful was a study in which I showed that a sex difference in preferences for shapes could best be interpreted in terms of psychoanalytic theory (Jahoda, 1956a); its publication later had quite unforeseen consequences.

One of my tasks was to give occasional talks to teachers on child psychology, and thereby I came across the notion that a child's character is partly determined by the day of the week on which he or she is born and given a particular 'day name'. From the height of my superior knowledge I dismissed this idea, until a headmaster whom I had learned to respect as a highly intelligent man defended it stoutly. Challenged to provide evidence, he said that he always recorded details of offences and had noted that *Kwakus* (Wednesday boys) were punished far more frequently than others for aggressive behaviour. This was in conformity with traditional Akan beliefs about the character of *Kwakus*. Duly impressed, I embarked upon an extensive study of the types of delinquency committed by boys with various day names. There was in fact a highly significant association of the kind claimed by the headmaster, though we would interpret this outcome rather differently, in terms of socialisation (Jahoda, 1954). It was a lesson for me to take indigenous beliefs seriously.

Although not yet independent, the Gold Coast had internal self-government, and elections were to be held in 1954. Walter Birmingham, an economist colleague, and I decided to conduct a pre-election survey in the capital, Accra. It was to be the first of its kind based on a random sample, which meant that great practical difficulties had to be overcome. We stuck our necks out and gave the results to the main newspaper, which published it. In the event we were, no doubt partly by good luck, extremely close to the actual voting figures and regarded almost as magicians (Birmingham and Jahoda, 1955). Such an attribution was hardly surprising in a culture where traditional beliefs about divination, witchcraft, and so on, remained powerful, an issue to which I shall return.

Among studies designed to test Western theories was one not unrelated to this topic, namely Piaget's postulate of child animism. The original questions were adapted for the African setting, and in addition children who had heard music and songs from a gramophone were asked to explain where the music comes from. It transpired that animism was to some extent built into the language: for instance, there is a word for an ordinary stone and another for a stone inhabited by a spirit. If one makes allowance for that linguistic feature, the level of animism was relatively low in comparison with findings from other non-Western cultures, and declined with age (Jahoda, 1958).

For over a century Africans had been regarded as being incapable of abstract thinking. During the 1950s there was still frequent mention of their 'concrete mentality', a view seemingly supported by test results. I was able to show that children from homes where at least one of the parents had some schooling performed significantly better on the Goldstein–Sheerer Cube Test (claimed to differentiate 'abstract' and 'concrete' normals) than those from an entirely illiterate background. It follows that, contrary to what had been assumed, such tests are by no means 'culture-free', and that performance levels are likely to rise with the spread of education (Jahoda, 1956b).

This brings me to another broad area of interest, namely the effects of the rapid social changes that were taking place. I tackled this issue in a variety of approaches that can only be briefly indicated. One was an attitude/opinion survey on a wide range of topics conducted with people of differing degrees of literacy (Jahoda, 1961–2). It anticipated on a very modest scale what was later to become the salient issue of 'modernity' (Inkeles and Smith, 1974). A small but amusing piece describes how young people sought to come to grips with what to them was the puzzling business of 'romantic love'. It was based on an analysis of letters to the advice column of a local newspaper. For instance, one asked: 'How can I make my mother understand the word "love"?', and another: 'Is this love really from Heaven?' (Jahoda, 1959). Lastly, some more extensive studies were carried out on the impact of change on the activities of traditional healers and on the emergence of new types of practitioners dealing with mental illness and other troubles (Jahoda, 1961b). For instance traditional healers, at one time concerned mainly with illness or barrenness, expanded their scope to deal (magically) with problems of pay and promotion in employment. One variety of the new breed tended to adopt some of the external trappings of medical science (e.g., a crude apparatus for the distillation of herbs, or specimens of toads and snakes in jam jars, supposed to have been vomited by witches), while others specialised in 'modern' problems such as passing exams; I saw letters from students in London requesting the sending of suitable 'vibrations' for their Finals!

After nearly five years in what was then about to become independent Ghana, we left – regretfully – for family reasons. My wife's mother, who was in poor health, complained that she seldom saw her or the grandchildren, and it was also partly a question of the children's schooling. A Senior Lectureship was advertisd at the University of Glasgow, close to my wife's home town. While far from optimistic about my chances, I decided to apply. Although called for interview, my doubts were confirmed on meeting the two other candidates, clearly much better qualified. In the course of my interview the professor questioned me at length about the study published in 1956 that supported the psychoanalytic hypothesis, and to my delighted amazement then offered me the job. Later I discovered him to have been one of the very rare academic psychologists who was also a fervent Freudian. At any rate, for a few years I was fully occupied not merely with teaching, but also with writing up my African data as well as conducting other studies, especially on the development of social cognition.

MANY RETURNS AND A CHANGE OF STYLE

In 1963 I was invited to set up a new psychology department at the University of Strathclyde, an administrative task which I found very burdensome. Already I was planning further research in Africa, and it was clear that on relatively brief visits of two or three months the work would have to be much more sharply focused, with greater emphasis on survey or experimental studies, the latter chiefly in the sphere of perception. Sometimes I obtained the help of colleagues with the testing of European comparison samples, and on several studies cooperated with my friend Jan Deregowski, himself a distinguished cross-cultural psychologist active in Africa.

My first project along these lines was inspired by the studies of Segall, Campbell and Herskovits (1963) on the factors influencing illusion susceptibility, a study which later became a classic. Theirs had been a world-wide sample, and I took advantage of the great variations in both 'carpenteredness' and natural ecologies in Ghana to find out whether their results could be replicated *within* a given culture area. The study concentrated exclusively on illiterate villagers, and special methods had to be devised for ensuring they understood the nature of the task. The expected differences between Ghanaian sub-groups were not found (Jahoda, 1966), and it emerged from subsequent work that the determinants of illusion susceptibility are a good deal more complex than Segall *et al.* (1963) had surmised (Jahoda and Stacey, 1970).

While the concern with illusions was theoretical, I felt it to be important to deal also with problems of potential practical relevance. My own observations of African children suggested that they experienced some difficulties with the perception of depth in pictures of the kind demonstrated by Hudson (1962), but that his test exaggerated them (Jahoda and McGurk, 1974). A later project carried out in several African countries as well as India indicated that at the secondary school level there is no longer a problem (Jahoda, Cheyne, Deregowski, Sinha and Collingbourne, 1976). The same cannot be said of other aspects of space perception, which cause difficulties even at the university level in fields like geology or engineering. This was explored in an extensive series of studies, too long to be detailed here, indicating that mental rotation is the key issue (summarised in Jahoda, 1988).

All this may sound as though I had made a complete break with my earlier research, but this was not quite the case. For instance, in 1955 I had given children the Piagetian task of drawing a bicycle – they were very common – and found relatively little grasp of the mechanism. On a return trip thirteen years later I repeated this task, discovering considerable progress, Ghanaian boys having caught up with Scottish ones (Jahoda, 1969a). The reasons for this are not clear, but a greater emphasis on the teaching of science during the intervening period was probably at least partly responsible.

One topic that fascinated me throughout was that of traditional supernatural beliefs, e.g, in witchcraft and sorcery, which in the 1950s I had taken to be mainly an African phenomenon; their psychological implications were of particular interest (Jahoda, 1970). For instance, people who had done well in life often feared that envy would lead others to direct evil forces against them, and obtained 'protection' from fetish priests and others. At one famous shrine I came across a prominent and highly educated politician, who was then in some trouble. The sudden death from a heart attack of an African professor was rumoured by his relatives to have been caused by witchcraft. It used to be an article of faith that education eliminates non-rational beliefs, but a study of university students at the outset and the end of their studies showed that this is not the case (Jahoda, 1968). Since then the imperviousness of non-rational beliefs to education has been confirmed by the spectacular spread of such beliefs in the West, with astrologers among the best-paid professionals. At any rate, the experience prompted me to think about the psychological nature of 'superstition' (Jahoda, 1969b).

The numerous research trips I was able to make testify to the generosity of the University in giving me leave, that of my colleagues willing to hold the fort in my absence, but not that of grant-giving agencies. Obtaining funds for what had long been a less than fashionable field was a continuous struggle. On several occasions I managed to get myself appointed external examiner in various places, which covered the main cost, and for the rest I had to put my hand in my own pocket. It will be gathered from the above that my research was not wholly confined to Ghana, but extended to some other African countries and, on a minor scale, to Hong Kong and India. The last stages of my active fieldwork were in Zimbabwe, and the outcome of one of these investigations gave me special satisfaction. Anyone informed about cross-cultural Piagetian studies will be aware of the so-called 'developmental lag', meaning that children in many non-industrial cultures are about two years behind compared with European ones. In my view this is because Piagetian tasks, even when adapted, are not necessarily 'culture-fair'. In seeking for something that would be fairer, I hit upon the idea of focusing on the development of the concept of 'profit'. My work with Scottish and Dutch children had shown that for them this is a difficult concept, arrived at only by about the age of eleven years. I reasoned that African children, usually involved in small trading from an early age, might be expected to do better than European ones in this sphere. And so it turned out: they were at least two years ahead of European children (Jahoda, 1983).

During the late 1970s I was beginning to feel that I was getting too long in the tooth for fieldwork. It had at times been very strenuous, and several bouts of malaria were taking their toll. When going to a village, one had to sit with the chief and his elders to explain one's 'mission'. A calabash of water circulated, from which everyone had to take a sip before a libation was poured. If that took place in broad daylight so that one could not cheat by merely pretending to sip, one ran the risk of dysentery. Incidentally, some prestation had to be offered – usually at least a bottle of gin, though at times a goat had to be sacrificed. The appearance of such items in the record of research expenses raised some eyebrows.

Anyway, it was time for me to phase out field research, though I still collaborated with a colleague in Zimbabwe (e.g., Jahoda and Neilson, 1986). I also continued to do some empirical studies at home until my retirement, though an increasing proportion of my writing came to be devoted to theoretical and historical issues. My interests in these spheres were of long standing. For example, in order to understand African images of Europeans it had been necessary for me to delve into the historical background of their relations. Similarly, I had long wrestled with the theoretical aspects of culture and psychology (Jahoda, 1980), and these two strands came together in a more recent volume (Jahoda, 1992). Thus the transition from being primarily an empirical researcher to becoming an armchair scholar was a gradual one.

THE RETREAT TO THE LIBRARY

Throughout my career I have greatly benefited from contacts with anthropologists, whose different ways of looking at problems of culture and cultural differences have often been illuminating. Over many years this contact led me to reflect on the relationship between these disciplines, and a one-year fellowship at the Netherlands Institute of Advanced Studies gave me the leisure and facilities to expound my ideas on this topic. It was my good fortune that A.L. ('Bill') Epstein, a prominent anthropologist, was a Fellow at the same time. The book that resulted (Jahoda, 1982) owes much to his wise counsel.

After my retirement in 1985 I was fortunate to be invited as a visiting professor to various universities in four continents. I continue writing on theoretical topics and the history of ideas about psychology and culture.

Looking back, I feel that I have been very fortunate in landing in so rich and vibrant a culture as that of West Africa, and recall the kindness with which I have been received. I was also lucky in having had a wife willing to take a plunge into the unknown, who cheerfully faced the difficulties, and occasional hardships, which that journey entailed.

Over almost half a century there have been great changes in cross-cultural psychology. Getting to the Gold Coast took nearly two weeks by boat; now one can fly to Ghana from London in less than seven hours. The modern researcher, equipped with lap-top computer and questionnaires in his baggage can, grant permitting, stay in air-conditioned hotels. We had to put up with rather more primitive conditions. Yet then it was something of an adventure, and not just an intellectual one; and perhaps the former helped to enrich the latter. For if one shares even to a limited extent the life of those in another culture, then one does not just see them as mere 'subjects', appearing in tables as numbers, but as real people.

This realisation had several consequences as regards both my practice of doing research and my theoretical outlook. It taught me not to accept the results of Western tests and experimental procedures at face value, especially where they conflicted with my personal observations, and to question the universal validity of some Western psychological theories. Today, of course, this position is no longer the heresy it was at the time. The testing of Western findings sometimes confirmed them, as with drawing styles (Jahoda, 1981a), or failed to do so as in relation to memory for verbal and spatial stimuli (Jahoda, 1981b).

Apart from such testing, I was led to generate culture-relevant hypotheses, sometimes inspired by the people themselves, as in the above-mentioned case of the influence of naming on socialisation (Jahoda, 1954). At that period African intellectual inferiority was still widely accepted, and the results of a Progressive Matrices Test with schoolboys appeared to confirm such a view. However, having personal knowledge of them made me doubt this conclusion, and lack of familiarity with the material suggested itself as an alternative hypothesis. Hence I administered the test to another sample for three successive weeks (without knowledge of results) and found a dramatic improvement (Jahoda, 1956b). One final example of this kind concerns the Kohs Block Test, on which the children performed very poorly. On close examination I noted that the reproduction of the patterns themselves was often correct, but this could not be credited according to the rules since the orientations did not correspond to those of the model. Hence it occurred to me that the instruction to 'make it the same' might have been interpreted by the children as referring solely to the *internal stucture of the patterns*, a hunch that was subsequently confirmed (Jahoda, 1978).

Although not averse to hypothesis-testing, it became obvious to me that for many interesting and important problems such an approach, drilled into me by my formal training, was not merely unduly narrow, but simply inapplicable. As already implicit in some of the examples, it is often essential to understand the *meaning* of behaviour, whether in artificial or natural situations. Sometimes a research style more akin to that of anthropologists is necessary, involving observation of everyday life and talking to *informants* rather than testing 'subjects' (cf. Jahoda, 1982). Let me illustrate this with a brief anecdotal example. At that time women in a northern part of the country were often dressed only in a kind of tail that hung down from a string around their waist. Some Europeans cited this to me as evidence of both their shamelessness and their stupidity, for why have covering on the back? This prompted me to ask some of the women, through an interpreter, 'Why?'; and the answer was perfectly simple and logical: 'When we work in the fields bent down,' they said, 'one can see much more than from the front.'

Patronising and derogatory views of Africans were by no means confined to the ignorant. For example, in 1953 a WHO-sponsored monograph was published whose author claimed that African children's 'thought modes do not progress beyond the level of those seen in European children at the age of eight' (Carothers, 1953, p. 100). On the basis of my experience this struck me as arrant nonsense, further undermining my faith in the received wisdom, and in the results of *particular* tests and experiments. My conviction grew of a need for a variety of converging approaches to problems, including unorthodox methods. I recall describing my work to a visiting American social scientist, who commented that my use of unstandardised instruments was 'unscientific'; my reply was 'too bad for science'.

Generally, one salient effect of my African experience has been a progressive disillusionment with the more pompous scientific pretensions and methodological obsessions of some mainstream psychology – there is in my view more to it than number-crunching. In fact, in some of my research, I had moved in the direction now known as 'cultural psychology' which complements the 'cross-cultural' version. Thus, the years in Africa constituted the most crucial formative period of my professional life.

REFERENCES

Beaglehole, E. (1931). *Property: A study in social psychology.* London: Allen & Unwin.

Beaglehole, E. and Beaglehole, P. (1938). *Ethnology of Pukapuka.* Honolulu, HI: Bernice P. Bishop Museum Bulletin No. 150.

Birmingham, W. and Jahoda, G. (1955). A pre-election survey in a semi-literate society. *Public Opinion Quarterly, 19,* 140–152.

Carothers, J.J. (1953). *The African mind in health and disease.* Geneva: World Health Organization.

Hudson, W. (1962). Pictorial perception and educational adaptation in Africa. *Psychologia Africana, 9,* 226–239.

Inkeles, A. and Smith, D.H. (1974). *Becoming modern.* London: Heinemann.

Jahoda, G. (1954). A note on Ashanti day names in relation to personality. *British Journal of Psychology, 45,* 192–195.

Jahoda, G. (1955–6). The social background of a West African student population. Part 1. *British Journal of Sociology, 5,* 355–365. Part 2, *British Journal of Sociology, 6,* 71–79.

Jahoda, G. (1956a). Sex differences in the perception of shapes – a replication. *British Journal of Psychology,47,* 126–132.

Jahoda, G. (1956b). Assessment of abstract behavior in a non-western culture. *Journal of Abnormal and Social Psychology, 53,* 237–243.

Jahoda, G. (1958). Child animism: A study in West Africa. *Journal of Social Psychology, 47,* 213–222.

Jahoda, G. (1959). Love, marriage, and social change. *Africa, 29,* 177–190.

Jahoda, G. (1961a). *White man.* London: Oxford University Press. Reprinted 1983, Westport, CN.: Greenwood Press.

Jahoda, G. (1961b). Traditional healers and other institutions concerned with mental illness in Ghana. *International Journal of Social Psychiatry, 7,* 245–268.

Jahoda, G. (1961–2). Aspects of westernisation, Parts, I and II. *British Journal of Sociology, 12,* 375–386; *13,* 43–56.

Jahoda, G. (1966). Geometric illusions and environment: A study in Ghana. *British Journal of Psychology, 57,* 193–199.

Jahoda, G. (1968). Scientific training and the persistence of traditional beliefs among West African university students. *Nature, 200,* No. 5174, p. 1356.

Jahoda, G. (1969a). Understanding the mechanism of bicycles. *International Journal of Psychology, 4,* 103–108.

Jahoda, G. (1969b). *The psychology of superstition.* London: Allen Lane.

Jahoda, G. (1970). Supernatural beliefs and changing cognitive structures among Ghanaian university students. *Journal of Cross-cultural Psychology, 1,* 115–130.

Jahoda, G. (1978). Cross-cultural study of factors influencing orientation errors in the reproduction of Kohs-type figures. *British Journal of Psychology, 69,* 45–57.

Jahoda, G. (1979). A cross-cultural perspective on experimental social psychology. *Personality and Social Psychology Bulletin, 5,* 142–148.

Jahoda, G. (1980). Theoretical and systematic approaches in cross-cultural psychology. In H.C. Triandis and W.W. Lambert (eds), *Handbook of cross-cultural psychology.* vol.1 (pp. 69–141). Boston, MA: Allyn & Bacon.

Jahoda, G. (1981a). Drawing styles of schooled and unschooled adults: A study in Ghana. *Quarterly Journal of Experimental Psychology, 33A,* 133–143.

Jahoda, G. (1981b). Sex differences in retention of verbal and spatial characteristics of stimuli: A cross-cultural replication. *Journal of Experimental Child Psychology, 31,* 424–429.

Jahoda, G. (1982). *Psychology and anthropology.* London: Academic Press.

Jahoda, G. (1983). European 'lag' in the development of an economic concept: A study in Zimbabwe. *British Journal of Developmental Psychology, 1,* 113–120.

Jahoda, G. (1988). Les études comparatives sur la perception de l'espace. In R. Bureau and D. de Saivre (eds), *Apprentissage et cultures* (pp. 143–158). Paris: Karthala.

Jahoda, G. (1992). *Crossroads between culture and mind.* London: Harvester Wheatsheaf.

Jahoda, G., Cheyne, W.M., Deregowski, J.B., Sinha, D. and Collingbourne, R. (1976). Utilisation of pictorial information in classroom learning: A cross-cultural study. *Audio-Visual Communication Review, 24,* 295–315.

Jahoda, G. and McGurk, H. (1974). Pictorial depth perception in Scottish and Ghanaian children. *International Journal of Psychology, 9,* 255–267.

Jahoda, G. and Neilson, I. (1986). Nyborg's analytical rod-and-frame scoring system: A comparative study in Zimbabwe. *International Journal of Psychology, 21,* 19–29.

Jahoda, G. and Stacey, B.G. (1970). Susceptibility to geometric illusions according to culture and professional training. *Perception and Psychophysics, 7,* 179–184.

Segall, M.H., Campbell, D.T. and Herskovits, M.J. (1963). Cultural differences in the perception of illusions. *Science, 139,* 769–771.

4 Raised in a collectivist culture, one may become an individualist

Harry C. Triandis

I was born and raised in Greece, at the time when it was a collectivist culture (Triandis, 1972). Yet many factors pushed me toward individualism. My grandfather was an industrialist, in Patras, Greece, where I was born. He had a large flour mill that distributed to most of Western Greece, and several ships that transported wheat from abroad. His was a collectivist household. He had twelve children, and most of them and their spouses lived in the huge house where I was born, on Maisonos Street 52. On a normal day forty people had lunch at grandfather's house! That included not only my grandmother, some of the children and their spouses and some of the grandchildren, but also governesses, cooks, chambermaids, chauffeurs, gardeners, and a sprinkling of employees from the factory.

From the time I was born in 1926 to the time my grandfather died, two years later, I lived in this real collective. When he died, my uncles took over the business and fortunately made a mess out of it. I say fortunately, because if they had not invested in new machinery just months before the Great Depression of 1929 started, I would have *had* to become a Patras industrialist. In collectivist cultures, duty comes before pleasure. I was the oldest grandson, and the one who bore my grandfather's name. In fact, in reaction to grandfather's immense family, his children had either one child or none. I was the only Triandis who emerged from this crop. There would not have been any other acceptable career.

Since later in life I studied engineering and business administration with success, I could well have become an industrialist. But my real love was revealed during my business administration studies, when I met psychology. I would not have been able to pursue that interest had I been forced into being an industrialist.

My first governess, at age two, was French. I have a vague recollection of her. The next one was German, and I remember her well. By that time we had moved to Chalandri, a suburb of Athens. Frau Friebe was about forty and believed in strict discipline! I had to be up at 6:30 in the morning to do gymnastics on the veranda of our house. The neighbourhood children thought that this was hilarious, a wonderful spectacle, and came daily to see it. Frau Friebe paid no attention to them. I soon learned that I should not pay attention to the opinion of my peers – a strictly anti-collectivist viewpoint! She also insisted that I learn to read German at age five. I still use German to find the letters of the Latin alphabet. She complained about Greek food, which she found horrible, and at the dinner table she would exclaim: '*Immer dieses Oel!*' (Always this oil!). Exposure to cultural differences around the dinner table aroused some interest on where they came from. Finally, after she beat me black and blue a few times my mother dismissed her, and hired another German governess.

Fraulein Schumann was sweet, but when I was naughty she also beat me. She told me that Greece was backward, and if I wanted to be anybody I should study in Germany. More cross-cultural conflict! She had an atlas that I was allowed to look at only under her supervision. She taught me much about geography and the wonders of travel. I probably developed my Odysseus complex at that point, and that comes in handy when one is a cross-cultural psychologist. The most wonderful city in the world, she said, was Dresden, where she came from. She talked of opera, concerts, theatres, universities, railway stations, broad avenues. It sounded like a dream. In fact, I remember dreaming about Dresden, and when I finally visited it in 1980 I was so sorry to see so much of it in ruins.

When my grandfather's business went under, we had to move from a house to an apartment. No more governesses; just German lessons twice a week. My father had a modest income. He was a mechanical engineer, and at that time he worked for the Ministry of Transportation, making sure that the railways of Greece functioned more or less as they should. He also had a second job at a technical college, to earn a bit more. Later, during the war with Italy, he was in charge of the distribution of energy for the country. Still later he became a consulting engineer.

I went to school for the first time when I was ten. Up to that time I had tutors at home. Of course, this did little to socialise me to peers and ingroups, so that was distinctly an individualistic influence.

In school, I got into a fight with no less than the son of the Prime Minister. I was much bigger than he was, and I gave him a push that landed him on a fountain, where he broke a front tooth. Punishment by the school's Principal was physical and swift, so much so that I became instantly a pacifist. That position is also hardly consistent with collectivism, which emphasises the wars of the ingroup against the outgroups. One of my friends at that school was the son of the Greek ambassador to China, and he told me wonderful stories about that mythical place, and made me follow the Chinese–Japanese war as if it were of vital importance to me. It was then that I developed a great desire to go to the Far East, which did not happen until thirty years later.

At age twelve I had to go to a high school. My family did not consider Greek high schools good enough (another cultural conflict!). I remember major family consultations about going to a high school that emphasised English, German, Italian or French. All these schools started with two hours of a foreign language and during the last year of high school all subjects were taught in that language, with only two hours of Greek included in the curriculum. The least expensive of these schools was the French one, run by the Marist brothers. In 1938 French was *the* international language. Thus, the combination of low cost and the importance of the language determined that I should go there.

I was happy in that school, because the priests believed in frequent re-inforcement. You would earn a red card for A, and a blue card for B, but no card for less than B work. For every lesson there was the possibility of earning a card. At the end of the year you could exchange the cards for books, or other valuables. At the previous school, with no reinforcements, I was at the bottom of the distribution. But at the French school I suddenly moved to the top. Thus, my experience was that I did not get along with the Greek school, while I did get along with the French school. That must have made me decidedly less ethno-centric, and open to understanding other cultures, since I felt quite good about my relationships with non-Greeks.

In 1941 the Germans occupied Greece. They paid no attention to the food needs of the population. On the contrary, they shipped what food they could to Germany. Within a month of the occupation I was hungry. My mother's family had a large farm on the island of Corfu. There was food there. I went to the Corfu Lyceum, a high school that emphasised the sciences rather than literature. I was good at maths and did not like ancient Greek, which was taught for fourteen hours per week at the regular high school. I would rather spend my time on maths and physics than on Homer. Ancient Greek is, of course, part of the heritage of the collective, and while a bit of it is fine, fourteen hours per week seemed excessive, and was one more factor in my rejection of the collective.

Corfu was occupied by the Italians. They fired the Greek teachers and substituted Italian teachers. We went on strike. No school for a year!

That was the year when I learned the most. I had private lessons: mathematics and physics, Greek, French, German, English, Italian. The private tutors were paid in oil, from my mother's property. This schedule was insufficient to keep me totally busy, so I spent much of my time reading the 24-volume encyclopedia that I found in the house. I loved that set! It was so interesting discovering concepts from psychology, sociology, political science, physics, mathematics, theology.

Being on strike is fine, but what would one do after the strike? I had to make sure that I could function at the next level of the school. Just in case the Italians did not lose the war, I had better learn Italian. But hoping that the Allies would win, I also started learning English. English was so easy! Maybe because I liked the Allies, or may be because it was my fifth language so I had learned how to learn, six months of twice a week tutoring by the lady who taught my mother a quarter of a century earlier had me speaking fluently.

Of course, I needed to practice. Fortunately, the local mental institution had a seventy-year-old fellow whose father was Greek but whose mother was English, and who spoke excellent English. He had recovered by that time, but the hospital did not want to expel him at that age. To earn a bit of cash he gave English conversation lessons. My English improved so much that after the liberation I got my first job as an interpreter for an American who was part of the United Nations observers of the referendum that brought back the King of Greece.

My world view was shaping up. All religions, I concluded, are systems of self-deception organised by power-hungry priests. People need to deceive themselves, because they feel better when they think that their prayers will change the course of events. They like to think that they will end up in paradise. Priests take advantage of this human proclivity, and kill those humans who disagree with them, as during the Inquisition, and send them to death so that the priests will acquire more power (the sacrifice of Iphegenia in Aulis; contemporary jihads). At age sixteen I debated the existence of God with no less than the bishop of Corfu, and developed the sense that I floored him. He probably had not met a person who was so disrespectful as to present such views before. Of course, since religion is a very important element of the Greek collective, the fact that I rejected it made me an individualist.

At that point it occurred to me that I should become a university professor. I loved studying, debating. Is that not what professors do? But the idea did not seem practical. I had to make a living. Thus, after the liberation I went back to Athens, and competed to get into the Technical University. That is the most selective institution of higher learning in Greece, and engineering has more prestige than most professions. But just after the war the higher education system was in bad shape. My father told me that I had to go abroad. The universities that were untouched by the war were in North America. Hence, McGill in Montreal, Canada.

In January 1948 I landed in North America. Moving from 50°F to minus 10°F was quite an experience. I fell several times each week until I learned to walk on the snow. Since I was good at maths and physics, I was able to complete the bachelor's degree in engineering with honours. At that point I had the inclination to go on to graduate work in engineering, but I had no money. I had to work for a while.

I interviewed with Procter & Gamble, and was offered a job in Hamilton, Ontario. Between the interview and the job offer, I also interviewed with a government research outfit in Ottawa. When the offer from P&G came it was too wonderful to believe: $275 per month! I accepted instantly. Then the Ottawa offer came, and it was $250, but it was research and more to my taste. I went to see the head of the department to ask for advice. He had no doubts. I had accepted the P&G job, and that was that! He told me that having accepted that offer was like 'swearing on a stack of Bibles'. I went to Hamilton.

My moving from collectivist Greece to individualist North America, of course, allowed me to make many cross-cultural observations. I noted, for instance, that my Canadian friends did not protect unfavourable information about their families the way Greek families did. Collectivists do not 'wash dirty linen' even in front of their best friends; individualists sometimes do. Social relations in Canada were friendly but superficial, while in Greece they were much more intimate. But one could not become friends as easily in Greece as in Canada. I also noticed that my fellow students were different. McGill is a very international campus, and I had fellow students from many countries. Some were very close to their parents, as I was, writing a letter every two or three days, with details about their lives. Others saw their parents only for Christmas. What was very surprising to me was that so many Canadian students would not go to see their parents though they lived only a few hundred miles away.

I did not see mine for six years, because travel to Greece was too expensive and also somewhat dangerous. When I crossed the Atlantic by air in 1948, three planes had crashed that very week. So, I was far away from home and very much on my own. What better regime for shaping individualism?

Now I will go back to the tale of what happened after I graduated from McGill. As I mentioned I went to Hamilton, which is only one hour from Toronto. The University of Toronto offered an executive Master of Commerce degree, very similar to the MBA that was just then emerging as a degree in North America. It required going to Toronto every Saturday and one evening during the week. It took me three years to complete that degree. One of the courses for that degree was a turning point in my life.

It was titled Human Relations in Industry. When six of us arrived at the appointed time and place, there was no professor. We introduced ourselves. One of us said: 'My name is Bob Joyner, and the university thinks that I will teach this course, but learning has to be active. You have to decide what to learn and how to learn it.' It took us quite a few sessions to get a reading list out of him. He came up with 200 books! Having nothing better to do, since the 8 to 5 job at P&G was not very demanding, I read quite a few of them. It was anthropology, psychology, sociology. I was fascinated. One could actually make a living dealing with this stuff!

At that point I wrote to a psychologist who had married an engineer: Lillian Gilbreth (of *Cheaper by the Dozen* fame). Would she advise a shift in careers? She answered in detail, and said 'Yes'. I decided to forget about graduate work in engineering and become a psychologist.

Of course, I had essentially no background in that field. I went to McGill and talked to Ed Webster, who taught industrial psychology. He told me I had to spend a year learning undergraduate psychology. He arranged for me to teach industrial engineering at McGill's extension programme. That made it financially possible.

The 1954–5 year was wonderful. I absorbed psychology the way a thirsty wanderer drinks out of a mountain spring. I had teachers like Hebb, Olds (discoverer of the Olds effect), and Wally Lambert, as well as Webster.

In December it was time to apply to graduate schools. My transcript, however, only listed engineering courses, because most of the McGill courses run until April. I applied to Princeton, Harvard, Michigan, and Cornell. Only Cornell accepted me, and it took Wally Lambert some time on the phone to convince Robbie McLeod, of phenomenological psychology fame, that I knew some psychology and that my English was good enough to do graduate work.

Cornell turned out to be the best choice for me, because the system assumes that the student is mature and can be guided by a committee of three people to do the right things to complete a degree. I did my PhD (1958) in three years. The Cornell system does not always work out for some students. Returning to Cornell, for a year as a visiting full professor in 1968, I found that one of the fellows who had entered at the same time with me was still looking for a dissertation topic. He had played a lot of tennis in the intervening years.

My committee chair was Bill Lambert, Wally's brother. He was doing the six-cultures study with Whiting and Child. He was a walking encyclopedia, from learning theory, which he mastered when he took his degree at Harvard with Dick Solomon, to anthropology and sociology. He is the only man I know who headed all three departments sometime during his career, and eventually became Dean of the Cornell Graduate School.

The other two members were Bill Whyte, of *Street Corner Society* fame, which I had read in Bob Joyner's course in Toronto, and Art Ryan, author of an important text on industrial psychology. Pat Smith, of the famous Job Description Inventory to measure job satisfaction, also talked with me a lot, and we had many pleasant evenings at her home.

Whyte insisted that I take cultural anthropology, which I did under Morris Opler and Alexander Leighton. He also put me into one of the best courses that I have ever had. It was a course on methods of social research, financed by a $25,000 grant from the Social Science Research Council. It included not only lectures from faculty about their particular way of doing research, from anthropology to statistics, but intensive 'do it yourself' experiences of every one of the methods – systemic observations, interviews, IQ tests, personality tests, unobtrusive methods, laboratory experiments, field experiments, surveys, translations of questionnaires, and the use of Human Relations Area Files. Later, when I read Don Campbell about multimethod research, I felt confident that I could do it, because I had done it in that course.

For each method, we read a stack of commentaries that were mimeographed and distributed to every student and provided guidance on dos and don'ts, and we actually collected some data. A Teaching Assistant for every six students ensured close supervision.

At a seminar I was given the job of reporting on Fechner's work. I found it so up-to-date that I wrote to E.G. Boring, who was 'Mr History of Psychology' at that time, suggesting that he should edit a volume of works from the past that had contemporary value. He answered in great detail, telling me that each study must be seen in its historical context, and the *Zeitgeist* of the period was essential for understanding it, so that a volume that has the content without the context would not be valuable. I was impressed that so famous a person would answer in such detail a letter from a graduate student. I resolved in the future to answer mail from students and young colleagues. Clearly, the lessons from Lillian Gilbreth and E.G. Boring had an effect on the way I dealt with my correspondence, as Michael Bond reminded me in 1995.

My savings during the years in engineering made it possible for me to spend my first summer in graduate school in Europe: France, Germany, Switzerland, Italy, Greece. I had been away for 6½ years, and it was wonderful to go back.

Europe was wonderful, because I felt so much at home. In Paris, for two weeks, I went to the *Comédie française*, and found that I could follow the theatre rather well. In Germany I went down the Rhine on a boat, seeing the Lorelei and the Black Forest just as in the German books I had read. In Switzerland I visited an aunt and she advised me on what to see. In Italy, Milan, Venice, Florence, Rome, Naples, Bari, Brindisi provided a month of contrasts, arguments with waiters about being overcharged, which I managed in my Italian, and opera performances that remain unforgettable. Finally, Greece. A delegation of relatives met my boat. After all these years of separation, it was one of the highlights of my life. The family collectivism was still in place!

But intellectually, Greece was not exciting. There were many things about the culture, such as the bureaucracy and high-power distance that I disliked. I decided that no culture is perfect. All cultures are flawed, and it would be an interesting task to figure out what 'works well' and what does not. There is too much cultural lag. Behaviours that were effective a few centuries earlier become encrusted as customs that are burdens on everyday life. While family collectivism was wonderful, the culture did not agree with me. I liked North America better. I had become an individualist.

That summer I had a small grant from the National Institute of Mental Health to replicate Osgood's work on the structure of meaning with monolingual subjects from Greece. Taking advantage of a two-week stay at a village in Corfu, I also tested people who had not been to the movies, showing the standard set of pictures of emotional expression produced by Schlosberg. Even though they had no experience of movies they recognised the emotions that were expressed in those pictures about as well as did American subjects. It showed that emotional expressions may be recognised the same way regardless of culture. Quoting this paper later, Ekman received a grant to study the phenomenon in New Guinea. Two papers came out of that cross-cultural summer, both in the *Journal of Abnormal and Social Psychology*, edited at that time by Brewster Smith (Triandis and Osgood, 1958, and Triandis and Lambert, 1958).

In the spring of 1957 I gave my first paper at the meetings of the Eastern Psychological Association in New York. It reported on the emotion study. Schlosberg was in the audience and was enthusiastic. Since he was the author of the most important text on experimental psychology at the time, that praise got me imprinted on going to conferences. In fact, I have been to all the international congresses of psychology, except one (the year my daughter was born), since 1960.

Osgood and I corresponded about the summer study, and after the data were analysed we met in New York and agreed on the wording of the paper. When I was about to complete my degree at Cornell, he went to Lyle Lanier, head of the department at Illinois, and told him that I was 'a real catch'. Lanier offered me a job, sight unseen. It was an unbelievable salary: $6,200 for nine months. When I told the Cornell faculty, they said, 'Take it!' McLeod told me that though he had a chair he was making only 50 per cent more than that! Given the lack of opportunities in psychology in Greece, and the attractiveness of the Illinois job, the possibility of returning to Greece was not even raised by anyone.

Illinois was very good to me. The department was full of famous psychologists – Cronbach, Eriksen, Humpreys, Hunt, Mowrer, Osgood, P.T. Young. Other contemporaries, like Bill McGuire, were available for lunch every day. Excellent students made it a pleasure to be there. I was free to explore, and explore I did. Eriksen invited me to a meeting of a society where psychologists under age forty congregated once a year. There I met Len Berkowitz who was starting his series of *Advances* volumes. He asked me to do one on culture. I read a great deal in preparation. That was my immersion into emics and etics and the like (Triandis, 1964) and the beginnings of the analysis of subjective culture.

The issue of how to develop equivalent measurements in different cultures was solved by using Thurstone standardisation in each culture (Triandis, Davis and Takezawa, 1965; Triandis, 1992). That meant that etic constructs, such as social distance, had to be operationalised emically and the items generated by focus groups in each culture had to be scaled locally.

In 1964–5 I had my first sabbatical, and I went around the world (thanks to a contract with the US Navy) collecting collaborators for what eventually became the *Analysis of subjective culture* (Triandis, 1972). It was a trip full of cross-cultural experiences. Japan, Hong Kong, Malaysia, and a month in India, Iran, Israel, and the rest of the time in Europe, provided a strong contrast between the collectivists and the individualists. By that time I was an individualist, but I understood collectivist cultures. Related themes emerged in the book.

The Navy contract had four principal investigators: Fred Fiedler, Charlie Osgood, Larry Stolurow, and myself. The idea was to see how to train Navy personnel to behave appropriately when in contact with members of other cultures. That meant that the Navy had to provide the correct leadership (Fiedler), learn how to teach Navy personnel about communication (Osgood), figure out what it is about culture that should be taught (that was my job) and put it into computers so they could learn it through Skinnerian programme learning (Stolurow). The idea of a 'culture assimilator' that would include episodes of interaction involving people from different cultures and would require judgements about why each person acted that way, with feedback to correct poor judgements involving such attributions, was generated over breakfast at a meeting of the four PIs.

The issue was what to teach about culture. Culture had to be broken down into categories, associations, role and self-perceptions, values. These elements of subjective culture take different forms in different cultures. Data collected in Japan, India, and Greece showed these contrasts clearly.

A portion of that sabbatical was spent in Greece at the Institute of Anthropos, with George and Vasso Vassiliou. The Institute was a Vassiliou private entity. It had, however, research associates, such as Jim Georgas, and research assistants, such as Maria Nassiakou. Money came from market surveys and the Navy contract, and I taught the Vassilious how to use a 60 per cent overhead to pay the rent, electricity, and the research assistants who were not working directly on the contract. It was a wonderfully productive period. Vasso did surveys ('What kind of toothpaste do you like?') with representative samples, of the population of Athens and Thessalonike, and we added questions that tapped subjective culture elements in between. The Triandis, Vassiliou and Nassiakou (1968) monograph came out of that year's work.

The analysis of subjective culture (Triandis, 1972) followed soon after, much of it written on the island of Aegina, with my wife Pola helping to make it come out in good English. In that book, I also tried to show how culture is related to social behaviour, which resulted in a model that links elements of subjective culture and behaviour (Triandis 1977, 1980). This model is now widely used by health psychologists and research nurses.

Looking at my total career, I feel very satisfied with the way things went. So many things could have led me astray from what the American Psychological Association said when they gave me their Distinguished Award in International Psychology. They obviously exaggerated when they said that I established cross-cultural psychology as a separate scientific discipline. Yes, I had something to do with it, but I certainly did not establish the field alone. The co-authors I mention above had a lot to do with it, and the many wonderful students I had in Illinois taught me a lot while I was teaching them. If luck had been different, I might have been a Patras industrialist, a professor of engineering, or a manager of a soap factory. I think I was fortunate to have escaped those fates and instead be able to satisfy my curiosity about what makes people from different cultures see the world, judge it, and evaluate it both similarly and differently. It has been such fun!

I think that because I became an individualist through my unique experiences across cultural lines, I was able to get into topics and areas of investigation that were not popular at the time I started them. For example, cross-cultural research in general, and the study of individualism and collectivism in particular, were not 'on the map' in a significant way when I tackled them. My personal journey liberated me for my intellectual journey.

REFERENCES

Triandis, H.C. (1964). Cultural influences upon cognitive processes. In L. Berkowitz (ed.), *Advances in experimental social psychology* (vol. 1, pp. 1–48). New York: Academic Press.

Triandis, H.C. (1972). *The analysis of subjective culture*. New York: John Wiley.

Triandis, H.C. (1977). *Interpersonal behavior*. Monterey: Brooks/Cole.

Triandis, H.C. (1980). Values, attitudes and interpersonal behavior. In H.E. Howe and M.M. Page (eds), *Nebraska symposium on motivation, 1979* (pp. 195–260). Lincoln, NB: University of Nebraska Press.

Triandis, H.C. (1992). Cross-cultural research in social psychology. In D. Granberg and G. Sarup (eds), *Social judgment and intergroup relations: Essays in honor of Muzafer Sherif* (pp. 229–244). New York: Springer Verlag.

Triandis, H. C. and Lambert, W. W. (1958). A restatement and test of Schlosberg's theory of emotion with two kinds of subjects from Greece. *Journal of Abnormal and Social Psychology, 56*, 321–328.

Triandis, H. C. and Osgood, C. E. (1958). A comparative factorial analysis of semantic structures of monolingual Greek and American students. *Journal of Abnormal and Social Psychology, 57*. 187–196.

Triandis, H.C, Davis, E.E. and Takezawa, S. (1965). Some determinants of social distance among Americans, German, and Japanese students. *Journal of Personality and Social Psychology, 2*, 540–551.

Triandis, H.C., Vassiliou, V. and Nassiakou, M. (1968). Three cross-cultural studies of subjective culture. *Journal of Personality and Social Psychology, Monograph Supplement, 8*, No.4, 1–42.

5   The Archimedes effect

Geert Hofstede

THE METAMORPHOSIS OF AN ENGINEER[1]

Some time in 1963 I took a walk with our eldest son, Gert Jan, who was then six or seven. I was a thirty-five-year-old manager in a Dutch textile firm, with a degree in mechanical engineering. I asked Gert Jan what he wanted to be when he was big. After some reflection, he said: 'I want to be a scholar' (*geleerde* in Dutch). 'Gosh, Gert Jan, that is what I would want too!' Gert Jan smiled: 'Yes, but in your case, of course, it's too late now!' As a matter of fact, it wasn't.

At that time I had already made up my mind not to remain an engineer all my life. I wanted to go back to university and get some kind of qualification in the social and economic side of organisations. As an engineering student I had been much impressed by a dissertation from a Dutch Jesuit priest, A.M. Kuylaars (1951). Kuylaars studied the impact of job content on the life of workers. He was inspired by, among others, the French sociologist Georges Friedmann (1946). Neither Kuylaars nor Friedmann ever became known in the USA, although Kuylaars's research led to similar conclusions as the US study by Herzberg and his collaborators eight years later (1959). Kuylaars distinguished between the 'external' and the 'internal' productivity of labour. The external productivity is based on the amount of goods and services produced. The internal productivity is related to human development and self-actualisation: Kuylaars used in Dutch the word *zelfverwerkelijking*, the exact equivalent of the term later to be popularised in the USA by Maslow (1954). Kuylaars's book had been a revelation to me; it integrated technology and humanity. Technology was the field I was being trained in; humanity was my deepest concern as a person, and a major theme in the programmes of a Christian student association in which I took an active role. That book put me on a track I have never left since.

Up till then the Dutch university system had granted doctorates only to persons having a master's level degree in the same field. Thus, with my master's level degree in engineering I would only have been able to get a doctorate in engineering. For any other doctorate I would have had to complete another master's study first, which was almost prohibitive. A change of the law in 1963 allowed departments to accept doctoral candidates from any field, subject only to the judgement of the faculty; that change opened my way to a doctorate in social science.

Doctorates in the Netherlands required the completion of a thesis under the direction of a Thesis Adviser (*Promotor* in Dutch), but no further courses or examinations. For a thesis subject I had started with some vague ideas about research into employee motivation. Gradually, remembering job experiences with incentive schemes and with standard setting, I narrowed my subject down to the psychological impact of standards and budgets on the people involved. After all, these techniques were intended as (among other things) tools for motivation.

A well-known professor of social psychology at the University of Groningen, Herman Hutte, accepted me as an external doctoral candidate and my subject as a thesis theme. Herman gave me a list of books to read to fill the gaps in my professional knowledge. One book in particular influenced me greatly: a Dutch textbook on social science research methodology by A.D. de Groot (1961). De Groot was both a mathematician and a psychologist; he wrote a famous doctoral dissertation on the thinking process of chess players, which inspired the work of, among others, Herbert Simon in the USA. De Groot's methodology book showed me the similarities and the differences between the exact sciences, in which I had been trained so far, and the social sciences which I now entered.

An unpaid 50 per cent leave of absence from my employer for two years and a 25,000 guilder stipend from the Dutch Productivity Committee (*COP*) created the marginal conditions to achieve my goal. We were a young family; Maaike Van den Hoek and I were married in 1955, and our third son Bart was born in 1964. Maaike had a masters' level degree in French language and literature, and in between babies she worked as a part-time secondary school teacher. She supported my study as a matter of course; on hindsight this contribution appears less obvious than it looked at the time.

My textile company was not a suitable place to do research, as I would not have been perceived as an impartial observer. With an introduction from the *COP* I was allowed to study experiences with standards and budgets in six manufacturing plants of five Dutch companies; one of them was the typewriter plant of IBM Netherlands in Amsterdam.

In early 1964 I made a four-week trip to the USA, my first. For my employer I visited modern textile plants in New England, the Carolinas and Georgia. Then, under my 50 per cent leave scheme, I set off to academia and visited the Institute for Social Research in Ann Arbor, Michigan; Cornell University in Ithaca, New York; Yale University in New Haven, Connecticut; and MIT at Cambridge, Massachusetts. I met many of the academics whose work I had read before; one was Chris Argyris at Yale, who gave me a copy of his earlier psychological study of budgeting (1952), as far as I know the first ever. I also met Andrew Stedry at MIT who had won an award with a PhD thesis on budgeting (1960) and from whom I borrowed the key concept of 'aspiration levels' as the link between the formal budget and the informal motivation.

After my return home I worked under high pressure, half time for my employer and the other half, plus vacations, on my thesis. I spent over 400 hours in the six plants doing semi-structured interviews with line managers of all levels and with staff employees in charge of standard setting and budget administration.

My research contacts with IBM led to a job offer in IBM World Trade, which I accepted. In September 1965 I became a trainer in the European Executive Development Department at Blaricum near Amsterdam, with the special assignment to set up a Personnel Research Department for IBM Europe.

So I quit the textile industry and my life as an engineer. As a family we moved to Blaricum; our fourth and youngest son Gideon was born there in 1967. Maaike found another secondary school, continuing to teach French on a part-time basis.

My doctoral thesis *The game of budget control* (1967) was finished in the summer vacation of 1966, and the public defence at the University of Groningen took place in March of the next year. I owe a lot to my *Promotor*, Herman Hutte. He built up my self-confidence; after all, I entered the field of psychology as an amateur; but he took me seriously, and taught me to think as a social scientist. The conclusion of my research was that budget systems potentially held a strong motivating power, because they affected the budgetees' performance aspiration levels. The motivation by budget systems was optimal if higher management maintained a game spirit around the achievement of budgetary targets by lower-level managers. Too much pressure led to evasive behaviour; not enough attention led to neglect. Participation in budget-setting, then an ideologically popular theme, had some influence on motivation, but less than the literature claimed. The idea of budgeting as a 'game' was, in fact, a cultural interpretation, although at the time I had not recognised it as such.

The thesis had been written in English, checked by an American colleague at IBM. I saw myself as communicating with the international community, not only with the tiny number of potentially interested readers in the Dutch language area. In the Netherlands we learn our foreign languages at secondary school – mine had been a *Gymnasium* which meant, next to our native Dutch, taking French, German and English, plus classical Latin and Greek. Languages have always fascinated me. I later taught in Dutch, English, French and German, and on odd occasions in Italian, picked up on the basis of my school Latin.

My thesis was well received. I got a *cum laude* qualification, a national award, and two publishing houses, one in the Netherlands (1967) and one in Britain (1968), distributed commercial editions of the study. Much later it turned out I had become one of the Founding Fathers of a new field called Behavioural Accounting: in spite of having deserted this field quickly after siring my intellectual offspring.

THE IBM WORLD

One of the characteristics of the IBM corporate culture was a strong concern of managers with employee morale. This grew out of the convictions of IBM's founder Thomas J. Watson Sr many decades before, and it was made one of the basic beliefs ('respect for the individual') in which newcomers were socialised. Given this concern with employee morale, employee attitude surveys were something natural. In 1966–7 I headed up an international team of six researchers who prepared IBM's first internationally standardised questionnaire, for the personnel of IBM's Development Laboratories in six European countries; it was issued in five languages. Strong support came from the new Personnel Research Manager at the IBM World Trade Head Office in New York, David Sirota. David had a vision of standardising and internationalising surveys throughout IBM worldwide, to create a comparability of results, over time, across countries, and across functions. Between 1967 and 1970 he and my team managed to survey virtually all of IBM's personnel outside the USA.

The international attitude surveys were not sold to IBM management as a research project, but as a tool for organisation development. I had to visit all the Country General Managers in the European area to convince them of the survey's usefulness. Considerable attention was given to providing data feedback to managers of different levels, as well as to the employees themselves.

In 1969 both David Sirota and I received an IBM Outstanding Contribution Award for our work on the survey programme. It was the first time the award had gone to someone in the personnel function. The international surveys had become an established practice in IBM. Personnel departments of all major parts of the organisation had appointed personnel research officers. Within this new personnel research fraternity we planned a survey approach for the next round, settling for a core set of sixty questions to be used in all surveys, and additional functional and national questions according to need. The core items were selected on the basis of an extensive study of the available literature, and of factor analyses of the results obtained in the first survey round (Hofstede, Kraut, and Simonetti, 1976). At the end of the second round, in 1973, some 117,000 questionnaires had been collected from all functions and levels in the company in seventy-two countries, using twenty different languages.

In the summer of 1971 our family moved to Switzerland. I had obtained a two-year leave from IBM in order to teach at IMEDE Management Development Institute in Lausanne (now called IMD). Our four boys shifted to French-speaking local schools. The eldest two attended a very good and progressive canton (public) *collège secondaire*. At the end of their first year at school they were present during an incident which I documented in a case study 'Confrontation in the cathedral' (Hofstede, 1977, 1994) – the conflict between a brilliant but critical student and an autocratic public authority system.

At IMEDE, besides teaching, I had time to do research, and with the help of a student assistant from the Technical University I started to do statistical analyses of the IBM attitude survey data base; trying to solve all the puzzles that had come to my mind earlier, but for which the IBM job did not leave me the time to work on them. I had recognised that the answers to some of the IBM questions differed from country to country, following a pattern that seemed to repeat itself from one employee category to the next. These were in particular the questions dealing with basic values of the respondents, rather than with their attitudes about daily events in the company.

In my IMEDE classes I administered a number of the same questions; and the answers by my management students, none of whom were from IBM, showed similar country differences as the IBM employees. This convergence of results proved something that I had suspected all along: the vast IBM employee survey material contained information not only about IBM, but about differences in attitudes between nationals of different countries, IBMers or not. The IBM population was a very specific sample from the national populations, but it was extremely well matched from country to country: same corporate culture, same education level, same kind of jobs, similar age and gender distribution. Serendipitously, the IBM data bank had become a major source of comparative information about the national societies these IBMers came from.

In the summer of 1973 I was due back at IBM. My boss, the European Personnel Director, wanted me to move to the Paris office now, again as Manager of Personnel Research, which had been my title since 1968. I offered a counter-proposal. Showing some results of my recent analysis of the IBM data bank, I proposed to step down to a researcher position, and to do a special study on the meaning of what I found for IBM management. My boss, however, said that he needed me in my manager role, and that the project I proposed was too academic for the company; I could give it to some university. Another issue was my date of return. We had planned the realisation of an old dream: a three months' expedition of the whole family to Greece and Turkey. My American boss had no sympathy with long vacations and wanted me back in August. This was the last straw; we agreed that I would quit IBM and find a university base to continue my research on the IBM data bank.

THE CREATIVE YEARS

I was offered a position at INSEAD, the international business school in Fontainebleau, France, but I hesitated, knowing that INSEAD was a teaching rather than a research institution. Then I had another offer from the European Institute for Advanced Studies in Management (EIASM) in Brussels, Belgium, which had been founded in 1971 as an international think tank. This suited my research objectives, but I did not want to quit teaching altogether. I ended up with a two-year contract for two half-time jobs, one teaching at INSEAD and one researching at EIASM. We would move our home to Brussels.

At INSEAD I became a staff member of CEDEP (*Centre d'Education Permanente*), providing post-experience training to managers from an international consortium of companies. Most of these, however, were French multinationals, and I was asked to teach part of my classes in French. I bribed a kind participant, promising him a drink at the bar every night if he kept a list of my recurrent language errors, and I think we succeeded in weeding out my worst mistakes this way. I enjoyed teaching high-calibre, experienced participants; I also enjoyed an eminent group of colleagues who stimulated my thinking, in particular André Laurent, Sami Kassem and Owen James Stevens.

In Brussels, at EIASM, I found the time and the quiet to really dig into the IBM data. There was a good library where I hunted for related literature; I had computer support from a service bureau, and access to a terminal where I could do the simpler analyses myself in timesharing. I exchanged views with colleagues from other European countries, and ventilated the progress of my own work through the Institute's Working Paper series – which was a way of getting feedback from the selected circle of colleagues who read them. I attended workshops, and served on the thesis committees of doctoral candidates from different countries.

My initial estimate had been that the two years of the contract would be enough to write up the conclusions from the IBM study. However, the job soon appeared much bigger than I had realised. I made fundamental discoveries and had to make fundamental decisions about the conduct of the study. One discovery was that I was no longer dealing with psychological issues; what I studied were manifestations of the national cultures of countries. Culture became a key word in my study. The relevance of culture for organisations and management was not as obvious in the 1970s as it later became. Using a metaphor from the then increasingly popular computer field, I coined my own household definition of what I meant by 'culture': 'the collective programming of the mind which distinguishes the members of one group or category of people from another' (Hofstede, 1980, p. 21; 1991, p. 5).

My own interest in culture was supported by the entire family. We had all become quite culture-sensitive. Cultural differences were not only an intellectual exercise – we lived them. After all, this was our third country, and we often discussed our daily experiences in culturally comparative terms, especially at the dinner table. I remember my telling about the relationship between authority and obedience – something I was exploring in relation to the emerging concept of power distance – and Rokus, who was about sixteen, remarking that he had just learned at school about a sixteenth-century French writer who had argued the same. This is how I found out about Etienne de la Boétie (1530–1563) and his *Discours de la servitude volontaire*: a tyrant has no other power than his subjects choose to allow him. But we also understood why this book had come to be written in France, and not somewhere else.

Focusing on culture, I left the field of psychology proper; I was practising the comparative anthropology of modern societies. The difference between a psychological and an anthropological approach to the data became operationally clear in the choice of the level of analysis. As a psychologist I had been accustomed to correlating the answers of individual respondents, that is to analyse at the level of individuals. In comparing countries I had to correlate mean scores for the respondents from these countries. This is not a trivial matter: the two approaches can lead to entirely different results. Other categories for aggregating the data, like occupation, again lead to different correlations, and therefore different conclusions. Correlating individual data appeals to psychologists, correlating social categories to sociologists, and correlating country data to political scientists and anthropologists. As a reformed engineer I had never been a complete psychologist, which must have made it easier for me than for fully fledged psychologists to switch my level of analysis. I still meet many psychologists who cannot mentally adjust to this switch.

Moving from an individual-level to a country-level analysis did simplify my analysis task tremendously: I was no longer dealing with 117,000 individual responses, but with responses from forty countries (from the total of seventy-two countries for which I had some data, I initially took only the ones with more than fifty IBM respondents per survey round per country, to be statistically conservative).

It was obvious that I would have to extend my research time beyond the two years of my contract with EIASM, and I applied for financial support from IBM's University Relations office. IBM granted US$50,000 to support my research. For the next four years, from 1975 through 1979, I spent most of my time researching, reducing my teaching at CEDEP/INSEAD to about 20 per cent.

It was around 1975 that I started to think of the country differences in the IBM data bank in terms of *dimensions*. I had first analysed the answers on questions related to the distribution of power. This led to the identification of a characteristic of national societies that I labelled power distance, ranking from relatively equal (like Denmark) to very unequal (like the Philippines). Answers to other questions in the IBM database also showed stable distribution patterns across countries, but not the same pattern as power distance. Searching further I identified three more dimensions: uncertainty avoidance, individualism–collectivism and masculinity–femininity. Across the forty countries, the last three were uncorrelated (orthogonal). Individualism was negatively correlated with power distance; but I hesitated to consider them as aspects of the same dimension because the two were conceptually distinct. In fact the reason for the correlation was external: country individualism scores were positively correlated with national wealth, and power distance scores negatively; and if I kept wealth constant (comparing rich with rich and poor with poor countries), the correlation between power distance and collectivism disappeared.

Finding significant correlations of individualism and power distance scores with wealth (per capita gross national product) meant external validation: it showed unambiguously that the responses of the IBM employees contained information about their countries not specific to IBM. I started searching the literature for other quantitative results of country comparisons that could be expected to correlate with the IBM country dimension scores. I had opened a Pandora's box: there was much more related literature than I had ever dreamt of, in sociology, anthropology, psychology, political science, market research, demography, economics, even comparative medicine. In the end I had found some forty studies external to the IBM study that showed country scores significantly and meaningfully correlated with the IBM dimensions. The pattern of external validations, of course, helped considerably in interpreting the dimensions. The greater part of my 1980 book is devoted to these validations and their interpretation.

The theoretical meaning of the dimensions is, I believe, that they reflect basic problems that every human society encounters, and for each of which a range of solutions is possible. Power distance stands for social inequality, individualism for the relationship between the individual and the collective, masculinity for the social role distribution between the genders, and uncertainty avoidance for coping with the unknown future.

My choice of the label masculinity–femininity has been criticised a lot, oddly enough almost exclusively in countries which I found to score 'masculine'. I think I had, and still have, good reasons for my choice. This dimension was the only one for which the country scores depended strongly on the gender of the respondents. Country scores on femininity correlate with several indexes of gender role distribution in societies, such as the percentage of women in elected political offices, women in higher professional roles, and the extent to which women and men pursue the same degrees in higher education. The resistance to the term in some countries showed that I had hit upon a culturally sensitive issue; fine, what else was to be expected?

Altogether, the analysis of the IBM databank during my six years at the Brussels EIASM filled seventeen working papers. At the end, I re-worked these into a book manuscript 'Dimensions of national cultures', and wrote to nineteen American publishers asking about their interest. Only half of them reacted, mostly by a letter in the sense of 'your manuscript looks very interesting but it does not fit our list'. One asked to see the manuscript. In the meantime, however, I had attended the fourth conference of the International Association for Cross-cultural Psychology, of which I had become a member. The conference was held at Munich, Germany, in the summer of 1978. There I met Professor Harry C. Triandis from the USA whom I told about my project. Harry, an eminent and broad scholar, immediately recognised the potential importance of what I had to offer. He spoke to Walter J. Lonner and John W. Berry who had been appointed series editors for a new series with Sage Publications, California, on 'Cross-cultural Research and Methodology'. Sage was also one of the nineteen publishers I had written to myself. By the same mail that I received their 'it does not fit our list' letter from a lower authority, there was another letter from the publisher and president, Sara Miller McCune, expressing her interest in publishing the book, on the recommendation of Lonner and Berry.

Sara and I met in London in 1979. We spent hours in an Italian restaurant discussing the project. One problem was that the manuscript was far too long for a regular social science publication, but Sara showed herself flexible: she believed in the book. We arrived at a compromise that I would leave out some appendices and Sara would use a smaller type size and a larger number of pages than normal (475, as it turned out). Also, Sara suggested another title: 'Culture's consequences'. The book appeared in December 1980.

In 1979 I spent most of the spring at the International Institute for Applied Systems Analysis (IIASA) at Laxenburg Castle near Vienna, Austria. IIASA was an East–West institute, hosting scholars from either side of the Iron Curtain that in those days still separated the communist from the capitalist world. Working and partying side-by-side with Hungarians, Poles, Czechs, East Germans and Russians opened new perspectives.

CULTURE'S FURTHER CONSEQUENCES

In many respects 1979 was a turning point. My book had gone to the printer, my contracts with CEDEP and EIASM would once more expire, the rent agreement for our house in Brussels ran out, and the family decided that after eight years they wanted to go home to Holland. There was only one small problem: I was fifty-one and I did not have a job. I tried for a professorship at one of the Dutch universities but, with cuts in the education budget, departments were not very interested in a compatriot returning from abroad.

For a living I made some money from guest teaching, among others at INSEAD, and from a research contract. Maaike had spent the years in Brussels studying Islamic Studies at the Université Libre de Bruxelles; as a foreigner in Belgium she was not allowed to teach French. She graduated with a second master's level degree, but in Holland she got back into teaching French, contributing to the support of the family.

One day in the autumn of 1979 a headhunter approached me with a job offer. At the beginning of 1980, I found myself back in the business world for three days a week, as a Director of Human Resources of Fasson Europe at Leiden, Holland; the other two days I could use for my own continued research. I was responsible for Fasson's personnel management in seventeen countries. It was fascinating to see the differences in functioning from one subsidiary to another. For example, our manufacturing plants in Belgium, Britain, France and Holland all had some form of joint consultation between management and employees. I sat in joint consultation meetings in all four countries, but the dynamics were vastly different, following the power distance distinction I had identified in my research: active involvement of the employees in the discussion in Britain and Holland, passivity in Belgium and France.

Going back to 1980 for a moment, with my two days a week off from Fasson I could continue to do research, but I needed an institutional umbrella for doing so. Then I met Bob Waisfisz. Bob was a Dutchman with a university education in business administration and anthropology, who had worked in Lebanon and Turkey for the International Labour Organization, and later had run a Dutch non-governmental organisation for development assistance. Bob recognised the importance of my work for intercultural communication even before my book had appeared. In fact I think he believed in it more than I did myself. Bob suggested we could create our own research institute, as a non-profit foundation. On 16 December 1980, the Institute for Research on Intercultural Cooperation (IRIC) was founded. Bob was Chairman and I was Director. Our secretariat was at the institute in Delft where Bob worked at the time and where we paid his secretary for the hours she needed for IRIC.

In 1983 I left Fasson to become Dean of the Senior Management Forum (Semafor) in Arnhem, a non-profit foundation offering residential courses for higher-level managers; IRIC moved with me, and I continued to run it as a side activity. In 1985 I was finally offered a professor's chair, at Maastricht University; I went there full-time in 1986.

IRIC was definitely non-profit. During the first years we were glad when we could pay the out-of-pocket expenses, and our own time was unpaid. When I moved from Fasson to Semafor in 1983, the IRIC secretariat moved with me, to a small cubicle in the Semafor office. We engaged an unemployed teacher as a volunteer secretary. In 1984 results had become so much better that we could pay her a salary. It was not until 1988 though that IRIC became a going concern, able to pay even its Director.

In late December 1980 I attended the fifth conference of the International Association for Cross-cultural Psychology, which this time was held at Bhubaneswar, India. It was one of the most remarkable conferences I ever participated in, held on the campus of a local university where students and holy cows shared the lawns. I found myself assigned as a discussant to a session in which a Dr Michael H. Bond from Hong Kong presented a joint paper on 'Human values in nine countries', based on students' answers to a US questionnaire, the Rokeach Value Survey. Looking at the paper I found it to contain a basic level-of-analysis flaw: countries had been compared on indexes designed for comparing individuals. In *Culture's consequences* I had called this the 'reverse ecological fallacy'. In the discussion I argued that the authors had committed this fallacy, although I was afraid that the presenter would not appreciate me for making this criticism.

During the session there had been no time for a rejoinder, but in the evening there was an open-air reception for the conference participants. In the darkness a tall figure emerged behind me; it was Michael Bond. 'I have reflected on your comments of this afternoon,' he said. 'I think you were right.' This was the historic beginning of an intellectual partnership that has lasted until the present day. Michael did a re-analysis at the country level of the data from his presentation, and found them to reflect all four dimensions from my work. We reported this supportive result in a joint article (Hofstede and Bond, 1984).

In the summer of 1981 I visited Michael Bond in Hong Kong, after a lecturing tour of Japan and China. Our discussions dealt with cultural relativity and with the way minds are pre-programmed by culture, including the minds of researchers. Michael then conceived his Chinese Value Survey project: recognising that the results of surveys designed by Westerners were biased by their Western minds, he asked his Chinese colleagues to compose a questionnaire with a deliberate Chinese mental bias, and administered this survey around the world in Asian and non-Asian countries. I helped by finding a translator from Chinese to Dutch, motivating a colleague to administer the questionnaire to a sample of students in Holland.

The Chinese Value Survey also produced four country-level dimensions. Three were significantly correlated with three of the IBM dimensions, but no counterpart of uncertainty avoidance was found using the Chinese questions; instead, there was a new dimension which Michael Bond called 'Confucian work dynamism' and that I later re-baptised 'long-term orientation'. Long-term orientation as a values complex correlated with national economic growth in the past twenty-five years; as far as we knew, this was the first values measure ever that did so. This was an exciting finding; it became the theme of our next joint publication (Hofstede and Bond, 1988).

IRIC also started to produce interesting research. In 1981–2 I did a study for a Dutch management consulting firm that had started an office in Jakarta, Indonesia.

Indonesia did not figure among the forty countries from the IBM database that I had studied for *Culture's consequences*. There was an Indonesian sample in the IBM data, but I had initially omitted it, because it was (just) below the limit I had set of fifty respondents per survey round. I decided to lower the limit to twenty, which meant I could get scores on the four dimensions for another ten countries, plus for three multicountry regions assumed to be culturally more or less homogeneous: Arabic-speaking countries, East Africa, and West Africa. The country scores obtained in this way aligned themselves perfectly with the scores of the other countries, both impressionistically and in their correlations with outside indexes. From this moment onwards, I used the scores for fifty-three (50 + 3), rather than for forty countries in my writings (Hofstede, 1983).

The newly obtained score for Indonesia served as the basis for an in-depth comparison with the Netherlands. I revisited Indonesia (I had been there as an engineering student working on a ship in 1947) and interviewed a number of Indonesians in Jakarta about their experiences with Dutch expatriates. The result was a booklet *Cultural pitfalls for Dutch expatriates in Indonesia*, issued by the consultant to its customers. It turned out that Indonesians found it useful to become aware of cultural pitfalls in dealing with the Dutch (Hofstede, 1982).

For IRIC, Bob Waisfisz did a study of the problems encountered by Dutch expatriates in Saudi Arabia. The study was commissioned by a large Dutch contractor, Ballast-Nedam, that was doing a huge building project for the Saudis. On the basis of his research, Bob designed a training programme for future expatriates that used the four IBM dimensions (he called it the 4-D model) as a basis. When Ballast-Nedam's project ended, the programme was opened for participants from other companies. These trainings became quite a big operation, and in 1985 we decided that Bob would found a separate training institute, ITIM (Institute for Training in Intercultural Management), located in The Hague, while I retained the research activities within IRIC in Arnhem. ITIM has since subsidised IRIC's continued research.

Culture's consequences sold well. Sage and I had the good luck that the theme of national cultural differences, which had been an exotic hobby before, just became popular at the time the book appeared; and there was little serious competition. The reviews were mixed, some ecstatic, some irritated, condescending, or ridiculing. I had really made a paradigm shift in cross-cultural studies, and as Thomas Kuhn (1970) has shown, paradigm shifts in any science meet with strong initial resistance. Sage published an abridged paperback version in 1984. Paperback and hardcover together were still selling well in the mid-1990s; the book has become a classic.

Another topic that became popular in the early 1980s was organisational, or corporate, culture. Paradoxically, the IBM studies, although based on data from a corporation, did not yield any information about IBM's corporate culture, for lack of comparison. Studying organisational cultures would mean studying many organisations in one country, rather than, as in IBM, studying one organisation in many countries. After considerable efforts to sell the project to the participating organisations, IRIC could do the study with twenty units from ten organisations in two countries, the Netherlands and Denmark, varying from two police corps in Holland to the Lego toy plant in Denmark. We leased two researchers from the University of Groningen, Geert Sanders and Bram Neuijen. In Denmark a friend from the Association for Cross-cultural Psychology, Denise Daval Ohayv, provided the local coordination. We did interviews in all twenty units, employing eighteen graduate students and young professionals as interviewers whom we trained. The next phase was a survey study for which the questionnaire was based partly on the interviews and partly on the IBM cross-national study.

The project ran in 1985 and 1986; it led to several publications, of which the most complete appeared in *Administrative Science Quarterly* (Hofstede, Neuijen, Ohayv and Sanders, 1990). The key conclusion was that organisation cultures are not, as the faddish management literature claimed, a matter of shared values among an organisation's members. They are a much more superficial phenomenon: shared organisational practices, developed on the basis of the values of founders and significant top leaders. They could be measured along six dimensions which did not resemble the four IBM dimensions of national culture; the new dimensions belonged to sociology rather than anthropology; examples are process vs. results orientation and professional vs. parochial orientation.

At the University of Limburg at Maastricht (now called Maastricht University), in the far south-eastern tip of the Netherlands, the Department of Economics and Business Administration had started up in 1984. I was one of the early hires, a part-time Visiting Professor in 1985 and full-time since 1986. I defined my subject as 'Organisational Anthropology' (in Dutch: *Vergelijkende Cultuurstudies van Organisaties*). Later on 'and International Management' was added to the title of my Chair. I rented a small appartment in Maastricht which is a beautiful old city, and commuted once a week from and to Velp, a three-hour train ride.

IRIC was initially left in Arnhem; I spent one day a week at the IRIC office before or after going to Maastricht. In 1988 we reached an agreement with the university that IRIC would be brought under their umbrella as a financially independent unit.

My professorship gave me the time to write a popular book on culture. *Culture's consequences* was a scholarly volume, too difficult for students and lay readers; this consideration applied also to the abridged 1984 edition, although some professors have used it as a textbook for lack of better. Having trained various publics in intercultural communication, I had some idea of the desired level of sophistication for the new book. It became an update of the message of my earlier research, plus the results of Bond's Chinese Values Survey study, plus IRIC's Organisational Culture study, plus an extended part on applications and implications. I had separate chapters of the manuscript read by non-expert friends and students for clarity. The result was *Cultures and organizations: Software of the mind*, published in hardcover by McGraw-Hill UK, London, in 1991, and in paperback by HarperCollins UK in 1994 and by McGraw-Hill USA in 1996. The book was well received, and up till the end of 1996 has been translated into twelve other languages.

In the academic year 1990–1 I was granted a sabbatical, teaching for one semester at the University of Hong Kong, and the second semester at the University of Hawaii at Manoa. In Hong Kong I was made an Honorary Professor, which meant I could continue to serve on thesis committees. With Michael Bond and his assistant Chung-Leung Luk I worked on a re-analysis of the Dutch–Danish Organisational Culture data. I had analysed those data at the organisational level and found sociological dimensions. We found that when we re-analysed the same data at the individual level, after eliminating the between-organisation variance, we found six dimensions of individual personality, of which five corresponded with the 'big five' of modern personality theory; a wonderful illustration of the power of multilevel understanding (Hofstede, Bond and Luk, 1993).

On 1 October 1993, the day before my sixty-fifth birthday, I became an Emeritus. In my Valedictory Address *Images of Europe* (Hofstede, 1993) I looked at European integration in cultural terms, arguing that only a unity in diversity is attainable. Since my retirement I have been an Honorary Professor at the University of Hong Kong, and a Fellow of the Centre for Economic Studies of Tilburg University in the Netherlands. I also act as the Chairman of IRIC, which under its new Director, Niels Noorderhaven, is now affiliated with two universities: Maastricht and Tilburg.

An analysis of citations (using the Social Sciences Citation Index) shows that my work on culture has reached a wide public; I have become one of the most cited non-Americans in the SSCI. About 40 per cent of the citations are from psychology, about 40 per cent from business administration (including marketing); the remainder is from a wide variety of disciplines: sociology, anthropology, political science, history, law, philosophy, psychiatry, medicine, computer science. This variety suggests that I hit upon a common foundation stone of the sciences of man, beyond the specifics of any particular discipline.

Different disciplines tend to cite different dimensions. Psychologists most often refer to individualism–collectivism. Current psychological theories were developed in individualist Western cultures. The assertion that most non-western cultures are collectivist and therefore expect people to behave as ingroup members rather than as individuals appeals especially to psychologists from newly industrialising countries. The introduction of the individualism–collectivism dimension has led to a contingency approach to various psychological theories previously assumed to be universal, like Maslow's model of human needs. Besides many articles, two books have been devoted to this dimension alone (Kim, Triandis, Kağitçibaşi, Choi and Yoon, 1995; Triandis, 1995). The masculinity–femininity dimension has been the theme of workshops in three successive bi-annual congresses of cross-cultural psychology. It has an obvious meaning for the psychology of gender and of sexual behaviour; there are also significant links with religion (Hofstede, 1998).

Sociologists and management researchers have spread their interest across all four or five dimensions; if they have a special interest, it is rather in power distance and uncertainty avoidance. These dimensions explain the different preferences in different countries for centralisation and formalisation. Development economists have been most interested in individualism–collectivism and long–short-term orientation, associated respectively with wealth and with economic growth.

Innovations in any science often come from outsiders. The dimensions of national cultures that I proposed do not belong to psychology proper, but they set the scene on which psychology has to play. The book has benefited from what I like to call an 'Archimedes effect'. Archimedes of Syracuse (287–212 BC) is best known for his *Eureka!* (supposed to have been said when he stepped into his bath and the water overflowed), but I now refer to his dictum about the principle of the lever: *Dos moi pou sto kai tèn gèn kinèso*: 'Give me a firm spot on which to stand, and I will move the earth'. By finding a firm spot in anthropology, this engineer's lever has moved psychology.

People are wholes: one cannot isolate what a person writes from what (s)he is and has been through. The life experiences described in this chapter were essential to allow me to make sense of the research data that landed in my lap. Work history, travels and family life have been key components of the eventual intellectual products.

In addition, the place and the time in which I grew up contributed greatly to my venturing into unknown intellectual territory. Being a citizen of a small country meant being uniquely conscious of the large world around, as well as learning to read and speak other languages. Growing up amongst the upheaval of World War II and reaching adulthood in the decade of postwar optimism meant strong support for seeking new ways. Ideas arise at specific places and times; this was as true for me as it once was for Archimedes.

NOTES

1   Parts of this autobiography were published before in Hofstede (1996a).

REFERENCES

Argyris, C. (1952). *The impact of budgets on people*. Ithaca, NY: School of Business and Public Administration, Cornell University.
de Groot, A.D. (1961). *Methodologie*. The Hague: Mouton.
Friedmann, G. (1946). *Problèmes humains du machinisme industriel*. Paris: Gallimard.
Herzberg, F., Mausner, B. and Snyderman, B.B. (1959). *The motivation to work*. New York: Chapman & Hall.
Hofstede, G. (1967). *The game of budget control*. Assen: Van Gorcum; and (1968). London: Tavistock.
Hofstede, G. (1977). Confrontation in the cathedral: A case study on power and social change. *International Studies of Management and Organization*, 7, 16–32.
Hofstede, G. (1980). *Culture's consequences: International differences in work-related values*. Beverly Hills, CA: Sage. Abridged paperback edition, 1984.
Hofstede, G. (1982). Cultural pitfalls for Dutch expatriates in Indonesia. *Euro-Asia Business Review*, *1*, 37–41; and 2, 38–47.
Hofstede, G. (1983). Dimensions of national cultures in fifty countries and three regions. In J.B. Deregowski, S. Dziurawiec and R.C. Annis (eds), *Expiscations in cross-cultural psychology*. Lisse: Swets & Zeitlinger. (pp. 335–355).

Hofstede, G. (1991). *Cultures and organizations: Software of the mind*, London: McGraw-Hill. Paperback editions London: HarperCollins, 1994; New York: McGraw-Hill, 1996.

Hofstede, G. (1993). *Images of Europe*. Valedictory address, Maastricht University. Reprinted in *Netherlands Journal of Social Sciences*, *30*, 63–82.

Hofstede, G. (1994). *Uncommon sense about organizations: Cases, studies and field observations*. Thousand Oaks, CA: Sage.

Hofstede, G. (1996). A hopscotch hike. In A. Bedeian (ed.)., *Management laureates: A collection of autobiographical essays* (vol. 4, pp. 85–112). Greenwich, CN: JAI Press.

Hofstede, G. (1998). *Masculinity and femininity: The taboo dimension of national cultures*. Thousand Oaks, CA: Sage.

Hofstede, G. and Bond, M.H. (1984). Hofstede's culture dimensions: An independent validation using Rokeach's Value Survey. *Journal of Cross-cultural Psychology*, *15*, 417–433.

Hofstede, G. and Bond, M.H. (1988). The Confucius connection: From cultural roots to economic growth. *Organizational Dynamics*, *16(4)*, 4–21.

Hofstede, G., Bond, M.H. and Luk, C.L. (1993). Individual perceptions of organizational cultures: A methodological treatise on levels of analysis. *Organization Studies*, *14*, 483–503.

Hofstede, G, Kraut, A.I. and Simonetti, S.H. (1976). *The development of a core attitude survey questionnaire for international use*. Working Paper 76–17, Brussels: European Institute for Advanced Studies in Management. Summary in *Catalog of Selected Documents in Psychology*, (1977), *7*, 21–22.

Hofstede, G., Neuijen, B., Ohayv, D.D. and Sanders, G. (1990). Measuring organizational cultures: a qualitative and quantitative study across twenty cases. *Administrative Science Quarterly*, *35*, 286–316.

Kim, U., Triandis, H.C., Kagitçibaşi, C., Choi, S.C. and Yoon, G. (eds) (1995). *Individualism and collectivism: Theory, method, and applications*. Thousand Oaks, CA: Sage.

Kuhn, T.S. (1970). *The structure of scientific revolutions*, 2nd edn. Chicago, IL: University of Chicago Press.

Kuylaars, A.M. (1951). *Werk en leven van de industriële loonarbeider, als object van een sociale ondernemings-politiek*. Leiden, Netherlands: Stenfert Kroese.

Maslow A.H. (1954). *Motivation and personality*. New York: Harper and Row.

Stedry, A.C. (1960). *Budget control and cost behavior*. Englewood Cliffs, NJ: Prentice-Hall.

Triandis, H.C. (1995). *Individualism and collectivism*. Boulder, CO: Westview.

6 Indigenising Westernised Chinese psychology

Kuo-shu Yang

THE MAKING OF A THOROUGHLY WESTERNISED CHINESE PSYCHOLOGIST

I have had a professional dream for about twenty years – to turn the unhealthily Westernised psychology in Chinese societies into a genuinely indigenous Chinese psychology. The dream began as an outcome of my temporary disillusionment with doing psychology as a lifelong profession, on which I had set my heart ever since my undergraduate years.

The difficult decision to take psychology as my undergraduate major was made more than forty years ago in a tiny island called Taiwan (or Formosa, literally meaning beautiful island). The island, at that time, was packed with more than half a million soldiers under the command of the late president Chiang Kai-shek who had just retreated from mainland China. As an underdeveloped, poor Chinese society with a population of about seven million, gradually recovering from the traumatic experiences of World War II, Taiwan then had only one small department of psychology at the National Taiwan University (NTU) after the termination of Japanese occupation. The number of psychologists was so small and the research activities were so meagre on the island that the late American psychologist Carl Murchison (1957), well known as the founder and editor of the *Journal of Social Psychology*, labelled Taiwan a 'military camp' without saying anything about psychology there in his report after trips to identify cross-cultural studies all over the world in the late 1950s.

It was under such circumstances that I made up my mind to major in psychology in the Psychology Department at the NTU simply for the reasons of helping others and improving the quality of life for Chinese people. In my undergraduate class, there were only nine students and I was the only male. In those years in Taiwan, taking psychology as a college major was something peculiar to most 'sensible' people and even considered crazy if the one who did it was a male. Almost every time I revealed my major to someone, he or she looked at me with a frown of disapproval.

During those undergraduate years (in the late 1950s), I found myself rather interested in the laboratory study of the formation and cure of experimental neurosis in animals. This approach, mainly under the influences of N.R.F. Maier,

J.H. Masserman, N.E. Miller, and O.H. Mowrer, held promise as a royal road to a better understanding of the basic processes and mechanisms involved in human psychopathology and psychotherapy.

After my graduation in 1959, I worked as a full-time teaching assistant for four years and then as an instructor for another four years in the same department. During those eight years, I switched my research interest from the study of experimental neurosis to that of learning in rats, monkeys, and children in the heyday of C.L. Hull's and B.F. Skinner's glory. I was particularly fascinated by Hull's (1943, 1952) two major works entitled *Principles of behaviour* and *A behaviour system*. Hull's hypothetico-deductive approach to systematically investigate learning phenomena offered a concrete exemplar of a beautiful psychological theory, which is now still influencing me in my conceptualisation of a good theory. However, my worship of Hull's S-R reinforcement theory did not last for long. My humanistic inclination finally awoke to such an extent that my research interest gradually shifted to the study of Chinese personality and social behaviour from both the psychometric and experimental perspectives.

I went to the USA for advanced studies in 1966, with the hope of becoming a well-trained personality and social psychologist. I spent three years completing my doctoral programme in the Department of Psychology at the University of Illinois (Urbana), where I received training from such eminent American psychologists as R.B. Cattell, C.W. Eriksen, F.E. Fiedler, M. Fishbein, O.H. Mowrer, C.E. Osgood, H.C. Triandis, and J.S. Wiggins. During my stay in Urbana as a graduate student, I tried very hard to learn whatever I could from Western (mainly American and British) psychology, just like a dry sponge absorbing water. Upon my graduation with a doctoral degree, I congratulated myself for having received probably the best training in scientific psychology available anywhere in the whole world. What I did not realise was that I had been thoroughly 'brainwashed', so to speak, to become an almost 100 per cent Westernised psychologist.

THE DISILLUSIONMENT WITH THE WESTERNISED CHINESE PSYCHOLOGY

In the late 1960s, most, if not all, young men and women from Taiwan who went to the USA for advanced studies and graduated with a doctoral degree would stay in the 'New Continent' to create a new career for themselves and their families. I myself, however, decided to go back to Taiwan as early as possible for several reasons. First, I felt I knew Chinese people and culture much better than American people and culture and I would be able to function much better as a research-oriented personality and social psychologist in a Chinese society like Taiwan. Second, so many psychological studies had been conducted with American subjects, but so few with Chinese subjects. As a Chinese psychologist, I felt obligated to devote my whole professional life to the psychological study of Chinese people rather than American people. Third, as a teacher of psychology, I would be much more needed in a psychology department at any university in any Chinese society than in American society.

Three months after I passed the final, oral examination in May of 1969, I went back to the Department of Psychology at the NTU, where I have been teaching and doing research ever since. During the first five years (1969–74) after I returned from the USA, I was enthusiastic and did a lot of psychological research with Chinese subjects and maintained a high level of productivity. Starting from 1974, however, I found myself gradually losing my appetite for doing empirical research. I felt that the studies I had completed and published did not have enough relevance or make much sense for the explanation, prediction, and understanding of Chinese psychological life. My heart had long been seriously set on the lifelong goal of becoming and functioning as a full-fledged research psychologist. But it turned out that I found my professional career as a Chinese psychologist shaky and unsatisfying.

To find out why, I asked myself whether or not psychology as an academic discipline was no longer attractive to me and it was time for me to transfer to another profession. My answer, however, was no. Then I chewed the matter over by rethinking all of my previous studies with Chinese as subjects and reflecting upon my own mental activities during the process of conducting those studies. Gradually I found that almost all the psychological topics I had investigated, e.g., authoritarianism, cognitive dissonance, individual modernity, self-concept congruence, social-distance attitude, repression-sensitisation, and test anxiety, were concerning phenomena that Western (especially American) psychologists had already studied. I had just followed in their footsteps without asking whether or not those topics were really important or relevant to the everyday life of the Chinese people in Taiwan. It was as if only those phenomena that Western psychologists had investigated were deemed legitimate ones for academic psychological research. Furthermore, in studying those phenomena I had uncritically accepted the concepts defined, adopted the theories developed, and utilised the methods (and tools) invented by American psychologists, without seriously caring whether or not those concepts, theories, and methods were sufficiently compatible with the studied local phenomena and their social-cultural contexts. To my dismay, almost all the other local psychologists had been doing research basically in the same manner. I suddenly realised that by then what we had in Taiwan was an extremely Westernised (mainly Americanised) psychology, in which Chinese investigators had been studying Western-valued psychological topics with Chinese as subjects by adopting concepts, theories, and methods constructed by Western psychologists. In the research process of such a Westernised psychology, only the investigator and the subjects were Chinese and all the other major elements were Western.

What were the investigator's thinking processes involved in doing a Westernised psychological study using Chinese as subjects? Through repeated reflections upon my own mental activities in the process of conducting psychological research, I found to my surprise that whenever involved in a research process I tended habitually to suppress my Chinese values, ideas, concepts, and ways of thinking so that research problems could be easily dealt with by relying upon what I had overlearned from Western psychology. It seemed that I had been so thoroughly 'brain-washed' by Western psychology, before and after I went to the USA for advanced studies, that my thinking in terms of Western psychological concepts, theories, and methods overwhelmed my thinking in terms of native Chinese ways. In other words, during the research process I was definitely not a Chinese-oriented psychologist. Instead, I virtually became a Western psychologist. The same was apparently true of most, if not all, of my fellow psychologists in Taiwan at that time.

After all those considerations and reflections, I finally found the reason why doing Westernised psychological research with Chinese subjects was no longer satisfying or rewarding to me. When an American psychologist, for example, was engaged in research, he or she could spontaneously let his or her American cultural and philosophical orientations and ways of thinking be freely and effectively reflected in choosing a research question, defining a concept, constructing a theory, and designing a method. On the other hand, when a Chinese psychologist in Taiwan was conducting research, his or her strong training by overlearning the knowledge and methodology of American psychology tended to prevent his or her Chinese values, ideas, concepts, and ways of thinking from being adequately reflected in the successive stages of the research process. Research of this kind resulted in an Americanised Chinese psychology without a Chinese 'soul'. Research findings in such an imposed, 'soulless psychology' would not do much good in explaining, predicting, and understanding Chinese behaviour, simply because the imported, Westernised concepts, theories, methods, and tools habitually adopted by Chinese psychologists could not do justice to the complicated, unique aspects and patterns of Chinese people's psychological and behavioural characteristics.

Here it is relevant to mention that, in the psychology classes I had taught, there were always students pointing out that what they had learned from my courses, and courses taught by my colleagues as well, was alien to their life experiences as Chinese. Some of my former students were repeatedly heard to complain that what they had learned from American psychology textbooks (original or translated) and research findings by local psychologists just did not fit what they actually observed in their patients, customers, pupils, or colleagues in the work place. Some of them even frankly admitted that the psychological knowledge they had learned was too *yanghua* (literally meaning Westernised) to be adequately applicable in everyday life.

It was my realisation that such a highly Westernised psychology was being reproduced in Taiwan that made me feel disillusioned. Starting from 1976, seventeen years after I did the first psychological study, I sincerely confessed to my close colleagues in the Department of Psychology at the NTU that I had been doing research in the wrong way and the only remedy was to Sinicise my research in the future. I further pointed out to them that all the other local psychologists had made the same mistake by doing research in the Western way and that they should Sinicise their future research as early as possible. What we needed was a new psychology that would make much more sense not only to Chinese psychologists but also to Chinese people at large so that Chinese psychological and behavioural functioning could be adequately conceptualised and understood.

THE SINICISATION OF PSYCHOLOGICAL RESEARCH IN CHINESE SOCIETIES

Once I found that the real cause of my disillusionment with psychology was doing the wrong kind of psychology (i.e. the extremely Westernised psychology), my heart lightened and my disillusionment suddenly disappeared. I convinced myself that it was my responsibility to let my fellow Chinese psychologists know that they had been doing research in a rather fruitless way. I considered it my lifelong mission to promote and help create a better psychology in Chinese societies, which would make better sense to Chinese people and be more applicable in explaining and predicting their psychological and behavioural functioning.

Once I had made up my mind, I began to take action in 1976. I knew definitely that it would be very difficult to sell my ideas to my colleagues in the Department of Psychology at the NTU, where almost all faculty members honoured the experimental tradition of Western psychology (especially American psychology). So, I decided to do it in a roundabout way. Instead of trying to convince my psychology colleagues directly, I first communicated my ideas about the Sinicisation of research in social and behavioural sciences in Chinese societies to my anthropology and sociology colleagues at the Institute of Ethnology, Academia Sinica in Taipei, where I had been jointly appointed first as associate research fellow and then as research fellow for quite some years. My worries about the over-Westernisation of social and behavioural science research in Taiwan were quickly echoed by two leading colleagues, Professors Y.Y. Li (anthropologist) and C.I. Wen (sociologist), successive directors of the Institute during that period. After many long talks and debates, we came to the conclusion that an academic movement of Sinicisation had to be seriously promoted among social and behavioural scientists in Taiwan and other Chinese societies as well.

In 1978, I moved to Hong Kong and was appointed Senior Lecturer and functioned as Head of the Psychology Section, temporarily under the umbrella of the Department of Sociology, at the Chinese University of Hong Kong. Before I took the position, Professors Li and Wen and I reached the agreement that the Sinicisation movement should also be promoted in Hong Kong. So, not long after my arrival at the Chinese University, eight colleagues including such leading figures as C. Chien (anthropologist), A.Y.C. King (sociologist), R.P.L. Lee (sociologist), and S.S. Liu (philosopher) from the Departments of Sociology, Psychology, Anthropology, Philosophy, and Business Administration began to meet once a month to exchange ideas and discuss issues about the Sinicisation of research in social and behavioural sciences in Chinese societies. I stayed in Hong Kong for only one year. At our last meeting before I returned to Taiwan, a consensus was reached among us that a Sinicisation movement was needed not only in Taiwan but also in Hong Kong, and that the Institute of Ethnology, Academia Sinica should take the responsibility to organise an interdisciplinary conference on the Sinicisation of research into the social and behavioural sciences in Chinese societies in the near future.

Such an interdisciplinary conference was actually held at the Academia Sinica in 1980, in which about sixty Chinese scholars from ten disciplines in social sciences and humanities from Taiwan, Hong Kong, and Singapore participated and presented papers. Two years later an anthology of the major papers, entitled *The Sinicisation of social and behavioural science research in Chinese societies* (Yang and Wen, 1982), was published in Chinese. This compilation has been quite influential in the promotion of the Sinicisation-indigenisation movement over the last fifteen years.

In my paper for that book, I made the first formal statement of the imperative need for Chinese psychologists to Sinicise their research. First of all, I pointed out that, according to relevant theoretical and factual analyses in sociology of knowledge (e.g., Curtis and Petras, 1970; Remmling, 1973), knowledge (including scientific knowledge) was an intellectual product that tended to be determined by certain social, cultural, philosophical, and historical factors. Moreover, research in the sociology of science (e.g., Barnes, 1972; Merton, 1973) had also indicated that science, as a social institution, was not created in a social vacuum; instead, it was constructed in a social-cultural-philosophical-historical milieu and therefore conditioned by factors in that milieu. This was especially true of social and behavioural sciences, including psychology. Sociological analyses by such psychologists as Buss (1975) and Coan (1973) argued persuasively that the selection of research topics, the definition of psychological concepts, the construction of psychological theories, and the designing of research methods (and tools) were substantially influenced by social, cultural, philosophical, and historical factors. Most of the examples used in those analyses to illustrate this point were from Western (especially American) psychology.

In my 1982 paper, I further proposed four major future directions for the academic endeavour of Sinicising psychological research by Chinese psychologists:

1 Empirically retesting the significant research findings obtained by foreign psychologists;
2 empirically studying important psychological phenomena that were unique among Chinese people;
3 revising foreign-origin theories and constructing new theories that were especially compatible with Chinese behaviour; and
4 improving foreign-origin research methods (and tools) and developing new methods (and tools) that were especially applicable to the study of Chinese people.

I also mentioned that the Sinicisation movement had nothing to do with Chinese nationalism and ethnocentrism and that it was not meant to reject uncritically psychological concepts, theories, methods, and findings of Western psychology or to forget about the literature of Western psychology altogether.

It is interesting to note that my 1982 paper suggested an unfavourable position for the conceptualisation of indigenous psychology. It was said that the aim of Sinicisation was neither to establish a 'Chinese psychology' nor to develop an 'indigenous psychology'. At that stage, I still insisted there was only one scientific psychology and that it was not legitimate to talk about indigenous psychology within that psychology. Apparently, what I had in mind for indigenous psychology was a kind of highly limited and descriptive psychology using only folk concepts such as those studied by cultural anthropologists (see, for example, Heelas and Lock, 1981). I implicitly thought that a Chinese indigenous psychology as such was not scientific enough to be part of psychology as an empirical science. This position continued until 1988.

The concepts, directions, and issues I advanced in the 1982 paper provided the first set of guidelines not only for myself but also for other Chinese psychologists in Sinicising our psychological research and they serve as an intellectual departure for those who are interested in understanding the Sinicisation (and, later, indigenisation) movement. From 1980 to 1988, I tried deliberately to Sinicise my own research and to require my doctoral students to do their research in the same way. During that period, my students and I began to devote our efforts to the Sinicised study of such culturally bound psychological and behavioural phenomena as *yuan* (predestined interpersonal affinity) (Yang, 1982; Yang and Ho, 1988), *mianzi* (face) (Cheng, 1982; Chu, 1983), filial piety (Yang, 1985; Yang, Yeh and Hwang, 1989; Yeh and Yang, 1989), social-oriented achievement motivation (Yu and Yang, 1987), and Chinese personality perception (Yang and Bond, 1985), which were unique and important to the psychological functioning of the Chinese. Without exception, the findings obtained from such studies tend to be highly meaningful and stimulating and to inspire us to construct theoretical concepts and frameworks that lead to further systematic research. It is fair to say here that during this stage our efforts to Sinicise psychological research in Taiwan were both partially influenced and partially reinforced by the conceptual analyses of face (Ho, 1976, 1980), *renqing* ('favour') (King, 1981), and 'relationology' (relationship orientation) (Chiao, 1982), and strategic behaviour (Chiao, 1981), made by our distinguished colleagues in Hong Kong.

THE INDIGENISATION OF PSYCHOLOGICAL RESEARCH IN CHINESE SOCIETIES

Starting from 1986 (see, for example, Yang, 1986), my colleagues and I have used the term 'indigenisation' to replace 'Sinicisation' in labelling our efforts to make our research more meaningful to our Chinese people. There were two major reasons for this change. First, the term 'indigenisation' is much more neutral and broader in its denotative and connotative meanings than 'Sinicisation', with the latter having the suggestion of Sinocentrism. Second, up to 1988, the three major Chinese societies Taiwan, Hong Kong, and mainland China, separated for more than forty years, have already developed their own respective political, economic, social, and cultural characteristics on the basis of the core Chinese culture during the process of social change induced by modernisation. As a result, people in these different societies had displayed both common and unique psychological and behavioural characteristics. For people in each Chinese society, both the common and unique psychological and behavioural aspects may be called indigenous, but only the common (especially the traditional common) may be called Sinicised. The indigenisation of psychological research with Chinese subjects means to reveal accurately both the common and the unique psychological and behavioural aspects of people in a certain Chinese society, whereas Sinicisation would reveal only the common aspects. From these and other points of view, indigenisation should be better than Sinicisation as a term to describe a more comprehensive research strategy.

However, advocating and adopting the research strategy of indigenisation is one thing, and formally claiming and actually striving to establish a Chinese indigenous psychology is another. As can be recalled, my 1982 position insisted that we had only one scientific psychology in the whole world and there was no room for indigenous psychology to fit in. In 1988, however, I changed this position as a result of my short visit to Harvard University. During my stay at Cornell University as a visiting scholar in the spring semester, I was invited by the renowned medical anthropologist Arthur Kleinman to go to Harvard to give a talk on my research on Chinese personality from an indigenous perspective as part of the Seminar on Personality in China, Japan, and India, organised for about ten professors from various departments in humanities and social sciences. In the discussion session after my presentation, the well-known developmental psychologist Jerome Kagan asked me the question: What kind of psychology would have been developed by Chinese psychologists if there had not been any Western psychology? I was shocked by his question and, after a moment of silence, I managed to reply that Chinese psychologists would have developed some kind of collectivistic-oriented psychology without the hegemonic influence of Western or American psychology. To be honest, I found myself, then and later, dissatisfied with my answer. I must admit that Kagan's question gave me a chance to look more closely and squarely at the naked reality that little was left in Westernised Chinese psychology after those elements that had been borrowed from, or influenced by, Western psychology were taken away. Moreover, through my exchange of ideas with the seminar participants, I began to realise that North American psychology, the most developed in the world, was an endogenous kind of indigenous psychology (Enriquez, 1989) in the sense that its major concepts, theories, methods, and findings have originally and spontaneously evolved partly from the European intellectual traditions but mostly from the cultural and social-philosophical matrix of the American society.

My 'Harvard experience' promptly stimulated me to consider seriously the possibility and legitimacy of developing a Chinese indigenous psychology. Much more strongly than ever, I felt that to treat American indigenous psychology as the psychology of all human beings, including non-Western people, was a big mistake made by non-Western psychologists. If American psychologists could have their own indigenous psychology, why did not we Chinese psychologists have our own indigenous psychology? American indigenous psychology had made its contribution to global psychology, why should not Chinese indigenous psychology also do so in the future? My answers to these questions were all in the affirmative. At that time, I still believed there was only one global psychology for all human beings, but the shortest road leading to this overall human psychology should be through the establishment of representative indigenous psychologies all over the world. Such a human psychology would never be accomplished by relying upon one single dominant indigenous psychology, namely, American psychology (or the broader Western psychology). Instead, local psychologists in various societies should develop their own respective indigenous psychologies, which would then be gradually integrated to form a genuine global psychology.

With the new dream of developing a Chinese indigenous psychology, I returned to Taiwan in August 1988. I vividly felt that it was my responsibility to promote, in collaboration with my interested colleagues, the development of an indigenous psychology in Taiwan and other Chinese societies. In that year I was already fifty-six years old. For the first time I realised that my time to accomplish such a big professional mission was running short and thought that I should have had that 'Harvard experience', say, ten years earlier. It is with such a psychological background that I set out to do anything I thought beneficial to the development of a Chinese indigenous psychology.

Starting from 1988, my colleagues and I have speeded up the tempo of promoting Chinese indigenous psychology and conducting psychological studies with an indigenised research strategy. We have done many things that we think are helpful in developing a Chinese indigenous psychology. The following are among the most important:

1 An indigenous research group or team consisting of about twenty professors from various local universities as core members had already been formed before 1988 and has been meeting regularly once a month in the Department of Psychology at the NTU to discuss our own indigenous studies or to exchange ideas about relevant theoretical and methodological issues with invited speakers.
2 A package of more than ten empirical studies with an indigenous perspective, supported by grants from the ROC National Science Council, has been carried out every two or three years by members of our indigenous research group.
3 A medium-size interdisciplinary conference on the study of Chinese psychological functioning has been held once every two or three years for the presentation of empirical, methodological, and theoretical papers by investigators from Taiwan, Hong Kong, and mainland China adopting an indigenous approach. Similar academic conferences have been occasionally held in Hong Kong and mainland China.
4 About seventeen academic books on the indigenous study of Chinese psychological functioning have been published in the Chinese language by local publishing companies.
5 A new academic journal in Chinese, entitled *Indigenous Psychological Research in Chinese Societies*, was launched in 1993 to provide a formal forum for Chinese scholars from psychology and other disciplines in humanities and social sciences all over the world. Two volumes, in book form, have been published each year and circulated in the three major Chinese societies.

6 Semester courses on Chinese indigenous psychology for graduate and senior undergraduate students have been offered in psychology departments of various universities in Taiwan.
7 In addition to frequent single speeches, seminars and workshops (each for one or more days in summer or winter vacations) on issues of Chinese indigenous psychology have been organised in Taiwan and mainland China for graduate students and faculty members from various universities. A six-week summer training programme in advanced personality and social psychology has been conducted by my colleagues and me from Taiwan and Hong Kong for seven years (from 1991 to 1997) for graduate students and young faculty members interested in the indigenous approach, from universities and research institutions in mainland China.

Through all these efforts, we feel that we have indeed made substantial progress in developing a Chinese indigenous psychology.

My major standpoints on Chinese indigenous psychology at this stage are detailed in a long paper (Yang, 1993) published in the inaugural issue of *Indigenous Psychological Research in Chinese Societies*. In that paper, I define Chinese indigenous psychology as an evolving system of knowledge about the psychological and behavioural functioning of the Chinese people that has been built up by utilising an indigenous or indigenised research strategy or paradigm. In such a strategy or paradigm, the concepts, theory, and method adopted have to be so developed or devised that they can accurately reveal, or effectively reconstruct, Chinese psychological and behavioural processes, mechanisms, and patterns closely embedded in the political, economic, cultural, and historical context of a Chinese society. Put differently, in order for a research strategy or paradigm to be indigenous, its concepts, theory, and method (a) have not only to reflect sufficiently the investigator's native cognitions, values, and ways of thinking (b) but also adequately to unravel the subjects' psychological and behavioural characteristics being studied (c). If both the investigator and the subjects are members of the same culture and the investigator consciously refrains from letting Western concepts, theory, and method inhibit or overwhelm his or her native ideas and ways of thinking, (a), (b), and (c) tend to be highly compatible with one another. I term this condition of (a), (b), and (c) being consonant with one another 'indigenous congruousness or compatibility' (for a detailed analysis of this concept, see Yang, 1993, pp. 24 – 26). I stress that indigenous compatibility can be relied upon as a standard for judging whether or not a study is indigenous or indigenised and how much it is so.

How can a Chinese psychologist effectively indigenise his or her psychological research? To answer this question, my 1993 paper sets forth seven nos and ten yeses. The seven nos represent seven things that a Chinese psychologist should not do so that his or her research can become considerably more indigenous:

1 not to habitually or uncritically adopt Western psychological concepts, theories, and methods;

2 not to overlook Western psychologists' important experiences in developing their concepts, theories, and methods;

3 not to reject useful indigenous concepts, theories, and methods developed by other Chinese psychologists;

4 not to adopt any cross-cultural research strategy with a Western-dominant, imposed etic or pseudo-etic approach (the only acceptable type of cross-cultural research strategy is that of the cross-indigenous method as advanced by Enriquez, 1979);

5 not to use concepts, variables, or units of analysis that are too broad or abstract;

6 not to think out research problems in terms of English or other foreign languages; and

7 not to conceptualise academic research in political terms, that is, not to politicise research.

The seven nos are insufficient to ensure the indigenisation of one's research. More importantly, a Chinese psychologist needs to do at least ten things in a more positive direction:

1 to tolerate vague or ambiguous conditions and to suspend one's decisions as long as possible in dealing with conceptual, theoretical, and methodological problems until something indigenous emerges in his or her phenomenological field;

2 to be a typical Chinese when functioning as a researcher and to let Chinese ideas, values, and ways of thinking be fully reflected in his or her research thinking process;

3 to take the psychological or behavioural phenomenon to be studied and its concrete, specific setting into careful consideration before assessing the possibility of adequately applying a Western concept, variable, theory, or method to Chinese subjects;

4 to take its local social, cultural, and historical contexts into careful consideration whenever conceptualising a phenomenon and designing a study;

5 to give priority to the study of culturally unique psychological and behavioural phenomena or characteristics of the Chinese people;

6 to make it a rule to begin any research with a thorough immersion into the natural, concrete details of the phenomenon to be studied;

7 to investigate, if possible, both the specific content (or structure) and the involved process (or mechanism) of the phenomenon in any study;

8 to let research be based upon the Chinese intellectual tradition rather than the Western intellectual tradition;

9 to study not only the traditional aspects or elements of Chinese psychological functioning but also the modern ones and the characteristic traditional–modern combinations formed under the impact of societal modernisation; and

10 to study not only the psychological functioning of contemporary, living Chinese but also that of the ancient Chinese and its relationship to the psychological functioning of contemporary Chinese.

Some of the above recommendations are similar to those made by such leading indigenous psychologists as Chu (1993) and C.F. Yang (1991, 1993).

Moreover, my 1993 treatise contends that a multiparadigm approach, as defined by Gioia and Pitre (1990), should be encouraged at the present stage of the development of Chinese indigenous psychology. Any research method or strategy, ranging from the quantitative approach with a positivistic orientation to the qualitative approach with a hermeneutic, phenomenological, or narrative orientation, may be used in doing an indigenous psychological study so far as it can produce culturally relevant or meaningful results. At the epistemological level, either realism or idealism may be fruitfully relied upon as a useful theory of knowledge in designing a research strategy or paradigm for the indigenous study of Chinese psychology. More recently I made an attempt (Yang, 1996) to deal with another interesting methodological issue – the inadequacy of the current Western-dominant definition of psychology, as found in most standard, English textbooks of introductory psychology, for the indigenous study of psychology in non-Western societies. Almost all such textbooks define psychology, in one way or another, as the scientific study of the individual's behaviour (and consciousness or experience). This is an indigenous definition of Western (especially American) individualistic-oriented psychology, which views the individual as an independent, autonomous, and self-reliant person conceptually isolated from his or her social, cultural, and historical contexts. Such a definition, unless properly liberalised or expanded, will be inapplicable to Chinese indigenous psychology and other indigenous psychologies with a collectivistic orientation. In my 1996 paper I did try to redefine psychology in such a way that it covered both collectivistic- and individualistic-oriented indigenous psychologies. The liberalised definition and its related issues, however, are too complicated to be treated here.

SOME CONCLUDING WORDS

I have told, in a rather over-simplified fashion, the story of my intellectual and professional transformation from a Westernised Chinese psychologist to an indigenous Chinese psychologist. In the last twenty years or so, my Chinese colleagues and I have been trying hard, especially in the last eight years, to promote the development of an indigenous Chinese psychology not only in Taiwan but also in mainland China and Hong Kong. We have made considerable progress not only in the clarification of conceptual and methodological issues concerning the indigenisation (including Sinicisation) of psychological research but also in the indigenous study of theoretical and empirical topics in about thirty research areas including relationship orientation, *pao* (reciprocation), fatalism and *yuan*, face psychology, familism and pan-familism, filial piety, paternalistic leadership, interpersonal suffering, value system, views of morality, views of justice, social-oriented achievement orientation, formalism, strategic behaviour, Chinese Big-Five, and individual traditionality and modernity. Now we are editing a book (two volumes) entitled the *Chinese indigenous psychology: A survey of theoretical and empirical accomplishments*, composed of more than thirty chapters being written by Chinese psychologists from Taiwan and Hong Kong. The book will first appear in Chinese and then be condensed to generate a volume in English. Such a book will be used not only as a textbook for graduate and undergraduate courses on Chinese indigenous psychology but also as an informative sourcebook for indigenous researchers to consult.

As never before, I feel very confident of establishing an indigenous Chinese psychology in the future, a psychology which will gradually replace the Westernised Chinese psychology. It is anticipated that more and more indigenous theoretical perspectives and empirical findings will be incorporated into textbooks of general psychology, social psychology, personality psychology, developmental psychology, educational psychology, organisational psychology, abnormal psychology, and so on for Chinese students. It is my humble hope that some time in the distant future a textbook of general psychology for Chinese students will be written with indigenous chapter titles and contents as the major coverage and with theories and findings from foreign indigenous psychologies (for example, American psychology) included only for comparative purposes.

Finally, I must say that since 1976 I have never regretted my decision to take the promotion of Sinicisation and indigenisation of psychological research in Chinese societies as my major professional mission. I still feel, more strongly than ever, that doing psychological research with Chinese subjects in an indigenous way is the only way out for Chinese psychologists to make really significant contributions to the global psychological science.

REFERENCES

Barnes, B. (ed.) (1972). *Sociology of science*. Harmondsworth, Middx: Penguin.

Buss, A.R. (1975). The emerging field of the sociology of psychological knowledge. *American Psychologist, 30*, 988–1002.

Cheng, C.C. (1982). 'Face psychology: A theoretical and empirical analysis'. Unpublished master thesis, Department of Psychology, National Taiwan University.

Chiao, C. (1981). A pilot analysis of strategic behaviour in Chinese culture. In Y.Y. Li and C. Chiao (eds), *The race, society, and culture of China* (pp. 57–91). Taipei, Taiwan: Shi-huo Publishing Co. (in Chinese).

Chiao, C. (1982). A preliminary analysis of *Guanxi* ('relationship'). In K.S. Yang and C.I. Wen (eds), *The Sinicisation of social and behavioural science research in Chinese societies* (pp.345–360). Taipei, Taiwan: Institute of Ethnology, Academia Sinica (in Chinese).

Chu, R.L. (1983). 'The psychological and behavioural processes of face: An empirical study'. Unpublished doctoral dissertation, Department of Psychology, National Taiwan University (in Chinese).

Chu, R.L. (1993). The indigenisation of psychological research in Taiwan: Retrospects and prospects. *Indigenous Psychological Research in Chinese Societies, 1*, 89–119 (in Chinese).

Coan, R.W. (1973). Toward a psychological interpretation of psychology. *Journal of the History of the Behavioural Sciences, 9*, 313–327.

Curtis, J.E. and Petras, J.W. (eds) (1970). *The sociology of knowledge: A reader*. London: Gerald Duckworth.

Enriquez, V.G. (1979). Toward cross-cultural knowledge through cross-indigenous methods and perspectives. *Hong Kong Psychological Society Bulletin, 3*, 7–21.

Enriquez, V.G. (1989). *Indigenous psychology and national consciousness.* Tokyo: Institute for the Study of Languages and Cultures of Asia and Africa.

Gioia, D. A. and Pitre, E. (1990). Multiparadigm perspectives on theory building. *Academy of Management Review, 15*, 584–602.

Heelas, P. and Lock, A. (eds) (1981). *Indigenous psychologies: The anthropology of the self.* London: Academic Press.

Ho, D.Y.F. (1976). On the concept of face. *American Journal of Sociology, 10*, 867–884.

Ho, D.Y.F. (1980). Face and stereotyped notions about Chinese face behaviour. *Philippine Journal of Psychology, 13*, 20–33.

Hull, C.L. (1943). *Principles of behaviour: An introduction to behaviour theory.* New York: Appleton-Century-Crofts.

Hull, C.L. (1952). *A behaviour system: An introduction to behaviour theory concerning the individual organism.* New Haven, CN: Yale University Press.

King, A.Y.C. (1981). The analysis of *renqing* in interpersonal behaviour. In *Proceedings of the International Conference on Sinology* (pp. 417–428). Taipei, Taiwan: Academia Sinica (in Chinese).

Merton, R.K. (1973). *The sociology of science: Theoretical and empirical investigations.* Chicago, IL: University of Chicago Press.

Murchison, C. (1957). Preface to the publication of cross-cultural research. *Journal of Social Psychology, 45*, 139–141.

Remmling, G.W. (ed.) (1973). *Toward the sociology of knowledge: Origins and development of a sociological thought style.* London: Routledge & Kegan Paul.

Yang, C.F. (1991). Introduction. In H.S.R. Kao and C.F. Yang (eds), *Chinese people, Chinese mind* vol. 1, pp. 9–43. Taipei, Taiwan: Yuan-liu Publishing Co. (in Chinese).

Yang, C.F. (1993). How to deepen the indigenisation of psychological research: Plus a review of recent research findings. *Indigenous Psychological Research in Chinese Societies, 1*, 122–183 (in Chinese).

Yang, K.S. (1982). The Sinicisation of psychological research: Levels and directions. In K.S. Yang and C.I. Wen (eds), *The Sinicisation of social and behavioural science research in Chinese societies* (pp. 153–187). Taipei, Taiwan: Institute of Ethnology, Academia Sinica (in Chinese).

Yang, K.S. (1982). *Yuan* and its functions in modern Chinese life. In *Proceedings of the Conference on Traditional Culture and Modern Life* (pp. 105–128). Taipei, Taiwan: Promotion Committee for the Renaissance of Chinese Culture (in Chinese).

Yang, K.S. (1985). New filial piety in modern Chinese societies. *Renaissance of Chinese Culture Monthly, 19(1)*, 56–67 (in Chinese).

Yang, K.S. (1986). Chinese personality and its change. In M.H. Bond (ed.), *The psychology of Chinese people* (pp. 106–170). Hong Kong: Oxford University Press.

Yang, K.S. (1993). Why do we need to develop a Chinese indigenous psychology? *Indigenous Psychological Research in Chinese societies, 1*, 6–88 (in Chinese).

Yang, K. S. (1996). 'Liberalising the definition of psychology: Also on family psychology and historical psychology'. Unpublished manuscript, Department of Psychology, National Taiwan University (in Chinese).

Yang, K.S. and Bond, M.H. (1985). Basic indigenous dimensions for the description of Chinese personality: An example of Sinicised psychological research. In Y.Y. Li, K.S. Yang and C.I. Wen (eds), *Proceedings of the Conference on Modernisation and Sinicisation* (pp. 155–190). Taipei, Taiwan: Guei-guan Publishing Co. (in Chinese).

Yang, K.S. and Ho, D.Y.F. (1988). The role of *yuan* in Chinese social life: A conceptual and empirical analysis. In A.C. Paranjpe, D.Y.F. Ho and R.W. Rieber (eds), *Asian contributions to psychology* (pp. 263–281). New York: Praeger.

Yang, K.S., and Wen, C.I. (eds) (1982). *The Sinicisation of social and behavioural science research in Chinese societies.* Taipei, Taiwan: Institute of Ethnology, Academia Sinica (in Chinese).

Yang, K.S., Yeh, K.H. and Hwang, L.L. (1989). The social psychology of Chinese filial piety: Theory and measurement. *Bulletin of the Institute of Ethnology, Academia Sinica, 65,* 171–227 (in Chinese).

Yeh, K.H., and Yang, K.S. (1989). The cognitive structure and development of Chinese filial piety: Conceptualisation and measurement. *Bulletin of the Institute of Ethnology, Academia Sinica, 65,* 131–169 (in Chinese).

Yu, A.B., and Yang, K.S. (1987). Social-oriented and self-oriented achievement motivation: Conceptual analysis and empirical study. *Bulletin of the Institute of Ethnology, Academia Sinica, 64,* 51–98 (in Chinese).

7 In search of my *Brahman*

Jai B. P. Sinha

As I look back over three decades of my search for who I am and what I am trying to realise through my research, I see many mountains and valleys, oceans and jungles, frustrations and failures as well as ecstasy and achievements. I am still not quite sure about myself, except that I enjoy what I do and how I relate to my milieu. And I intend to keep on doing so. Let me start from the beginning.

YATRA[1]

I drifted into psychology by a sheer chance. My first love was literature. But my best friend prevailed upon me to accept that a knowledge of people's mind is the most appropriate way to enter into creative literature. At that time I thought that I was being more influenced by his friendship than the argument. Soon I found myself enjoying what I was doing. I was getting fascinated by the theories and the concepts which were popular in the late 1950s. All of them were Western in origin. I wanted to learn first hand from those great psychologists who had such deep insights in human nature. A dream started taking shape: I was treading on a strange land of psychologists with large laboratories and lots of students! Gold medals for topping the list of psychology students both at Bachelor (Honours) and Master levels turned the dream into a life goal.

A Fulbright travel grant and a fellowship from Ohio State University lifted me into a journey for which I was craving but was not quite prepared. Leaving behind ageing parents, a fourteen-month-old son, and my pregnant wife began taking their toll as soon as I landed on the campus. My puritanical background and the resultant orthodox mind-set were hardly any help. I was born into a family of freedom fighters under strong Gandhian influence. I hardly saw my father during my childhood. Whenever he was home, he was invariably surrounded by the people of his own kind who endlessly talked about what they were doing and how great their leaders were. My childhood memories were filled with these little-understood ideals and unknown names. I myself wanted to do something equally great to make my people talk about me. Inadvertently, I was picking up a world view which was idealistic with a ring of fixed notions regarding what was right or wrong.

In America, my self-confidence soon started tumbling as I tried to cope with reading assignments, speed, accent, and the colloquialism of teachers and students, and a totally unfamiliar environment. The food, the people, their lifestyles – all strained me. A near nervous breakdown was averted only because of a deadly fear that if I failed, I would disgrace all those who had pinned such high hopes on me. I was the first in the community who had ventured so far away from home with so much academic fanfare. I also had the role model of my father who preferred to go to jail and suffer harassment, but never compromised his pursuit of his country's independence. How could I let him down! How could I let my people down!

Once pushed to the wall, I fought like hell and bounced back as a straight A-grader – floating through advanced statistics, research design, experimentation, simulations, and what not. On my way, I picked up a few publications in collaboration with my professors – all involving experimentation, simulation, and quantitative methods. My outlook was changed too. I was no longer rejecting Western food or condemning American lifestyles. Rather I was enjoying, without any scruples or regard for my puritanical background, all that the campus life had to offer. In a way I was becoming a part of the world view where the lifestyles and the types of research were interrelated and supported each other. I still vividly remember the satisfaction I had in subjecting successfully a sample of naive freshmen to the pressure from a stooge to violate a norm. I had even greater satisfaction in violating some of the Hindu's codes of conduct because I considered them orthodox and dysfunctional. I was learning how to manipulate variables as well as to control my life events. It all was working well. But as the day of my departure came closer, I started feeling uncomfortable: a number of disturbing questions were cropping up.

NETI, NETI [2]

I was getting aware of my home culture. I asked myself: Can the Western world view be transplanted to India? Should it be transplanted? Should I continue doing research the way I did at Ohio State? Shall I feel comfortable running rats or undergraduates like rats in the maze of verbal instructions or in multifactorial designs? Can I replicate meaningfully the simulations I have been doing? Are we Indians authoritarian in Adorno's way of conceptualisation and must we change into high achievers or become participative managers in order to develop the country faster? Should I join McClelland's bandwagon to train Indian business-men to acquire high need for achievement (nACH). Should I get involved in training for participative leadership? Do our people have to wait for a couple of decades for their hygiene factors to be taken care of before they can experience any motivators? The answer in each case was no. Then: What have I learnt which I can use back in India? Maybe the rigour of research and sophistication of quantitative analysis will help me identify which of the current concepts and theories are irrelevant or even harmful. I shall have to distinguish substance from superficialities.

ASTHIR CITTA [3]

My two days of intensive discussions with McClelland and a seminar at Harvard on the eve of my departure set my priority to focus on the theory of need for achievement. Following my training in experimental research, I conducted a study which showed that groups of high nACH individuals, when placed in a limited resource condition, failed to maximise their collective outputs. They also developed interpersonal dislike for each other. When I brought the draft of my paper to the notice of McClelland, he commented:

> Your findings seem unequivocal to me, clear cut and highly significant – but I do have difficulties in seeing their applicability to the economic development problems. This is always the problem with 'model' experiments . . . I hope you will think a bit more along these lines before publishing too widely the results of your excellent experiment because they may help contribute to the self-defeating tendency in India's thought about how limited her resources are.[4]

I still published the study (Sinha, 1968) followed by another (Sinha and Pandey, 1970) which showed that high nACH people tend to maximise their achievement by any means and are less concerned about the justifiability of the means used. Altruistically oriented persons, on the other hand, use resources less selfishly, but fail to maximise their individual outputs. I did not have any problem in publishing these papers along with three others on ethical risk taking (which was the continuing interest of my professor) in foreign journals because they were parts of a highly published chain of studies which served as reference points to the reviewers. The reviewers did not find any flaw in the methodology. They were all experimental studies with checks on manipulations and standardised operation-isation of the variables. They added small bricks to the body of knowledge in a particular area.

It was, however, I who was getting uncomfortable again. What I was trying to accomplish was to retain my commitment to the canons of experimental method, but to simulate a reality which was bigger and more complex than the ones which I had studied so far. I was less and less sure that our findings had external validity. McClelland had already commented on the limitations of such simulations of the business world. The more I thought the more I felt confronted with two choices: to stay with the previously tested methods and to study only those fragments of Indian reality which the methods could cope with or to explore the bigger chunk of real-life issues which seemed to be more relevant but less amenable to the strait-jacketed methodology I had employed so far.

There was another concern in my mind: I was being negative in my approach. All I was saying was that nACH is detrimental in Indian conditions because of our resource constraints. Its benefits can be harvested in a culture where resources are in abundance. I was not sure that altruism by itself works either. I argued, should I not start afresh and identify some of the most critical psychological factors of rapid economic growth and select the one which seems to be the most critical for conducting research as well as for making interventions? What is the most viable entry point in the interplay of the complex growth process? I thought and thought, and suddenly recalled that a decade back I used to blame excessive dependency in Indians for their problems. At that time, this was my casual perception based on intuitive feeling without being tempered by any systematic investigation. Now it posed itself like a real research issue. It is this dependence proneness, I along with my colleagues argued, that needed to be examined and changed[5] if Indians are to develop faster.

Over a dozen studies were conducted by the end of the 1960s (Sinha, 1970) and many more thereafter. In these studies, dependence proneness was operationalised, measured, and related to antecedent and consequent variables. We tried our best to stick to what we thought to be acceptable courses of investigation. Our methods encompassed surveys, interviews, as well as experiments.

However, we ran into problems when we tried to publish in foreign journals. The reviewers were quite discouraging: the variables were unfamiliar to American readers, they were not adequately operationalised, control groups were not enough, checks on experimental manipulations were not appropriate, so on and so forth. The Indian journals, on the contrary, loved them. Their format was Western with all the high-sounding psychometric properties and rigour, and yet they looked like local products. Indian journals in fact were so receptive (to the point of being gullible) that we published even exploratory studies, often without being very careful. The stream of publications brought name and fame too: a nice place to work where all possible facilities were provided for research without any teaching or administrative obligations, a guest lectureship in the neighbouring graduate school without any strings attached, a full professorship at a relatively young age (relative to the Indian norm), a place in the executive of the Indian Council of Social Science Research (ICSSR) – the apex body for funding social science research, a national lectureship of the University Grants Commission, (later on) a national fellowship of the ICSSR, and so on. The system bestowed on me all that it could!

This tough-abroad and easy-home combination initiated a process of gradual transformation in my research interests. I was focusing more on compelling societal problems. I felt an obligation to contribute to the collective efforts towards nation building. I started believing that 'Our social psychological research will need to have a symbiotic relationship with the social milieu and that the demands of the latter will have to be reflected in the former and the findings of the former should influence the latter' (Sinha, 1981, p. 249). I was often carried away by the raw enthusiasm of hitting upon an idea and explored it in a way which defied stepwise operationalisation, systematic investigations, and statistical sophistication. I saw and felt as part of a milieu which was in a real hurry to be explored. There was not enough time or a sufficient number of psychologists to patiently decompose the real life problems into small researchable pieces and to investigate them in sequential order. I was tempted to develop profiles of some of the realities no matter how many pieces hung loosely here and there. The aim was to make as many scratches as I, with the help of my colleagues, could make, hoping that the missing links would be accounted for by us or others at a later date. I loosely talked about an *aram* (rest and relaxation not preceded by hard work) culture, of a 'poverty syndrome' where even the not-so-poor people imagine too much scarcity which then induces them to hoard and monopolise resources by any means for their own and their children's use, of status consciousness, of a preference for personalised relationships, and so on. As I now reflect on my research endeavour in the 1970s, I see a number of flashes of ideas which were not immediately subjected to thorough scrutiny but were necessary to prepare the ground to 'outgrow the alien framework' (my favourite expression at that time!). Some of them did catch others' attention and were incorporated in Indian psychological vocabulary later on.

Some of them were indeed followed up systematically. For example, we rigorously defined dependence proneness, refined its operationalisation over a period of time, developed multimethods for assessing it in a variety of samples, reviewed literature to identify its antecedent and subsequent variables, and conducted a series of experimental and field studies in order to develop its nomological net. In one such study, we found that highly dependence-prone persons took greater initiative and higher risk than low dependence-prone persons if they were placed under a leader who expected them to do so (Saha and Sinha, 1973). This led in the 1970s and 1980s to a series of studies on leadership. Probably, my exposure to Shartle and Stogdill at Ohio State had a sleeper effect on me. I was turning to leadership to identify ways of changing Indian's dependence proneness. Our studies revealed a number of culture-specific findings. For example, participative leaders were perceived to be weak and to abdicate their responsibilities, authoritarian leaders were disliked and were found to be ineffective, and nurturant superiors were liked but were not necessarily effective. It was a blend of nurturance and task-orientation (NT) that seemed to render the leader effective, but only for those subordinates who preferred dependency and personalised relationships, and accepted the superiority of the leader. Furthermore, a phase of NT leadership was found necessary to prepare subordinates for acquiring expertise, skills, experiences, and so on, which in turn induced them to assume a participative role. Thus, the NT model drew on the Indian ethos of nurturance, dependency, personalised relationships, and status consciousness. Simultaneously, it adopted the contingency approach and the principle of reinforcement from Western literature. The model was a blend of the East and the West.

It was this kind of work which was probably making me visible in the West. There were two critical events which again made me stick my neck out and return to the USA. Hunter College of the City University of New York invited me to teach during 1971–3 and for a number of subsequent summers. Second, I was asked to write an article for a special issue of the *International Review of Applied Psychology* (Sinha, 1973). I reported my findings from a comprehensive survey of climate, leadership, reward systems, etc., in comparable public and private sector organisations. Teaching at Hunter was exciting and taxing. I had to stretch at times to provide Indian perspectives on social psychology which at that time was totally Western in its coverage. In order to do so effectively, I read carefully all kinds of psychological and non-psychological materials on Indian culture. For the first time, I could appreciate the psycho-philosophical roots of the Indian psyche (Sinha, 1982) and my own embeddedness in it. I also felt my core identity making claims on my Western lifestyle: I was engaged in a process of transformation in reverse to what I had experienced in the Ohio days. This helped me in sorting out many of my tangled ideas. While the ground work for the NT leadership was started towards the end of the 1960s, the experiences at Hunter certainly contributed to give them a publishable shape (Sinha, 1980).

I started participating in international congresses of psychology from 1974. Whenever I was invited to do so, I felt that I was being used as a 'decorative piece'. The organisers needed someone from a physically different background and appearance to make their forum look international. Teaching at Hunter had certainly given me some confidence. I used to have mixed feelings about being recognised as a viable Indian who was denied entry in Western journals but was acceptable in an international forum. So, I decided to use these opportunities: the 'decorative piece' will talk – loud enough to be listened to! Now it was possible to engage my Western as well as other international counterparts in dialogue. The resultant experiences proved to be very enriching to me. They challenged my assumptions, expanded my perspectives, generated ideas, and granted greater acceptability. I was nominated as a Vice-President of the World Association for Dynamic Psychiatry, elected as a member of the executive of the International Association for Applied Psychology, invited as a visiting professor to two North American universities, and called upon to deliver addresses at international conferences. I was contributing chapters to volumes edited by top psychologists and published by reputable publishers (Sinha, 1994, 1995, 1996). Implicitly, I concluded that I was being recognised because I was different and was filling the gaps in their international map. They recognised my supplementary role, but did not consider it necessary to incorporate my contributions into their own work.

This conclusion led me to believe that the more I conducted culture-specific research, the more I would be valued both by my compatriots and international colleagues. Thus, there developed a sense of congruence between what I really wanted to do and what my colleagues at home or abroad valued. This belief freed me from the compulsion to publish in Western journals, except when asked to do so. I was more and more inclined to let my research problems decide the contents as well as the methods to study them. Simulations, manipulations, and so on were left far in the past. Concepts were still being operationalised and measured through surveys and interviews. As some of the operationalisations were new, factor analysis remained a favourite method. Regression analysis was now used more often than before to take care of a large number of variables in the surveys and interviews.

It was about that time that I got the shock of my life. My investigators often told me that respondents' behaviour did not always match with their responses to the items. Furthermore, it was not always possible to separate out individuals in order to ask them questions. There were others who hung around and often interrupted or contradicted the respondents. In many cases, respondents kept asking for the situation to which the items referred. It seemed to us that they probably could not think of their responses unless a context was provided. There was another interesting observation. Respondents often went back to the items of a questionnaire as if they were revising their previous responses in the light of the subsequent items and were trying to give an integrated set of responses. As I was more interested in constructing the realities than blindly following the dictates of a particular methodology, I had no choice but to ask my field investigators to collect secondary source data and to record observations of their respondents' behaviour, comments, and not-so-overt expressions. Whenever there were gaps or discrepancies in the information, I insisted on more data to arrive at any conclusion. As a result, I gradually moved towards supplementing quantitative data with more qualitative observations, secondary sources data, critical events, and so on. I was now looking for a more holistic picture of complex realities (Sinha, 1990).

SWANTAH SUKHAE[6]

While the new paradigm of my research was quite absorbing to me, it made systematic collaboration with my international counterparts increasing difficult. There was sporadic sharing of authorships or collective efforts. But we invariably ended up writing parallel reports or going our own ways. We have not been able to realise comparability in the whole complex of interrelated concepts and consequently in the choice of methods.

Many of my international colleagues have a full-grown theory, a well-computerised research strategy, a comprehensive plan, and a grant or contacts to get data collected at several points of the globe. When they approach me, I find myself in a difficult position. Neither our approaches, nor our methods, nor our priorities match. Their concepts and theories are at best only partly applicable in the Indian setting. I do not have the need to carry the cross of someone's theory or approach; nor do I have resources to try mine in some other cultures. My hunch is that even if I try, I will be imposing my emic under the delusion of realising an etic. Maybe the best I can do is to try to be a cultural rather than a cross-cultural psychologist. Maybe the route to a universal science of psychology is through many indigenous psychologies forming overarching patterns.

I now have a different world view of psychologies: we all have our own islands – psycho-historically and culturally determined. They form clusters, some being closer while others are more distant. It is unrealistic to think that some day the clusters will join to form one big monolithic mass. All we can do is to explore our own islands and build bridges to communicate and share. These crisscross bridges will some day assume patterns which we may call the facets of universal psychology. I am happy on my own island and shall be ready to join others in such pattern discovery. I would indeed love to do so. Anyone from any island can give me a call and I shall respond. But the bridges have to be built simultaneously from both sides. I have been to other islands. They are wonderful and exciting. But I have my own where I have plenty to do. And I enjoy doing my work.

NOTES

1 Literally means 'journey'. It also symbolises efforts towards inner transformation by religious and spiritual pursuits.
2 There is a mythological story about Lord Indra (the king of gods and goddesses) who asked a sage: 'What is my real self?' The sage said: 'It is you.' 'Is it my body?' The sage said: '*Neti, Neti* [No, this is not it; no, this is not it].' 'Is it my thought or feeling?' '*Neti, Neti.*' The dialogue continued till Lord Indra realised what his true self was.
3 It means a state of turbulence and instability arising out of the confusion regarding one's dispositions, conducts, desires, and expectations.
4 Personal communication, 26 May 1967.
5 We were still subscribing to the Western view that dependency is a manifestation of one's weakness and lack of worth, and therefore undesirable. It was much later that Doi (1986) and Kakar (1978) highlighted its positive role.
6 The expression is taken from the great epic, *Ramayan*, by the most popular medieval poet, Tulsidas, who stated that he composed it for his 'self-satisfaction/self-fulfilment'.

REFERENCES

Doi, T. (1986). *The anatomy of self: Individual versus society.* Tokyo: Kodansha.
Kakar, S. (1978). *The inner world: A psychoanalytic study of childhood and society in India.* New Delhi: Oxford University Press.
Saha, S. and Sinha, J. B. P. (1973). The transfer of model effects on dependence proneness. *Indian Journal of Psychology, 48,* 23–29.
Sinha, J. B. P. (1968). The nAch/cooperation under limited/unlimited resource conditions. *Journal of Experimental Social Psychology, 4,* 233–248.
Sinha, J. B. P. (1970). *Development through behaviour modification.* Bombay: Allied Publishers.
Sinha, J. B. P. (1973). Organisational climate and problems of management in India. *International Journal of Applied Psychology, 22,* 56–64.
Sinha, J. B. P. (1980). *The nurturant task leader.* New Delhi: Concept.
Sinha, J. B. P. (1981). In search of research identity. In J. Pandey (ed.), *Perspectives on experimental social psychology in India* (pp. 241–252). New Delhi: Concept.
Sinha, J. B. P. (1982). The Hindu identity. *Dynamic Psychiatry, 15,* 148–160.
Sinha, J. B. P. (1990). *Work culture in the Indian context.* New Delhi: Sage.
Sinha, J. B. P. (1994). Power dynamics in Indian organizations. In R. N. Kanungo and M. Mendonca (eds), *Motivation models for developing countries* (pp. 213–229). New Delhi: Sage.
Sinha, J. B. P. (1995). Socio-cultural factors of organizational behaviour in India. In K. K. Hwang (ed.), *Easternisation: Socio-cultural impact on productivity* (pp. 97–126). Tokyo: Asian Productivity Organisation.
Sinha, J. B. P. (1996, in press). A cultural perspective on organizational behaviour in India. In P. C. Earley and M. Erez (eds), *New perspectives on international industrial/organisational psychology.* San Francisco: Jossey-Bass.
Sinha, J. B. P. and Pandey, J. (1970). Strategies of high nAch persons. *Psychologia, 13,* 210–216.

8   The making, unmaking and remaking of a psychologist

Edward E. Sampson

I sometimes wonder how my ideas about psychology came to take the shape they have. Why am I, a psychologist, so distrustful of psychology? Why am I inclined to reject psychology's preferred kinds of analysis in favour of probing more deeply into culture and history? Why, when I consider a piece of psychological work, do my first thoughts turn to questions of politics and ideology rather than accepting psychological findings as interesting 'facts' about human nature?

As someone who was trained rather rigorously in the 'science' of psychology, first in UCLA's undergraduate Psychology Program and then in the University of Michigan's Graduate Program in Social Psychology, by most reckoning I should not be thinking in this manner. In fact, with this background, I should be lodged rather comfortably in the centre of the mainstream of psychological inquiry, either carrying on those inventive little studies that define what the field is, or sitting comfortably, tenure secure, resting after some thirty-five years in the profession. But I am neither lodged in that mainstream nor am I able to rest. I am marginal to my field, considered by some not even to be 'doing' psychology. I no longer conduct those inventively complex little experiments designed to test hypotheses using college students as subjects for which I had been so carefully trained. (What would my mentors – Katz, Newcomb, Cartwright and French – say?) Nor am I able to sit back, laurels in hand, and contemplate some thirty-five years of noble if not Nobel work.

Certainly, I am unlikely ever to be given an award for my contributions to psychology, because for these last twenty-five or so years, most of those contributions have been designed to undermine the conventional version of psychology – hardly a basis for receiving my colleagues' plaudits. And when I receive a new textbook in the mail, sent by some publisher eager for my adoption, and page to the 'Ss' in the name index, I rarely encounter 'Sampson'. Hoping not to warp young minds by planting seeds of doubt about the enterprise on which they are soon to embark, textbook authors have no reason to cite 'Sampson's' subversive writings.

When I was a bit younger, I recall wondering why I couldn't simply do what everyone else was doing and leave things well enough alone. Why did I insist on spending all my time locating the margins of my field and then embracing them when the mainstream beckoned? This chapter is an attempt to discover how someone set for a career within the normal routines of his conventional science moved so steadfastly away from that centre: the making and unmaking of a psychologist. I will conclude, however, by focusing on my efforts to remake the field so that I can be the mainstream and those currently seen as central will live as I now do – off on the margins, names rarely seen in future indices.

PREVIEW

To anticipate this process of unmaking and remaking, I think that my social location as a professor of psychology at Berkeley during the 1960s forced certain experiences upon me that shaped the kind of psychologist I have become. I was compelled to see both the academy and psychology as political subcultures that served dominant social interests even while professing scientific neutrality. I met people sufficiently different from those I had been accustomed to encountering that I was compelled to consider the impact of cultural socialisation on the kinds of people we become. But perhaps most significantly of all, my doubts about psychology's political functions led me increasingly to examine the cross-cultural literature. Unlike typical psychologists, however, for whom cross-cultural work represents a test of the universality of their own findings, I turned to cross-cultural work to demonstrate the hidden biases contained within US psychological work and thus to confirm my suspicions about the political role that much of psychology played. These are the items that I explore in this chapter.

THE MAKING OF A PSYCHOLOGIST

I will be brief, as there are only a few points of interest in this process by which I initially became a member in good standing of my field. As I stated at the outset, I was trained first at UCLA and then at Michigan in the normal routines of being a psychologist: several years of statistics, research design and experimental methodology followed by several more years of conducting laboratory experiments in social psychology, first as a graduate student, then as an Assistant Professor of Psychology at UC Berkeley, using these little laboratory encounters as the stepping stone to achieve publication and tenure.

The only noteworthy feature of my schooling is that it was so normal, so routine, so uneventful. I had some excellent professors, some of the top names in the field, presenting psychology to me as it then was. We spent none of our time together questioning psychology itself, only the bits and pieces within the already given field that one might challenge: e.g. was the impression formed of another person an additive or Gestalt-like reconfiguration? And so I never paused, even for a fleeting moment, to have doubts about my field. I was compliant and friendly, a bit shy, never one to speak out in seminars to challenge the entire enterprise; definitely not like some of my fellow students, disruptive to the core, I thought.

Dutifully, I absorbed everything that was offered to me, without question or critique. My task, as I understood it, was to learn what the people I read or heard were saying, not to wonder about it. Needless to say, with this attitude, I was a generally excellent student, both undergraduate and graduate, and received my PhD in 1960 from the University of Michigan after having completed a decent if not exciting experimental study within the research programme on power developed by Jack French at the Research Center for Group Dynamics. In short, I seemed to be heading for an exemplary, traditional career. I was especially fortunate to have my degree from Michigan as it paved the way to my first academic position in psychology at UC Berkeley, where I began in autumn 1960.

When I arrived at Berkeley in the Fall of 1960, a fresh young kid of twenty-five with my PhD in hand, the Department Chair sat me down along with the two other new kids and informed the three of us: 'We are all good teachers here, so don't worry about that if you want to remain. Publish at least two papers each year and your future here is set.' As an aspiring beginner, I heard the call of the small laboratory experiment and heeded that call as diligently as I could. I even managed to get a grant for a series of laboratory studies on 'status congruence', never knowing that besides the tenure this enterprise would eventually bring me, it would also lead me to ask questions the answers to which would press me towards the margins, never again to embrace the conventional science of psychology.

THE UNMAKING OF A PSYCHOLOGIST

It should come as no surprise that my unmaking as a psychologist had its beginnings at Berkeley in the 1960s. Nor should it be any surprise that someone who passed through so many years of education without critique, challenge or doubt should be especially ready to be transformed by that place in those times – when questioning everything and trusting nothing or no one in authority had become the watchwords for an entire generation.

Role change

As I took the podium for my first stint as a professor of psychology, I discovered that for the first time in my life I was genuinely responsible for other people's well-being, and not just my own. I will never forget looking down at my notes, then up at the class, hundreds just sitting there waiting for my words, pencils poised, notebooks at the ready, to record everything I uttered. As shy as I was, I was nevertheless the consummate performer whose momentary jitters helped shape an even better performance. Yet I was profoundly worried. Here they were busily writing down every word I had to say, as though what I was saying was important enough for someone to write down. To me this meant that what I said had to be important. Sadly, of course, all that I had to say was what I had been taught to say: 'Hull's learning theory was different than Tolman's'; 'While some argued that we formed impressions additively, others argued that it was . . . '.

Of course, when I was a student, I had dutifully recorded these same tidbits of knowledge, fascinated by the kinds of challenge they posed for the theorist/investigator. But now, I was the purveyor of this material who was shaken by watching others so intent on capturing every last word. The doubts that I never had for myself when I was the student came cascading down upon me now that I was the professor in charge of others' education.

Something was beginning to change in me. It was as though I began to hear things for the very first time as they were, not as I had always imagined them to be. I began to wonder just what it was I was giving away to my students. Were these the lessons they most needed to know? Too many questions; too many doubts. But there was no turning back now.

Fallen idols

A second eye-opener, at least for me, was to have as colleagues and professional peers the very people that I had been so assiduously studying in my student days. No names, please, but these were some of the major contributors to psychology; and now, rather than dutifully studying what they had to say, I sat next to them in meetings and watched them perform. And I was shocked and disappointed. These men (only one woman then!) may have been considered great psychologists but I had some serious questions about just what psychology had taught them about humanity, especially their own. I watched them romp through department meetings like selfish little children pursuing self-interest, and squabbling incessantly about who should get more space, who had too much already, who was the better, wiser, more famous.

One item that they could all agree on, however, was their disdain for their undergraduate students and their abiding suspicion of anyone who was a popular undergraduate instructor. I must admit to being somewhat puzzled in that I naively thought we were here to teach these students, not to consider them with such disrespect that anyone who worked well with them could not thereby be a serious Berkeley professor.

The many conflicts within Berkeley's psychology department eventually became so destructive that the administration felt compelled to divide the department into three relatively autonomous groupings, established sociometrically rather than in terms of any overall disciplinary plan. People in one group would not even look at those in the other group let alone chat with them when passing in the halls. Collaboration on anything was out of the question. Petty squabbling ruled, and not just between groups, but within each group as well. I felt I was living among children competing for the favour of some distant parent, though I was never sure just who this parent was, other than perhaps reputation and fame, the very kind of parent who could never be satisfied.

What kind of people were these?, I wondered. Did I really want to become one of them and carry on in *this* manner? Even more significantly, I had naively thought that a field such as psychology might work wonders in giving its practitioners insights which they could use in their own lives and even make them better or more concerned teachers. But if these folks, once my idols, had any insights into improving the human condition or in teaching undergraduates, they never employed them in their daily interactions with one another or their students.

I know that these indictments are rather harsh and made too broadly. Of course there were exceptions. But to a hopeful young professor, the Berkeley role models were profoundly disappointing. Not only did I have difficulty accepting their view of undergraduate education, but I also found their manner of relating to one another (and to me) something I simply did not want to emulate.

My worry over ever becoming one of them almost ended in my third year at Berkeley. My qualifications for tenured membership in what was generally considered a rather exclusive 'club' and a real plum of an academic position were seriously questioned. One afternoon, a group of sombre men met to give me feedback on my future prospects at Berkeley. The future did not look very good, they said; I did not quite measure up to their standards for a 'Berkeley Psychology Professor'. But, on the positive side, as they reminded me, I still had two more years to shape up before they would have to ship me out.

I was furious. These men were telling me that I did not fit their world, when from everything I had seen of their actions, I was not sure that any decent person should want to belong to that world! If this little lecture by these sombre men was designed to transform me into one of them, it had just the opposite effect. Oh, yes, I wanted membership and so produced enough over the next two years to gain tenure. But I vowed not to become one of them. My students deserved better than that and so too did I.

During the two pre-tenure years of struggle, I finally 'came out'. I began to challenge this plum of an academic appointment. In fact, it would come to pass that in 1970 I resigned from my tenured position at Berkeley, not to accept a comparable position at an even more prestigious university, but for a mere lectureship at a British red-brick polytechnic. People simply do not do such things. After all, to have tenure at Berkeley as I did, if not everyone's dream, is at least the dream of many in the academic world. And here I was, not only challenging the significance of that dream, but packing my bags and rejecting it entirely.

Of course, there were many complex reasons for my departure, not the least of which was simply burnout from the 1960s. But I like to believe that it is also the case that I had to reject Berkeley in order to follow the directions my work was now leading me. Had I stayed at Berkeley, I might have become the very person I sensed I should never be. Even before leaving, however, my work began its transformation. Two themes that have continued with me to this day began to emerge. Initially, they were poorly formed; increasingly, they became clarified and defined the kind of psychologist I would become.

Psychology not

First, I reacquainted myself with my preference, the origin of which continues to remain obscure, to favour social and cultural understandings over the purely psychological. In my initial contact with the disappointing character of my Berkeley colleagues, I located the problem in the personalities of the people, thereby overly psychologising the predicament I had encountered. Perhaps the jolt of being told I was not cut of the same cloth as these 'great figures' led me to remember why I had abandoned clinical psychology during my one graduate year at UCLA. I left clinical once I realised that probing individual psyches was of much less interest to me than probing the broader socio-cultural domain within which those individuals carried on their tortured lives. And now at Berkeley I again found myself rejecting a psychological analysis of individual character in favour of a more culturally situated understanding.

The unappealing qualities of my colleagues' character, but especially their overly inflated self-importance and inability to put psychology into practice in their own lives, worried me because I came to suspect, correctly I think, that anyone hoping to be successful within that academic culture would have to acquire precisely those same qualities. I began to realise that my colleagues' character, while annoying, was less the real problem than the culture of academe and of psychology itself that made these qualities so valuable an asset. It was this culture from which I had to escape, lest I too became like them. That same theme has continued throughout my professional life: rejecting the purely psychological and searching for answers within the domain of the social, the cultural and the historical (see, e.g., Sampson, 1983 for a useful summary).

Politics and ideology

The second theme that also runs throughout my published works and that animates my teaching involves probing the political and ideological dimension of psychology. It struck me, vaguely at first and then more clearly later, that psychology was a political discipline that occupied a definite place within the fabric of contemporary US culture. This was not the pristine 'science of psychology' that I had been taught and that I had heard endlessly praised by my esteemed colleagues; this was not a value-free, neutral discipline with its only allegiance being to the 'facts'. Where others saw empirical findings, I saw political messages. It became my self-appointed job to unearth the political and the ideological that lay just beneath the surface of psychology's theoretical concepts and empirical findings. My questions shifted dramatically from inquiring about the latest exciting discoveries of psychological science to wondering why those 'discoveries' were appearing now and, most importantly, whose interests did they serve (see, e.g., Sampson, 1977, 1978, 1985, 1988, 1989, 1991, 1993a, 1993b, 1994 for a sampling of this work). Needless to say, engaging in this kind of work did little to endear me to my colleagues who clearly got the message: I was not only questioning the purity of others' works but of theirs as well.

It seems that when my colleagues questioned my qualifications to join their exclusive club, they created a dedicated radical, not a loyal follower. It became my task to undermine their world by revealing its hidden secrets. Simultaneously, I found myself also helping to give voice to those interests that had been systematically denied by the shape of the existing field.

I should note that I had most of these subversive thoughts well before they became more broadly popular as African-American, feminist, and gay and lesbian groups voiced similar concerns about how psychology represented them. I am not asserting this in order to claim primacy – the history of such ideas preceded even their popularity as a social critique in the USA. Rather, I mention this in order to indicate the degree to which early on I had moved outside my field. Be that as it may, this second theme, unearthing psychology's political face, has remained with me and is central to all of my scholarly endeavours.

The Cuban missile crisis

In 1962, the relations between the USA and what was then the Soviet Union had deteriorated so far that war seemed inevitable. It was October. I was teaching a course in cross-cultural psychology, appropriate for someone for whom the purely psychological never held that much appeal. As I began my lecture, I was aware that Soviet ships were heading towards Cuba carrying missiles aimed at the USA while American warships were prepared to interdict their movement, possibly setting off World War III. What meaningful knowledge could I be teaching my students when tomorrow might never come for any of us? Somehow, telling my students about the child-rearing practices in Samoa seemed irrelevant at this key moment. And so I stopped talking about Samoa and began a collective conversation about all of us and what the future, if there were to be one, held.

This departure, not only from my prepared script, but also from what I still believed was the proper neutrality of a professor, placed me in a delicate position. Was I simply using the podium that had been given to me at the University to engage in personal politics or was there something more to it? Only later would I come to realise that there was no way to use that podium that was not a political act. On the way to that realisation, I found myself walking very tentatively and with great unease. But it was a step that I simply had to take. Nothing else made sense in that October of 1962. Samoa faded. Our shared fate became central.

The Free Speech Movement

In 1964, the Free Speech Movement descended upon Berkeley, bringing me into contact with people I had never really known: campus politicos, radical types, culturally marginal persons, later to be called hippies. I got involved in this movement, but not initially through any political motivation – I was still the nice 'boy', unaware of politics in general and still not clearly aware of the political face of the science of psychology. But the compliant patina was beginning to wear thin. I had been informed by a few students that a group had captured a police car on Sproul Plaza in which one of their own had been placed after being arrested for collecting money on campus for a political cause. Clearly, they intended to spend the entire night out there. I became worried more about feeding them than about their politics. And so I helped to organise a delivery of coffee and some snacks. Thus began my involvement in 'politics' and my further estrangement from my field with its professions of neutrality and its insistence on remaining disengaged from the very people it studied.

My presence at the beginnings of the Free Speech Movement had brought me into prominent contact with campus politicos. Soon I joined them in some of their meetings and planning sessions. I listened as they referred to the University as an oppressor, not as a source of enlightenment. What about psychology, I wondered?

Whatever else I thought about some of my colleagues in the department, most of whom were card-carrying liberals, I simply could not consider them to be oppressors. That was foolish. Yet, as we each carried out our jobs in compliance with the demands of our field, the University and our society, I came to see that we were participating in a political culture that expressed certain collective interests while denying others.

In thwarting students' political organising, the University was clearly taking a political position, and no matter how much it claimed neutrality, its stance was hardly neutral. Psychology itself was part of this same culture. The campus politicos and radicals saw psychology as part of the problem, not the solution. For them, and soon for me as well, psychology was a bit too lily-white, too male, and, in its tendency to reduce social issues to psychological concepts, too conservative. These claims resonated with my own emerging consciousness about myself and my field. My vocabulary of analysis began to shift from a mere acceptance of psychology to a forceful effort to transform it towards the role that I believed it should play. After all, if psychology was not neutral, then why not develop a psychology that helped give voice to those persons usually not clearly heard?

The radical professor

As I became more involved with the campus politicos, seen by them as an ally and by my colleagues as a threat to the neutrality of the field and to the reputation of the department, I became even more alienated from my departmental colleagues (with some very noteworthy exceptions). For them, this mixing of politics with psychology was anathema. Meanwhile, I became the darling of my students, who lined up in the hundreds just to get into my classes and to hear my 'wonderfully wise' lectures.

I think that what I had to say had in fact become much wiser. I had found ways of organising and presenting psychological material that made it relevant to the political concerns of the day. I had become a radical professor who was trying to give away a psychology that I hoped was not only relevant to our times and these students' lives, but was less an oppressive apology for our society than an ongoing critique of that society. And, needless to say, given the negative correlation assumed by most of my colleagues between attractiveness as an instructor and scholarly repute, my growing popularity was taken as a sure sign of my lagging scholarly potential.

At long last, I was accorded the same disdain within my department that I had earlier seen others receive: I too was passed in the corridors of Tolman Hall without a nod, a hello, a smile. The vacant stares told me that I had finally made it. I will never forget that look given to me by one of my colleagues – a very well-known, highly respected international scholar with a rather substantial list of publications and major grants – who watched me walk a picket line around Tolman Hall, the departmental home. If looks could kill, my life would have been over then.

It would come to pass that one level of involvement led easily to another and another, so that soon I was almost entirely a radical professor. Students would seek me out to support or join with them in the latest uprising. I found myself unable to say no. The press also sought me out. I began to think that my opinions were much more important on nearly every issue of the day than, in fact, they deserved to be. And as all of this moved onwards, my investment in mainstream psychology lessened and I found myself looking for a new kind of psychology. After all, no self-respecting radical professor could teach psychology as it then existed and still maintain radical credentials. A differently cast psychology was required; and I set about to discover and practise it.

REMAKING PSYCHOLOGY

The new kind of psychology that I sought did not exist in the mainstream of my field nor had it ever been part of my own education. But it did exist out there just waiting for someone to pick it up. I had the good fortune one day to find Martin Jay's (1973) excellent introduction to the contributions of the Frankfurt group. Shortly thereafter, and motivated by the new doors opening up to me, I happened upon Derrida's (1974, 1978, 1981) writings and encountered both deconstructionism and the entire postmodern movement. And then, of course, I ran into Foucault's (1979, 1980; also Dreyfus and Rabinow, 1982) distinctive challenges to psychology and to the very nature of human subjectivity.

I was not weird. I may have become marginal to the US mainstream, but here was a thoughtful tradition of scholarly inquiry to which I belonged. I found myself turning away from US sources and increasingly employing these and other European sources for inspiration, solace or direction. I found a similar comfort in the emerging feminist tradition. In each case, I discovered a kind of psychology that seemed to suit my growing radicalisation and need to ground that radicalisation in a substantively new understanding of psychology.

Unlike conventional psychology, these various approaches were often unashamedly political, recognising clearly what I had finally come to understand: even those who claimed to be neutral in their science were involved in a political act. The Frankfurt programme, Foucault and the feminist contributions helped me see that neutrality was impossible. If the only way to be neutral is to stand outside of all time and all culture, then to claim this impossible feat is to engage in a rhetorical tactic designed to avoid the very political entanglements which one can never avoid.

The professions of neutrality that continued to permeate US psychology became even more offensive to me. I saw clearly how they helped to disguise the particular group interests that were at work by insisting that the neutral observer had no interests at all (see, e.g., Sampson, 1994). One's opponents are thereby put down for their excessively interested arguments, while one claims no interests for him or herself. For example, a colleague's Marxist publications are not considered scholarly but rather only like religious tracts, while articles published in the

Journal of Personality and Social Psychology are considered to be the model of truly disinterested scholarship.

The idea that *JPSP* articles were the ideal model of good psychological science led me to probe beneath their surface seeking to understand whose interests were being paraded about in the guise of dispassionate science. I read *JPSP* less as a document in psychology than as a cultural map. I found it enlightening to select article after article and observe the underlying cultural values they served even while claiming simply to be reporting the facts. The Frankfurt programme and the others' works all confirmed for me the idea that facts do not live in a pristine way outside culture and history. These critiques helped shape my own writings and my suspicions about any and all claims to have discovered something true about human nature.

One of my early papers, 'Psychology and the American ideal' (1977), for example, took a then popular psychological concept, androgyny, and probed it critically for the underlying ideology that it reflected. As I had done previously for the concept of justice as equity (e.g. Sampson, 1969, 1975), I sought to expose the cultural and historical assumptions underlying androgyny that were hardly a neutral portrait of the individual's psyche. I reached conclusions about the individualistic cultural ethos that marked Western societies in general and the USA in particular and so questioned the universality of all psychological concepts. Increasingly, I turned to the cross-cultural literature, most of which clearly revealed that the individualism that lay behind androgyny, equity and almost every other psychological concept was unique and perhaps even a bit aberrant when viewed on the world's larger stage. So what then was psychology doing in presenting concepts derived from its own underlying culture of individualism as though these were universal features of the human psyche? All of this became fuel for my agenda seeking to reveal the political face of current psychology.

Each new issue of *JPSP* and our other journals provided me with a rich source of data. I conducted a series of critical investigations of so-called psychological truths (e.g. Sampson, 1978, 1981, 1987, 1989), in each case doing a critical, cultural reading of psychology's publications, employing them much as an anthropologist might use a culture's folktales as a device for unearthing the underlying assumptions and values of a culture.

Not only was I rapidly changing my views of psychology, but I now had strong support for the new kind of politically aware psychology that I had already been practising. Occasionally I would wonder why these European approaches had never been mentioned in my otherwise fine education. I did not believe that the answer to my question lay in the difficulty in finding English translations of works originally written in German or French. Rather, it was clear that conventional psychology simply did not consider these European challengers appropriate, in great measure, as Thomas Kuhn (1962) helped us to see, because their challenge was to the very rules of the game that psychology employed, not to the outcomes when the game is played by conventional rules. To understand this truth is already to embark on a journey towards a very different kind of psychology.

Social constructionism

I soon found myself turning towards a more constructionist view of psychology. Facts were social constructions. And each construction typically helped justify one group's claims over another's. The tentative steps of my earlier days were replaced by a more self-confident understanding of psychology, psychologists and their place in modern Western society. Not being in the mainstream of that enterprise was a mark of distinction that I came to wear proudly.

A consideration of my more recent writings, for example, reveals the extent to which I not only locate my works within a constructionist framework, but have adapted that framework to suit my concerns with the political face of psychological science (e.g. especially Sampson, 1991, 1993a, 1993b, 1994).

I believe that herein lies the basis of my ongoing interest in cross-cultural studies. I must be clear on this point, however. I have not turned to cross-cultural work in order to extend the universality of key Western concepts. For me, cross-cultural work offered alternative, viable frameworks for constituting reality, much as the constructionist thesis maintains. That we in the USA are fascinated by psychological discourses and could not live the forms of life we do without such discourses is something we can finally grasp only when contrasted with cultures in which psychologising is not central to their structuring of their world. In short, cross-cultural work became a way to demonstrate the diverse constructions of reality that are possible and to cast further doubt, therefore, about the functions that the currently dominant US formulations serve. The guiding question for me, then, is which groups benefit and which groups are harmed by the currently dominant forms of US psychologising.

CONCLUSION

As I reflect back on my career, I am increasingly aware that what invariably appears to be a personal account is in truth a cultural story as well. I was born white and male in a culture in which those very qualities opened doors that were closed to others. I used these qualities to enter through those doors only to decry publicly the privilege they permitted me and denied to others. I was a member of the academy, offered a life of great privilege, but even while embracing the academy, sought to undermine that special privilege. I was *in* psychology, yet never quite *of* psychology once it became clear to me what being *of* psychology really meant.

I had all the accoutrements to belong, to fit in, not to question. And yet, when given the chance, I could not embrace the comfort zone temptingly offered to me. I have outlined some of the reasons why I had such difficulty remaining an insider; yet I suspect that there is much more here than I have yet discerned.

Why have I challenged everything that I also embody? Why did I not choose the fame, fortune or comfort that I suspect could have been mine if I only had played the game as it was designed?

I have no answers to any of these questions. But, in reviewing the story of the

Frankfurt group, I am struck by some compelling similarities. Susan Buck-Morss (1977, p. 48) describes Adorno, one of the prime movers of the Frankfurt Institute both in Germany and then later in the United States (once even at Berkeley), as being involved in a never-ending effort 'to fight against the spirit of the times rather than to join it'. Distrusting any one place to stop, a spot where the ongoing process of critique seems to end, in an Adorno-like manner, I too work to sustain a 'critical distance from the gravitational pull of the prevailing reality' (Jay, 1973, p. 279).

I think that the core of my mission remains: to locate the centre and then move away from it. I distrust all of those centres, even those to which I have made my major contributions (see, e.g., Sampson, 1996 for a challenge even to the constructionism I embrace). The moving process that never settles for long seems a better approach to me, and for the psychology I hope someday yet to see (even if I have to return in some 200 years to check things out), than any approach that settles permanently anywhere. Although I am unlike the Frankfurt group who had to flee their country (Germany) in order to continue their work, I nevertheless share with them the same horror about the consequences that have occurred in the name of every centred system of belief and understanding. Only by never stopping, perhaps, can such horrors be avoided.

The gerunds of my title reveal this sense of ongoing process, movement, change: perhaps that is my story, whatever its worth may be to others.

REFERENCES

Buck-Morss, S. (1977). *The origin of negative dialectics*. New York: Free Press.
Derrida, J. (1974). *Of grammatology*. Baltimore, MD: Johns Hopkins University Press.
Derrida, J. (1978). *Writing and difference*. Chicago, IL: University of Chicago Press.
Derrida, J. (1981). *Dissemination*. Chicago, IL: University of Chicago Press.
Dreyfus, H. L. and Rabinow, R. (1982). *Michel Foucault: Beyond structuralism and hermeneutics*. Chicago, IL: University of Chicago Press.
Foucault, M. (1979). *Discipline and punish: The birth of the prison*. New York: Random House.
Foucault, M. (1980). *The history of sexuality*, vol. I: *An introduction*. New York: Random House.
Jay, M. (1973). *The dialectical imagination*. Boston, MA: Little, Brown.
Kuhn, T. S. (1962). *The structure of scientific revolutions*. Chicago, IL: University of Chicago Press.
Sampson, E. E. (1969). Studies in status congruence. In L. Berkowitz (ed.), *Advances in experimental social psychology* (vol. 4, pp. 225–270). New York: Academic Press.
Sampson, E. E. (1975). Justice as equality. *Journal of Social Issues, 31*, 45–64.
Sampson, E. E. (1977). Psychology and the American ideal. *Journal of Personality and Social Psychology, 35*, 767–782.
Sampson, E. E. (1978). Scientific paradigms and social values: Wanted – a scientific revolution. *Journal of Personality and Social Psychology, 36*, 1332–1343.
Sampson, E. E. (1981). Cognitive psychology as ideology. *American Psychologist, 36*, 730–743.
Sampson, E. E. (1983). *Justice and the critique of pure psychology*. New York: Plenum.
Sampson, E. E. (1985). The decentralization of identity: Toward a revised concept of personal and social order. *American Psychologist, 40*, 1203–1211.

Sampson, E. E. (1987). A critical constructionist view of psychology and personhood. In H. Stamm (ed.), *The analysis of psychological theory* (pp. 41–59). Washington, DC: Hemisphere.

Sampson, E. E. (1988). The debate on individualism: Indigenous psychologies of the individual and their role in personal and societal functioning. *American Psychologist, 43*, 15–22.

Sampson, E. E. (1989). The challenge of social change for psychology, I: Globalization and psychology's theory of the person. *American Psychologist, 44*, 914–921.

Sampson, E. E. (1991). The democraticization of psychology. *Theory and Psychology, 1*, 275–298.

Sampson, E. E. (1993a). Identity politics: Challenges to psychology's understanding. *American Psychologist, 48*, 1219–1230.

Sampson, E. E. (1993b). *Celebrating the other: A dialogic account of human nature*. London: Harvester Wheatsheaf; Boulder, CO: Westview.

Sampson, E. E. (1994). Justice and the neutral state: A postmodern, feminist critique of Lehning's (1990) account of justice. *Social Justice Research, 7*, 145–154.

Sampson, E. E. (1996). Establishing embodiment in psychology. *Theory and Psychology, 6*, 601–625.

9 Tales that wag the dog

Globalisation and the emergence of postmodern psychology

Kenneth J. Gergen and Mary M. Gergen

In his historical review chapter of the second edition of the *Handbook of social psychology*, Edward E. Jones (1985) took aim at the handful of scoundrels and ne'er-do-wells challenging the dominant tradition of experimental research in American social psychology. Borrowing from William Butler Yeats, he privately equated this critical work to 'dogs barking in the night . . . while the caravans move on'. This statement was particularly stinging to us in that Jones was the dissertation adviser for one of us (KJG) and a personal friend to us both. While the experimentalist caravans have indeed moved on with scarcely a sideward glance, the yapping breed (of which we have counted ourselves) has increased in numbers. From all corners of the globe scholars have joined in producing new forms of psychology, new ways of thinking about theory, research and practice, and new ideas about the relationship of the profession to society. While it is too early to know whether integration across these various pursuits is possible (or even desirable), the sense of excitement among the mongrel breed is everywhere and unmistakable.

This chapter is an account of at least some of the perturbations generated with our colleagues over the past twenty years or so. Much of our own work during this period – on historical psychology, generative theory, narratives, social constructionism, feminist postmodernism, relational theory, and performative psychology, for example – has been born in the wild.[1] By 'wild' in this case we not only mean outside the domesticated confines of experimental social psychology, but outside the specifically American orbit of behavioural science. In our view, most of our work over this period has been both stimulated and enriched by our experiences in cultural contexts that are distinctly non-American. It is in this respect that we view these various developments as contributing to a *postmodern* consciousness in psychology (also see Kvale, 1992). That is, we move toward a psychology no longer dominated by the cultural modernism of the USA.

Over the past several decades, we have had the great privilege of residing and/or travelling in many different locales around the world. Liberal sabbatical policies at Swarthmore College and at Penn State opened the door, and invitations from friends and colleagues, along with grants, fellowships, and awards from various institutions and foundations, provided the essential support. An enormous amount could be said about the many individuals around the globe who have directly stimulated and enriched our thinking. These relationships of love and respect deserve a chapter in themselves.[2] However, in the present offering our focus is on the more mundane aspects of immersion in the global flow. We wish to bring to life some of those otherwise unsung moments when fissures erupt in the intellectual ice, and it is no longer possible to go on in just the same way. In effect, we wish to pay tribute to the significant stimulation of the unplanned and unexpected encounters that have altered our intellectual paths.

SOCIAL PSYCHOLOGY AS HISTORY

One of the first howlings in the night occurred in 1973 with the publication of 'Social psychology as history'.[3] This paper was a principal fixture in what was then called 'the crisis in social psychology'. The central thesis of this work was that the subject matter of social psychology is historically contingent. That which we study – patterns of aggression, altruism, attraction and the like – acquire their character within particular historical circumstances. Thus, the attempt of social psychology to accumulate knowledge, in the sense of building on the findings of past experiments in order to make increasingly accurate predictions about the future, is misguided. While giving the impression of being ahistorical, experimental predictions can only be useful in so far as the scientist is immersed within the particular cultural/historical circumstances relevant to the experiment. Further, the very communication of psychological insights into the culture itself can shape the future patterns of conduct. In this sense, experimental study is reflexive, influencing the very culture it attempts to study.

It is very doubtful that these arguments would have originated without earlier sojourns in England and Sweden, where the contrasts between early traditions and contemporary upheavals were everywhere apparent. We were also buoyed by our later participation in a highly consequential meeting arranged by Lloyd Strickland of Carleton University in Ottawa, which brought together leading social psychologists and graduate students from Europe and North America to talk over the growing alienation from the hegemonic expansion of US social psychology[4] into Europe and Canada. In these circumstances we were bathed in the ethers of historical transformation – shouting, recriminations, demonstrations, and even tears – evidencing traditions now in trouble. The virtual renting of the fabric of twentieth-century understanding seemed in process. Two additional 'moments of insight' bear recounting.

It was a fateful year in the century for many people, 1968. For us, it was the beginning of our life together as a couple. We were for the first time away from the United States for an extended time, cut away from friends, family, and familiar surroundings, and feeling, at times, the great need for connections with our pasts. Yet, phone calls were prohibitively expensive and email had not yet reached even the stage of fantasy. The postal system was our umbilical cord, but at times this link was tenuous at best. All of Rome was in upheaval, in ways we continued to discover on a daily basis. Alas, our institutional association in Rome was the Istituto Nazionale de Psicologia, and the building – like most others connected to the University of Rome – was occupied by student revolutionaries. Further, transportation to the university was virtually impossible as municipal transportation systems were crippled by striking workers. In a frantic desire to collect the mail, I (KJG) set out on foot, determined to walk the five miles or so from home to the University. As I approached the barricaded doors of the Institute, I was struck by the historical disjunction before me: majestic white marble columns ascending to great heights above me, symbols of Rome's glorious tradition, authority, and order, and beneath them, the flotsam and jetsam of the revolution, posters, signs and trash, barricades piled between columns, and the hostile faces of late adolescents peering out between the crevices. I thought to myself: these columns commemorate a way of life that was to be everlasting; yet, they guaranteed nothing. If such a rich and sumptuous tradition could be so trammelled, how could social psychology presume that its subject matter – relations among people – was transhistorical and universal? No, life changes as it goes on. Truths of one time and place do not travel unchanged to other times and places. The psychologist's claims of universality and timelessness are as empty as those of the Roman Caesars.

But let us end this tale in proper fashion. As I approached the barricades, I puzzled over what might be the proper etiquette for such a circumstance. I politely knocked at the magnificent portal, chained and locked to prevent intrusion. Voices within shouted '*Sciopero*', '*sciopero*', but for me the words were insignificant. With a show of deference mixed with desperation I asked if they would locate mail from America. Astonishingly, after some rustlings behind the doors, they politely passed the cherished packets to me through the barricades.

A second drama of historical disjunction gave rise to our edited book, *Historical social psychology* (1984). In a sense the book resulted from a traffic jam. We had been travelling on the German–Austrian border, and ended up on the autobahn one Sunday evening with thousands of like-minded weekenders returning to their city lives. Unfamiliar with the landscape and the roadways, we decided to take a shortcut to Tübingen, the home of very close friends, Maggie and Wolfgang Stroebe. Soon we found ourselves on dark and lonely roads with snow ever slowing the pace of travel. The impending solitude was interrupted now and then by a small town, with the neon glow of a gas station, pizza parlour or small business often illuminating the ascending spire of a medieval church or castle. As we moved through the lonely night, the striking contrast in these juxtapositions gave us food for fantasy. Why not a psychology, we asked one another, that itself focused on historical transformations? Rather than attempting to transcend or ignore history, the discipline should give historical change a central place. What after all has happened psychologically between knights and neon? We began rattling off possible contributors to a work that might set such study in motion; the kilometres rapidly disappeared into the past as we were finally welcomed into the warmth of our Tübingen sanctuary.

THE SOCIAL CONSTRUCTION OF KNOWLEDGE

If psychological knowledge is historically situated, a second major shift in thinking begins to take wing. We have inherited in the USA a view of science as a truth-generating process. As commonly put, the sciences, including psychology, should attempt in so far as possible to describe, explain, and predict phenomena. Thus, as presumptuously put by Francis Bacon, scientific understandings should 'carve nature at the joint'. Our experiences in other cultural settings have not only brought this view of science into critical reflection, but have helped us to participate in broad-ranging discussions of an alternative to this view, namely a social constructionist conception of knowledge.

From a constructionist standpoint, the world-as-it-is makes no demands on the words by which we characterise it. Rather, our characterisations grow from human interchange itself. Our languages of description and understanding – scientific and social – reflect the nature of our relationships and that which we hold significant within them. Knowledge – all that we take to be true or good – is a cultural construction. Because knowledge, in an important sense, is local and because there are many localities, we should anticipate multiple truths – diverse modes of characterising the seemingly 'same' situation. Because of the diversity of truth claims around the globe, it is very difficult to participate with any depth in another culture without emerging with a constructionist sensitivity. We could scarcely emerge from our own experiences without a deep appreciation for the multiplicity of entirely reasonable and fully antithetical interpretations of any behaviour. Several illustrations will suffice.

During a year's residence in Japan we conducted research projects with several professors and a young assistant from the USA. One line of research took us into a private company. Over time we found a very congenial relationship was developing between our assistant and one of the senior partners in the firm, an esteemed and honourable gentleman. They shared a deep love of music and talked for long hours together, during which she improved her fledgling Japanese. Yet, after the two had attended several concerts together, he grew distant, even chilly in his relations with us, and hostile in his relations to her. With effort we learned that in the Japanese tradition, consent to a relationship of the kind she had granted signified a form of passionate commitment. When our assistant failed in the expression of such commitment, she unknowingly insulted her senior. What for her was proper decorum was for him a signal of shallow exploitation. Much sensitive conversation was required to restore tranquillity. Thereby hangs another tale.

In Cardiff, Wales, we watched in fear as a speaker was bitterly attacked by his audience, complete with *ad hominem* derision, including a comment by a very prominent psychologist who said, 'This is so much rubbish.' After the blood-letting had subsided we rushed to our friend's side, only to find him in a quite amiable mood. How could he be so buoyant, we inquired? He failed to understand the question. When we described the public execution we had seen, he laughed. 'No,' he said, 'this is just normal jousting, good fun for all. One isn't to take it personally you know. If someone becomes too nasty, you simply don't invite him around for tea.'

In Bremen, Germany, a sociologist friend told us about the severe un-employment in the surrounding area. A large industrial plant had been forced to close down, and there were no other manufacturing jobs available there. At the same time, he described the great opportunities in southern Germany, where industrial jobs were plentiful. However, the potential labour force from Bremen would not move to Bavaria. They preferred to stay where they were, impoverished and pessimistic. We were provoked by what seemed to us a tragic lack of ambition. Our friend, who had spent many hours in interviews with these workers, was not at all surprised by their lassitude. As he pointed out, the German worker is traditionally rooted in a given geographical locale; the family name often extends back for centuries; close and intricate interdependencies exist among family and friendship networks. The jobs in the south are not squandered opportunities; they are simply irrelevant to their notions of a proper life. We were led to ponder our unacknowledged values that seemed to honour career before family and friendship solidarity.

In all these cases our own clear and obvious understandings were found circumscribed and unserviceable in other cultural settings. Is this not also the case in terms of understandings generated within the social sciences? Each culture employs its own vocabularies, traditions, and values in describing and explaining human action, and the practising psychologist can scarcely step out of his/her own culture. A constructionist science requires, then, reflexive evaluation of traditional commitments, and exploration of the ways in which they are (and are not) serviceable.

THE POLITICS OF SCHOLARLY WORK

To the extent that psychologists resonate with social constructionism as an epistemological form, they will also increasingly recognise their role in the political and moral issues of society – if not the world. The dominant tradition in American psychology makes strong claims to value neutrality. Science, it is said, is about observing and recording what is the case; what *ought* to be the case is not the business of science. To be sure, one may apply the results of psychological science to various political or moral issues in society, but this is not the chief task of the scientist *qua* scientist. As the tradition expresses it, science itself is not political. However, for the constructionist there is no neutral ground; science is inherently value saturated, and therefore political. In large measure this is so because in doing research scientists construct the world under study, giving it certain meanings and not others, and placing value on certain kinds of categories, while ignoring others. Various 'findings' from research projects wend their way into the public domains. Science reports that drug abuse is mounting among youth; drinking alcohol causes premature and sickly babies; males and females have different brain structures; and homosexuals have bigger cerebella than the norm. As these constructions enter society, they undergird rationales for action. They contribute to shaping the societal future – for good or ill.

Having grown up in the traditional milieu, it required a number of bracing experiences abroad to bring the political significance of psychological research to painful recognition.

In the early 1970s we attended a peace research conference in Denmark. With the Vietnam war in full progress, strong and rigorous research on the peace process seemed imperative. At one symposium we listened to what we viewed as highly competent and optimistic papers on the possibilities of enhancing the peace process. Anticipating a lively discussion on the work, we were shocked to find an audience almost united in its animosity toward the speakers. The speakers, they argued, were not solving political problems with their research; they were contributing to them. By reducing the problems of injustice and oppression to pallid questions of theory and findings from laboratory studies, no moral stand was taken. By presuming that the aim of research is to locate means of generating peace, no account was taken of the way in which peace would simply mean returning to the status quo. Perfect peace is the equivalent to perfect oppression. After the shouting subsided, we faced significant rethinking.

We were in Greece carrying out research on reactions to help.[5] At the time, the challenge was for us primarily 'scientific': we hoped to generate a transcultural and transhistorical theory enabling predictions to be made of reactions to assistance. We hoped the work would have real world application, and were specifically interested in how nations might build positive relations through international aid. In this case we were hoping that the study of reactions to international assistance in several countries would supply useful data to build and test our theory. In our visit to Greece we were only marginally interested in the political situation – a military junta had brought a loss of democracy to the country. For us as scientific researchers, the regime was more of an unfortunate inconvenience than a personal concern. Our interviewees revealed to us our naivete. As we learned, the problem of international assistance could not be abstracted from the political situation. One's reactions to assistance were thus comments, for good or ill, about one's government, and about other governments which lent it support. In the most dramatic case, our 'research subject' refused to answer questions about foreign aid in her office; rather, she led us to the streets, out of range of the listening devices possibly hidden in her quarters, and revealed in a whisper her passionate feelings about the government in power. We were no longer the same researchers, who could readily separate the scientific from the political or from the personal. There were no hiding places in which scientists could claim a special exemption from social responsibility.

Before 'the wall' came down, we were visiting scholars at the Max Planck Institute for Human Development in West Berlin. The Institute itself is an emblem of scientific purity – a glossy modern structure, with all the latest research equipment and extensive library facilities. One Sunday morning, we went to the Institute to pick up a set of papers we needed that afternoon. We entered the rear door and were dismayed to find that everything was covered with a thick dust. How could the normally spotless interior have become so soiled? It was only later that day we learned that the front door of the Institute had been blown apart by a bomb. The bomb had been planted by a radical political group that accused the administration of the Institute for giving way to a capitalist/American research agenda. The research, they maintained, would serve as an instrument of exploitation and suppression. Our own research could not be separated from the attack.

In Buenos Aires, Argentina, I (KJG) was asked to speak to a voluntary organisation committed to causes of democracy in Argentina. As this interchange proceeded I again learned that 'a talk is not a talk'. Democracy was not for them an issue of polite intellectual inquiry. Rather, under the preceding government – a military dictatorship – many of the volunteers I met that night had family members removed from their homes by police, never to be seen again. Spouses, children, parents joined the ranks of thousands of 'the disappeared'. This organisation was deeply invested in monitoring government activities, publishing a newspaper, and setting up training facilities for ensuring the continuation of the shaky democracy. During these conversations I also recalled the Jesuit priests in Nicaragua – psychological scientists – who were murdered for their 'scientific' teachings. The message became clear: my role in this case was not that of neutral scientist, but of a partisan to the cause.

As these experiences made clear, there is no neutral ground. Every professional commitment functions as advocacy for some way of life. The chief results of this emerging consciousness in our own work have been twofold: first, we have become far more reflexive about our writings; what causes do we silently champion, who benefits from our particular theories and methods, and who is silenced or oppressed? At the same time, we also find ourselves more willing to give our values a place of prominence in our work. If we are to advocate, we feel, why attempt to hide the fact? Given that we must inevitably advocate, we believe it is an act of good faith to articulate our guiding values and assumptions. This has been most obviously the case in our work on relational theory and practice (to be treated below), as set against the tradition of cultural individualism. It is also manifestly evident in Mary Gergen's contribution to feminist psychology (see especially M. Gergen, 1988; M. Gergen and S. Davis, 1997).

BEYOND THE PAROCHIAL-AS-UNIVERSAL

This process of political sensitisation is linked to another significant breakthrough in our own thinking and development, again with significant implications for the conception of a psychological science. If we accept the possibility of multiple constructions of persons and worlds, lodged within different traditions, useful for different purposes, and inherently ideological in implication, then any attempt to establish universals flirts with tyranny. To replace all accounts, traditions, and values with a single set of concepts runs the risk of obliterating all that does not fit the vernacular. This line of argument stands against the tendency of the scientific tradition in the West and against psychology as a universalising science. Western psychology has not only presumed the universality of the experimental method as a truth-generating device, but as well the content of its theories. Looking back at our own graduate school indoctrination, the presumption that one's cloistered experiments with American college students speak for-all-people-for-all-times strikes us as an unfathomable arrogance.

In so many contexts we have been made painfully aware of these tendencies to treat the parochial as universal, and of their demeaning if not destructive implications. This is so even when the perpetrators fully believe they are doing good, enlightening others, and contributing to a better world.[6] Here are only a few experiences that have sharpened our sensitivity.

Many years ago, with two small children in tow, we drove around the Mediterranean Sea, from Rome to North Africa, returning through Spain and France, to gather data on reactions to aid. In Tunis, we interviewed a cabinet minister concerning his views of the foreign aid given by the USA to his country. After a brief and polite interchange, he harangued us for over forty-five minutes on the arrogance and rigidity of the US aid mission, and the hardships it created in his country. We sat in his office, mesmerised and yet terrified at his impassioned attack. The climax of his talk featured a parable in which a man gives a piece of bread with honey to his friend: 'The giver does not say, "Here, take this bread, but do not eat it all now, and give half of it to your son, and save half of the honey for next year, and so on." He says, "Here is some bread, eat it and live."' After this unstinting critique, the minister mellowed. Transforming his words into practice, he crossed the room, opened a cabinet and withdrew a handsome clay pot from the pre-Christian era. It had been discovered during an excavation on a construction project for which he was the director. He now made it a gift to us. No strings attached!

We attended a professional meeting in Caracas, Venezuela. Here we were introduced to psychologists from Central and South America who, in such gentle and kind ways, described the history of the previous decades, even centuries, in which their citizens had been oppressed by American capitalists, with the support of our government. The strength and endurance of these people, and the poetry of their words – deep with conviction, their faith in the future, and their willingness to reach out – even to those who were coming from the North, were enthralling and unsettling to us. We learned to listen with new ears. And, too, with our own eyes we could see the struggles of the poor, living in acres of makeshift shanties, while armed guards patrolled the corridors and grounds of the luxurious hotel in which the conference was held. We, the privileged, entered taxis bound for elegant restaurants; the restaurants booked taxis for the return. We were warned never to take an unauthorised taxi – and surely to take no walk in the city – if we wanted to remain unharmed.

During a year-long residence in Heidelberg we had several opportunities to hear American psychologists deliver colloquia at the Department of Psychology. These were difficult occasions for us, as we tended to be identified with the speakers. Thus, when speakers waxed self-assured in their presumptions, and spoke to the audience as if to untutored school children whose work was sub-standard, we wished we were elsewhere. Unlike the visitors, however, we were very much part of the local culture, and thus privy to their after-hours comments on the visitors. These only confirmed our suspicions. To them, the speakers' imperious attitude was particularly ironic, because, from their point of view, the research was typically so trivial, without conceptual sophistication or sensitivity to its place in history that it did not warrant serious attention. Our most respected scholars 'at home' were targets to be lampooned abroad.

At the outset it was important to realise, first, that the problem of the parochial-turned-universal is far more general than one of psychology alone, and second, that we can never separate ourselves from the problem. We are always 'from somewhere'. However, these kinds of experiences have had a marked impact on our own work. Our interest in 'indigenous psychologies' has been deeply stimulated, and in particular, we have attempted to locate ways in which theory and practice can be enriched through intercultural exchange (see, for example, Gergen, Gulerce, Lock and Misra, 1996). We have also helped to launch international conferences and organisations (such as the International Society for Theoretical Psychology), and one of us (KJG) serves on the APA Committee on International Relations in Psychology.

FROM METHOD FETISHISM TO THEORY AS ACTION

The tendency to presume the universality of Western psychological science is closely tied to another problematic feature of the profession: the glorification of methodology in general and the experimental method in particular. One of the chief features of our academic training in psychology was its emphasis on methodology. Our graduate programmes required several courses in advanced statistics, additional courses in research methods, and still other practicums in individual research. Interestingly, there was only a single course required in theoretical, philosophical, or historical issues in psychology. So secure was the profession in its belief in 'truth through method', that any critical reflection on research practices was so much waste of time. Nowhere in the standard curriculum was there training in the construction of theories – which is to say, serious immersion in intellectual or conceptual dialogue. Because truth was to be derived from facts (as generated through methods), it was said, then theory would grow naturally from observation. All else was mere conjecture.

Yet, from the constructionist standpoint, this emphasis seems wholly misguided. From a constructionist standpoint, the data generated from experimental techniques say nothing in themselves. They only begin 'to speak' when one approaches them with a theory in hand. It is not data that determine theory, but theory that determines what we count as data and how we interpret it. Further, because theory is a form of intelligibility with world-making implications, one cannot take lightly the responsibility of theorising. Theory is essentially a form of political and moral action, and should be subjected to the most astute forms of reflection. Again, these possibilities were dramatised for us on numerous occasions around the world.

While living in Marburg, Germany, for a semester, we received a letter from two academic assistants from a university in the south of the country. These young men had been reading about the historical and constructionist movements and wanted to come for an overnight visit. To us it seemed like quite a long journey – five hours by car – to speak about theoretical and metatheoretical matters, and especially to travel that distance for only a single evening's talk. For them, however, it was a pleasure. They arrived in mid-afternoon, and we conversed until mid-evening. After dinner, they were eager to continue the conversations. So deeply engaged, so thrilling was the immersion in the domain of ideas, that they pressed the dialogue on until 4 a.m. Early the next morning, glowing with energy, they departed. It would be difficult to imagine such an event in the USA.

During a year's stay at the Sorbonne we encountered similar energies. Scholarly life in Paris seemed to revolve around cafés and restaurants. A colleague might wish to have coffee with us at 10 a.m. Animated theoretical discussions might then last until almost noon. Another scholar, from across town, would then arrive for lunch together. Often we wouldn't return to the office until the afternoon was virtually departed. These discussions were seldom calm and dispassionate. As ideas were developed and elaborated, so were counter positions triggered; soon there were antagonisms, and voices became increasingly intense. Intellectual exchange was essentially a form of participatory drama.

For the '*Portingas*', the denizens of Buenos Aires, ideas are symbolic mainstays to cultural identity. Highly cosmopolitan, highly identified with European intellectual life, yet dramatically separated geographically, intellectual interchange is a major means of confirming a tradition and affirming a future. Speakers from outside the country are festive events. A common social event is to build a day of discussion around a visitor, with each participant paying a fee to support the event and the food and drink accompanying the intense activity. During one workshop which I (MMG) gave on feminist theory and research, I met three women who were working at a community centre in an outlying district with very poor women in traditional family settings. A day after the workshop we met in a café, where they tape-recorded our conversation so that they could take back details in order to begin emancipatory research projects that I had discussed in my presentation with these women. Their struggles on all levels were profound, but with discussion they grew enthusiastic about the possibilities. We continued to correspond, to exchange photos, and to think through ways in which these 'foreign ideas' could be adapted to their needs. They continue to 'grow' a feminist community in very barren soil.

Experiences such as these have galvanised our commitment to theoretical and conceptual work. Putting data ahead of theory seems myopic. The challenge has been to generate theoretical intelligibilities that are not only cemented to the longstanding dialogues within our traditions, but which attempt to press these dialogues forward in new and more promising ways. Occasionally we carry out research to illustrate or vivify these ideas. The following section illustrates one of these theoretical investments.

ON THE VISION OF RELATIONAL COORDINATION

Although a social constructionist stance liberates the psychologist from the demands of any particular logic, epistemology or ontology – thus setting the stage for a global dialogue among diverse participants – it does not itself prescribe any particular theory, method, or practice. Certain professional investments are more congenial or compatible with a constructionist view of science than others, but constructionism demands no adherence to them. To reduce the riches of the world's intelligibilities to a univocal voice is contrary to the approach.

With these views in mind, much of our professional investment in recent years has been focused on expanding a specifically *relational account* of human action, and developing practices (dialogic, therapeutic, organisational, etc.) that might realise its implications. The attempt is to move away from the methodological and theoretical individualism that has so captured the imagination of traditional Western psychology, and to develop a reconceptualisation of human action in terms of relational processes. The hope is to cast such traditional concepts as reason, emotion, perception, intention, and memory, among others, in terms that render them inseparable from social process. In keeping with constructionist views, work on relational processes is not attempting to 'tell the truth' about human action; rather it seeks to generate alternative resources (both linguistic and otherwise) for carrying out such actions.[7]

Given the political and societal challenges at hand, we are constantly asking ourselves about the action implications of our work. We are sensitised in particular to potentials for coordination – as a specialised form of relatedness. If all that is meaningful grows out of coordination, then it is forms of coordination that importantly fashion our future. Particularly on a planet where the distances between us continue to shrink, where our political interests increasingly clash, often brutally, we are drawn to instances of successful coordination. It is precisely these kinds of experiences that can fuel theories and practices of relational selves. Removing oneself from the comfortable traditions of one's home environment dares such experiences to occur. Let us share several of these which have been most significant in pressing our ideas and ideals forward.

When living in Kyoto, I (MMG) took Ikebana lessons from a teacher who did not speak English; my knowledge of Japanese was also scant. Each week I followed the example of the five young Japanese women in the course and knelt on the tatami mat before a vase, with a small pile of sticks and fresh-cut flowers on a newspaper at my side. Immediately I felt a sense of failure; the awkward form of my kneeling was no match to the fluid grace of the others (and it was painful to remain in such a position). The teacher moved from one student to another, arranging each item in the vase as the student observed. She then removed the flowers. The student's task was then to replicate her actions. After I was finished, she would come to my side and look with me. She would deftly rearrange the flowers until they looked exactly as she had done them before. Again, the disappointment was stinging – so rough and rude were my arrangements compared to the spare beauty which she generated; so clumsy were my fingers in comparison to the rapid and knowing movements of her hands. Then I had to draw in coloured pencils in my notebook what I saw, another effort without refinement. Was she secretly laughing at this American bull in a Japanese shop?

Yet, as the weeks drew on, with one new challenge after another, I sensed a gradual shift in our relationship. Modelling the teacher, my fingers began to sense the possibilities of a stem or the relationship of forms within the arrangement; I also seemed to forget the pain in my knees. I was acquiring some feeling for the 'rightness' of things, the relationship of vase to plants, arranger to occasion, arranger to teacher. Once, when my teacher had transformed my work to perfection – which now seemed effortless – she smiled at me as we said goodbye with a bow. The day the classes ended, our gaze was mutual and long-lasting. Without words, through mutual movement in a world of beauty in the making, we had become as one. The departure was painful for me and, I rather think, for her as well.

I (KJG) had agreed to give lectures in St Gallen, Switzerland, for two months. The only furnished quarters that could be located in this small town consisted of a single bedroom in the apartment of Frau F, an eighty-seven-year-old widow. The news of the quarters was most disagreeable, as it meant my freedom would be drastically curtailed, a continuous countenance of courtesy would be required, and I would face daily struggles in a language with which I still wrestled. My fears were only intensified as I realised that the old woman was very lonely and longed for company. At first I resented her attempts to weave me into her life-web, the breakfasts and dinners she would prepare even when I was not a boarder – all requiring my listening uncomprehendingly to unending stories delivered in a rapid-fire admixture of Hoch and Switzer Deutsch.

However, as the winter cold intensified, and I realised that this little town virtually came to a halt in the early evening, I began to appreciate Frau F's warmth and vitality. I began to listen more attentively, and to ask questions in German. Slowly we struggled toward dialogue. Frau F was then moved to break out bottles of evening wine from her well-stocked cellar, and the animated conversation continued. I began to feel guilty for all the hospitality I was accepting, and offered to take her to an opera. She gracefully accepted, but when we arrived at the box office, she rushed ahead of me so that I could not pay for the tickets. At the end of the first month, she would not accept my rent. The weekends sometimes yawned ahead, and I offered to take Frau F to the countryside where she was raised. She gave me a fascinating introduction to rural living – from the inside. As the days moved on, I would find the corners of my bed turned down at night; sometimes my shoes were polished; in the mornings she would examine my attire to ensure that I looked every bit 'Herr Doktor Professor'. As I departed one morning, I looked up at her apartment from the street below, and saw her staring at me in the window. We waved and smiled – and did so every morning for the remainder of my stay. When I finally departed, my gift to her was a replenishment of her wine cellar. The most significant gifts for both of us were the tears we shared at departure.

After a country-side conference in Israel, we travelled for several days. One late afternoon we were approximating a swim in the buoyant warm waters of the Dead Sea, when we noticed nearby a group of pre-adolescent girls playing in the water as their care-takers watched from the shore. They were especially interesting to us as they were the first Duise (an ethnic minority living in the North of Israel, typically poor, and noted for their colourful dress) we had seen at such close quarters. As one of the group came closer, I (KJG) smiled and skimmed a small plastic plate in her direction. She was startled, then paused, and finally smiled; the plate was returned in like manner. Soon an active game had begun, and her friends joined in. Later, amidst friendly waving, we departed. That evening we found an unpretentious outdoor café in Jericho for dinner. As we were eating, a school bus pulled up, and suddenly the entrance was filled with young girls – the Duise cohort had arrived carrying lunch boxes; they dispersed through the restaurant. Finally we spotted our Dead Sea friend at a table across the garden. We beckoned our waiter and asked him to take Coca-colas to the girls. We watched as the drinks arrived, and they turned their heads to laugh and wave. As we were finishing our meal, two of the girls shyly approached our table, bearing a small plate of sweets and fruit: a gift from their lunch pails. Culture, age, gender, language, class . . . all gave way to our coordination.

Experiences such as these have fired our work on relational theory in many important ways. At the very personal level, they affirm the significance of relatedness over isolation; there is a certain thrill that emerges in the location of affinity. They also reinforce our optimism in the potential of human coordination, even when there has been a lifetime of difference. Finally, such experiences stand as particularly interesting challenges to theory. How can we account for the emergence of such affinities, and how can these conceptualisations be used to foster practices for the future?

A FINAL BARK

Over twenty years ago we met by chance a young, dynamic psychologist in Kyoto, Japan. He was fresh from a PhD programme at Stanford University, but he scarcely viewed this experience as the culmination of his education. Rather, he actively threw himself into 'the Japanese experience', or should we say, the inter-cultural experience, for this man's keen sensitivities were polymorphically tuned. We spent many hours speaking of cultural differences, similarities, and indeed the reasons for thinking in these terms. The decades passed, and in February 1996 we were visiting the University of Hong Kong. After KJG's talk a lovely dinner was held in the faculty club. Among the invited guests was this same scholar, Michael Bond, from the Chinese University. Soon fond reminiscences were conjoined with cross-cultural concerns, and we found ourselves spinning into the stimulating dialogic matrix we had so enjoyed in the past. Yet, these conversations differed from the past in important ways – and most prominently in their richness. We now spoke with myriad voices from far corners of the world, and their presence multiply laminated our exchange.

As but one byproduct of this chance occasion – and especially Michael's invitation – we now find ourselves attempting to bring these relationships into articulation. In the end we do feel a vast sense of incompletion in the challenge. Absent from the present account are savoured experiences in Slovakia, Russia, Yugoslavia, Korea, Indonesia, Malaysia, Thailand, Australia, New Zealand, Norway, Finland, Israel, Chile, Portugal, and more. Looking back we also worry that we have been too selective in our travels – too oriented, perhaps, toward 'the good life', and insufficiently open to the full range of human existence. Why are there not tales here from India, China, Egypt, Africa south of the Atlas, or the less-fortunate regions of Central and South America? Experiences in these climes would surely press theory and practice forward in important ways.

For us, the global immersion of the past has fostered a 'relational stance' to life: we carry the echoes of countless voices into the present. And as these voices enter new and different dialogues, so will new and different patterns of relationship – including professional discourse and practice – emerge. Surely anxiety must accompany the sense of impending change, but for the most part, we look to the future with excitement and wonderment.

NOTES

1 See, for example, K. Gergen (1982, 1991, 1994), M. Gergen (1988), K. Gergen and M. Gergen (1984) and M. Gergen and S. Davis (1997).
2 In an autobiographical piece we jointly authored – a 'duography' – we describe some other aspects of our life together 'on the road' (Gergen, M. and Gergen, K. 1993).
3 See K. Gergen (1973).
4 See Strickland, Aboud and Gergen (1976).
5 Gergen and Gergen, 1983a, b.
6 It is important to stress that among the hundreds of social psychologists in the USA and elsewhere we have known, and continue to regard as our colleagues and friends, one of the guiding impulses that characterizes their commitments to social psychology has been a concern with promoting the societal good, moral betterment, a more peaceful and equitable world through their work. At the same time, we regard the experimental method as a deeply flawed methodology which, refigured as an ideology, hampers social psychologists in achieving the very ends they seek. The experimental method creates a schism between the knower and the known, the experimenter and the 'object' of study; it relies on manipulation to achieve its ends; and it established a hierarchy of power in which the research scientist is king.
7 The interested reader is directed to K. Gergen (1994) and K. Gergen and M. Gergen (1988).

REFERENCES

Gergen, K.J. (1973). Social psychology as history. *Journal of Personality and Social Psychology, 26*, 309–320.
Gergen, K.J. (1982). *Toward transformation in social knowledge.* New York: Springer Verlag. 2nd edn (1994), London: Sage.
Gergen, K.J. (1991). *The saturated self.* New York: Basic Books.
Gergen, K.J. (1994). *Realities and relationships.* Cambridge, MA: Harvard University Press.
Gergen, K.J. and Gergen, M.M. (1983a). The social construction of helping relationships. In J. Fisher, A. Nadler and B. DePaulo (eds), *New directions in helping*, vol. 1. New York: Academic Press.
Gergen, K.J. and Gergen, M.M. (1983b). Interpretive dimensions of international aid. In J. Fisher, A. Nadler and B. DePaulo (eds), *Applied research in help-seeking and reactions to aid*, vol. 2. New York: Academic Press.

Gergen, K.J. and Gergen, M.M.(eds) (1984). *Historical social psychology.* Hillsdale, NJ: Lawrence Erlbaum.

Gergen, K.J. and Gergen, M.M. (1988). Narrative and the self as relationship. In L. Berkowitz (ed.), *Advances in experimental social psychology* (pp. 17–56). San Diego, CA: Academic Press.

Gergen, K.J., Gulerce, A., Lock, A. and Misra, G. (1996). Psychological science in cultural context. *American Psychologist, 51*, 496–503.

Gergen, M.M. (ed.) (1988). *Feminist thought and the structure of knowledge.* New York: New York University Press.

Gergen, M.M. and Gergen, K.J. (1993). Let's pretend: A duography. In D.J. Lee (ed.), *Life and story: Autobiographies for a narrative psychology.* Westport, CN: Praeger.

Gergen, M.M. and Davis, S.N. (eds) (1997). *Toward a new psychology of gender.* New York: Routledge.

Jones, E.E. (1985). Major developments in social psychology during the past five decades. In G. Lindzey and E. Aronson (eds), *The handbook of social psychology,* vol. 1. New York: Random House.

Kvale, S. (ed.) (1992). *Psychology and postmodernism.* London: Sage.

Strickland, L., Aboud, F. and Gergen, K. (eds) (1976). *Social psychology in transition.* New York: Plenum.

10 The double life of a bilingual

A cross-cultural perspective

Anna Wierzbicka

MY 'DISCOVERY' OF AUSTRALIAN CULTURE

I live in Australia. I have lived here for more than twenty years. But I am not an Australian. I was born in Poland, and I am Polish. Australia is an open 'multicultural' society, and people like me are widely accepted here as what was once termed 'new Australians', while being at the same time allowed to maintain their 'ethnic identity', defined in terms of their country of origin. I could say, therefore, that I am both a Pole and an Australian. To my ear, however, this would sound phoney. Although I am an Australian citizen, I don't have two nationalities, as I don't have two native languages. My native language is Polish, and so is my native culture.

At the same time, Australia is now my home, and my ties with this country are very strong. First of all, my husband is Australian (which was why I came to live here in the first place), although he learnt Polish and speaks it so well that Poles have often mistaken him for a Pole, and knows, understands, and appreciates Poland better than I would have ever thought possible for a so-called foreigner.

Second, my two daughters are Australians, although they, too, speak Polish very well, and although of them it could be truly said that they are both Australian and Polish.

Third, having lived and worked in Australia for twenty-odd years, and being a member of, one might say, an Australian family, I have developed a deep professional interest in Australian culture, and have studied it over the years in a number of articles and book chapters (see Wierzbicka 1986, 1991, 1992a, and 1997).

Fourth, although in my basic cultural identity and in my basic emotions I have remained Polish, I have come to cherish Australia deeply: its landscape, its cultural heritage, its characteristic style of interpersonal relations, and its characteristic ways of speaking. Since it is fashionable in Australian intellectual (especially academic) circles to characterise Australian culture and history (in a thoroughly ahistorical way) as, above all else, 'racist' and 'sexist', I have invested a great deal of professional energy into trying to oppose this fashion and into writing, as a linguist, 'in defence of Australian culture'.

The 'discovery' of traditional Australian culture, and the study of Australian

English as an expression of this culture, became for me an exciting intellectual adventure. It taught me, for example, that words are a society's cultural artefacts, and that they serve as transmittors of social attitudes and cultural values. I became fascinated with characteristically Australian words and concepts such as *dob in* (roughly, betray someone by 'informing' on them), *whinge* (complain and whine at the same time), or *shout* (pay for other people, in a spirit of good-humoured generosity and good fellowship); in characteristic Australian abbreviations such as *mozzies* (for mosquitoes) or *Aussies* (for Australians); in peculiarly Australian interjections such as *good-o, right-o*, or *good-on-ya*.

I came to realise that, for example, the words *dob in* and *dobber* reflect the traditional Australian cult of loyalty and solidarity, especially solidarity *vis-à-vis* authorities, and the words *whinge, whinger*, and *sook* reflect the Australian cult of toughness and resilience; that the word *larrikin* (defined by the *Shorter Oxford English Dictionary* (1964) as 'the Australian equivalent of the "Hoodlum" or "Hooligan"') expresses a positive evaluation of irreverent wit and defiance of social norms and conventions; that the word *Aussie* (noun and adjective) expresses the capacity of 'traditional Australians' for combining an attachment to and pride in their country with a self-deprecating dislike of pathos, pomposity, and 'big words'; and that it also reflects some important aspects of the traditional Australian self-image, with an emphasis on being brave, tough, practical, good-humoured, and cheeky.

I also came to realise that the expression *good on you* (which implies admiration for the addressee's attitude and not necessarily for achievement or success) reflects the value placed on attitudes rather than on success or achievement as such; that the response words *goodo* (*good-oh*) and *righto* (*right-oh, rightio*), whose very meaning signals a good-humoured willingness to cooperate on an equal footing, reflect the value placed on egalitarian relations and on a relaxed atmosphere in social interaction; that the exclamation *you bloody beauty* reflects among other things the Australian value of anti-sentimentality, as does the use of the word *bastard* when used to express positive feelings; and that Australian names such as *Tez, Tezza* (for Terry), *Bazza* (for Barry), or *Shaz, Shazza* (for Sharon) reflect the traditional Australian combination of values: solidarity, equality, and anti-sentimental ('rough') affection.

All these discoveries had for me a deeply personal significance. It wasn't just the Australian literary hero, Bazza Mackenzie, who was called 'Bazza', it was my own daughter, Mary (for me, Marysia, Marysieńka, Marysik), who came to be referred to and addressed (by her friends) as 'Muz'. Australian humour was part of our family life, and I had to learn to cope with Australian 'jocular insults', the Australian practice of 'chiacking' (making fun of people in a spirit of congenial fellowship and good humour), the Australian use of sarcasm, the Australian spirit of independence and defiance . . .

How did it happen, it might be asked? Well, this may not apply to everyone, but in my personal experience learning to cope was linked with a search for understanding: it was intellectually exciting to discover 'on one's own skin' (a Polish idiom) the reality of different cultural norms (so often denied by monolingual and/or monocultural theoreticians), and to try to articulate these norms in clear and coherent ways.

Thus, I became engrossed in the study of Australian culture (through the study of Australian English and the Australian 'ethnography of speaking'), and everyday life provided me with constant tutorials and with tests in the subject, not all of which I passed, but from which I always tried to learn.

But my life in Australia opened the door for me to other interesting intellectual discoveries as well.

MY 'DISCOVERY' OF POLISH LANGUAGE AND CULTURE

One of the most important of these personal discoveries which I owe to my life in Australia was the discovery of the phenomenon of Polish culture. When I lived in Poland, immersed in Polish culture, I was no more aware of its specialness than I was of the air I breathed. Now, immersed in the very different Anglo (and Anglo-Australian) culture, I gradually became more and more aware of the distinctiveness of Polish culture.

To begin with, I became aware of Polish words which had no equivalents in English, and each of which epitomised something very special: an emotion, an attitude, a belief, a relationship, a colour, a time, a type of experience.

I noted that time was structured differently in Polish and in English. In English, the structure of the day in general seemed determined by the structure of a working day, with a lunch-break time in the middle, and two equal halves before it ('morning') and after it ('afternoon'). In Polish, on the other hand, the day was seen as a whole, extending from the end of one night to the beginning of another, with an *obiad* ('dinner') roughly in the middle, and with a 'morning' (*rano*) seen as a first part of the day, extending till no later than 11 a.m., and with an 'afternoon' (*popołudnie*) starting after the *obiad*, that is, roughly after 3.30 or 4 p.m. (The very important Anglo concepts of 'a.m.' and 'p.m.' had no equivalents in Polish at all, and played no particular role in Polish culture.)

Social practices associated with the Polish-speaking and English-speaking parts of my life were also different. For example, speaking Polish in Australia I couldn't find Polish words for such commonplace new realities as 'babysitters' or 'parties'; whereas common Polish words such as *imieniny* ('nameday celebrations') disappeared from my life, together with the social rituals which they stood for.

But if the outer world associated with the English language was different from my accustomed Polish world, the inner world was even more so. For example, I came to realise that the most important everyday emotions in Polish had no place in English. For instance, in Polish, I used to say often '*strasznie się cieszę*', '*strasznie się martwię*', or '*okropnie się denerwuję*', but none of these things were really sayable in English. First, the English equivalents of the Polish intensifiers *strasznie* and *okropnie* ('terribly') would sound excessive in an English-language conversation. Second, the Polish durative reflexive verbs suggest an on-going emotional process and an active attitude (similar to that reflected in the atypical English verb to *worry*, and in the archaic verb to *rejoice*), and so they were quite different from the English adjectives describing states such as 'happy' or 'upset'. And third, the lexical meaning of the Polish words in question was different from any corresponding English words: *cieszę się* was closer to the archaic *rejoice* than to *happy*, *martwię się* combined something like *worry* with elements of *chagrin* and *sorrow*, *denerwuję się* suggested a state of great agitation and 'fretting' (but without the negative connotations of the latter word) as well as something like being *upset*, and so on.

Similarly, everyday 'Polish' emotions described in Polish by the expression *zła jestem* (lit. 'I am bad', 'I am mad/angry/cross/furious'), or *bardzo mi przykro* (lit. 'to me, it is hurtful/unpleasant/painful/sorry') could simply not be expressed or described in any straightforward way in English; not to mention the key Polish emotion of *tęsknota* (homesickness/nostalgia/heartache-caused-by-separation).

What applied to emotions applied also to religion, to the everyday philosophy of life, to values, to social relations, to history. For example, I noticed that English had no word corresponding to the Polish word *Boży* (an adjective derived from *Bóg* 'God', but unlike *divine*, very colloquial and not neutral but embodying a positive attitude of faith and devotion); and also, that the literal English equivalents of Polish exclamatory expressions such as *mój Boże* (my God!), *o Jezu*! (Jesus!, lit. oh Jesus!) or *Chryste Panie*! (Christ!, lit. Christ Lord!) expressed quite different emotions from those embodied in the Polish expressions: the English expressions sounded angry and disrespectful, whereas the Polish ones sounded like prayerful invocations (see Wierzbicka, 1996b).

The Polish philosophy of life seemed to be best expressed in the common Polish word *los*, whose primary meaning is 'a lottery ticket', and a secondary one, 'a fate/destiny', but seen somewhat in terms of a lottery: unpredictable, uncertain, risky, and yet full of unforeseeable possibilities (see Wierzbicka 1992a).

Some traditional Polish values, shaped by Poland's historical experience, were clearly reflected in the positive connotations of adjectives such as *nieugięty* ('inflexible' – in English, pejorative), *szalony* (lit. 'mad, foolhardy'), or *śmiały* ('daring').

History seemed to be everywhere: in the resonant Polish word *niepodległość* (national independence, distinct from simply 'independence', that is, *niezależność*), in the word *wolność* ('freedom', but with connotations of national freedom, that is freedom from oppressive foreign powers), in the important Polish verb *wynarodowić się* (lit. to lose one's allegiance to one's nation, to cease to be a member of one's own nation, with implications of shameful betrayal and irreparable loss) (see Wierzbicka, 1997).

The historical frame of reference in my Polish world was defined very largely by expressions such as *przed wojną* ('before the war', that is, in Poland, before 1939), *w czasie Powstania* ('during the Uprising'), *po Powstaniu* ('after the Uprising', referring to the Warsaw uprising against the German occupying forces in 1944), *w czasie okupacji* ('during the occupation', referring to the German occupation of Poland from 1939 to 1945), and so on. That was how people spoke in Poland, and how they thought about their lives. Naturally, in English, people's temporal frames of reference were different.

Interpersonal relations associated with and reflected in Polish were also different from those linked with English. For example, when I tried to soothe my children in the first weeks of their lives with anxious Polish invocations of '*Córeńko! Córeńko!*' (lit. 'little daughter! little daughter!') my husband pointed out how quaint it sounds from the point of view of a native speaker of English to solemnly address a new-born baby as 'little daughter'. Now, when my daughters are university students, I still say to them *córeńko!*, and this typical Polish invocation reflects something important about Polish family relations and traditional cultural attitudes.

Like many other newcomers to the Anglo world, I was struck by the elasticity of the English concept of 'friend', which could be applied to a wide range of relationships, from deep and close, to quite casual and superficial. This was in stark contrast to the Polish words *przyjaciel* (male) and *przyjaciółka* (female), which could only stand for exceptionally close and intimate relationships. What struck me even more was the importance of the concept embodied in the Polish word *koledzy* (female counterpart *koleżanki*) as a basic conceptual category defining human relations – quite unlike the relatively marginal concept encoded in the English word *colleague*, relevant only to professional elites. It became clear to me that concepts such as '*koledzy*' ('*koleżanki*') and '*przyjaciele*' (*przyjaciółki*) (plural) organised the social universe quite differently from concepts such as 'friends' (see Wierzbicka, 1997).

Polish grammar, too, emerged as a world of conceptual distinctions quite different from those suggested by English. One example of this has already been provided in the preceding discussion of social relations: Polish grammar demanded that a great deal of attention should be paid to gender distinctions. Thus, while in English one could speak about a 'friend', without revealing this 'friend's' gender, in Polish this was not possible: one had to always distinguish between a *przyjaciel* (male) and a *przyjaciółka* (female), or between a *kolega* (male) and a *koleżanka* (female). Another conceptual distinction which I discovered was consistently drawn by Polish but not by English grammar was that between 'normal size objects' and 'small objects'. Thus, one couldn't speak in Polish simply about a bottle, a box, or a bag, one always had to make a distinction between, for example, *butelka* ('bottle') and *buteleczka* ('small bottle'), *pudełko* ('box') and *pudełeczko*, or between *worek* ('bag') and *woreczek* ('small bag'). In fact, in many cases one was also forced to distinguish 'normal size objects' from 'oversize objects' (e.g. *butla* 'big bottle', *pudło* 'big box', and *wór* 'big bag').

The constant attention to size required by Polish grammar was clearly related to the importance of 'affectionate' diminutives in Polish discourse, whose frequent use gave Polish interpersonal interaction a quite different flavour from that characteristic of, or indeed possible in, English. For example, in English one couldn't urge one's guests to eat some more *śledzika* ('dear little herring') or to drink some more *herbatki* ('dear little tea'), for such diminutive forms of nouns were simply not available. Nor could one coax a child to do something *szybciutko* ('dear-little-quickly') or *cichutko* ('dear-little-quietly'), for English adverbs don't have diminutive forms even in baby talk (cf. Wierzbicka, 1991).

But of course it wasn't just certain grammatical forms which were 'lacking' in English (from my Polish perspective); what was different was the whole style of interpersonal interaction. To put it crudely, diminutives like 'dear-little-herring' were not needed in English speech for in Anglo culture it was not seen as appropriate to urge guests to eat more than they wanted to; and a constant flood of diminutives in interaction with children was not only not needed but it would have seemed inappropriate, given the prevailing ethos of personal autonomy, independence, and self-reliance.

When I heard people express their satisfaction that their children (in their late teens) were leaving home and going to live elsewhere, and to study in another city, I was initially shocked and astonished: the hierarchy of values reflected in such declarations was very different indeed from that to which I was accustomed in Poland. But these and other similar differences in attitudes and in the prevailing hierarchy of values seemed to be quite consistent with the differences in ways of speaking that I was constantly observing.

Thus, a whole new field of inquiry opened before me: cross-cultural pragmatics. I developed a new university course on 'Cross-cultural communication', and a new theory: the theory of 'cultural scripts', which aimed at providing a universal 'culture notation' (cf. Hall, 1976) for the description and comparison of cultures (cf., e.g., Wierzbicka, 1994a, b, and c; 1996c).

MY DISCOVERY OF 'CULTURAL PSYCHOLOGY'

In his essay 'Cultural psychology – what is it?' which opens the important collective volume entitled 'Cultural psychology', Richard Shweder (1990, p. 1) writes:

A discipline is emerging called 'cultural psychology'. It is not general psychology. It is not cross-cultural psychology. It is not psychological anthropology. It is not ethnopsychology. It is cultural psychology. And its time may have arrived, once again.

Cultural psychology is the study of the way cultural traditions and social practices regulate, express, transform, and permute the human psyche, resulting less in psychic unity of humankind than in ethnic divergences in mind, self, and emotion. Cultural psychology is the study of the ways subject and object, self and other, psyche and culture, person and context, figure and ground, practitioner and practice live together, require each other, and dynamically, dialectically, and jointly make each other up.

Since my '*los*' (fate/destiny/lottery of life) has led me to live a deeply bicultural life, 'cultural psychology' as presented in the passage above was for me a matter of intimate and vital personal experience. It wasn't just in my life that the two cultures – Polish and Anglo (and, more specifically, Anglo-Australian) – met (or should I say, collided?), it was also in my 'psyche', in my 'self', in my 'mind', my emotions, my personal relations, my daily interactions. I had to start learning new 'cultural scripts' to live by, and in the process I became aware of the old 'cultural scripts' which had governed my life hitherto. I also became aware, in the process, of the reality of 'cultural scripts' and their importance to the way one lives one's life, to the image one projects, and even to one's personal identity.

For example, when I was talking on the phone, from Australia, to my mother in Poland (15,000 km away), with my voice loud and excited, carrying much further than is customary in an Anglo conversation, my husband would signal to me: 'Don't shout!' For a long time, this perplexed and confused me: to me, this 'shouting' and this 'excitement' was an inherent part of my personality. Gradually, I came to realise that this very personality was in part culturally constituted. But to what extent was it desirable, or necessary, to change it, in deference to my new cultural context?

Early in our life together, my husband objected to my too frequent – in his view – use of the expression 'of course'. At first, this puzzled me, but eventually it dawned on me that using 'of course' as broadly as its Polish counterpart *oczywiście* is normally used would imply that the interlocutor has overlooked something obvious. In the Polish 'confrontational' style of interaction such an implication is perfectly acceptable, and it is fully consistent with the use of such conversational particles such as, for example, *przecież* ('but obviously – can't you see?'). In mainstream Anglo culture, however, there is much more emphasis on 'tact', on avoiding direct clashes, and there are hardly any confrontational particles comparable with those mentioned above. 'Of course' does exist, but even 'of course' tends to be used more in agreement than in disagreement (e.g. 'could you do X for me?' – 'Of course'). Years later, my daughter Mary told me that the Polish conversational expression *ależ oczywiście*: 'but-Emphatic of course' (which I would often replicate in English as 'but of course') struck her as especially 'foreign' from an Anglo cultural point of view; and my close friend and collaborator Cliff Goddard pointed out, tongue in cheek, that my most common way of addressing him (in English) was 'But Cliff . . .'.

Thus, I had to learn to avoid overusing not only 'of course' but also many other expressions dictated by my Polish cultural scripts; and in my working life at an Anglo university this restraint proved invaluable, indeed essential.

I had to learn to 'calm down', to become less 'sharp' and less 'blunt', less 'excitable', less 'extreme' in my judgements, more 'tactful' in their expression. I had to learn the use of Anglo understatement (instead of more hyperbolic and more emphatic Polish ways of speaking). I had to learn to avoid sounding 'dogmatic', 'argumentative', 'emotional'. (There were lapses, of course.) Like the Polish-American writer Eva Hoffman (1989) I had to learn the use of English expressions such as 'on the one hand . . ., on the other hand', 'well yes', 'well no', or 'that's true, but on the other hand'.

Thus, I was learning new ways of speaking, new patterns of communication, new modes of social interaction. I was learning the Anglo rules of turn-taking ('let me finish!', 'I haven't finished!'). I was learning not to use the imperative ('Do X!') in my daily interaction with people and to replace it with a broad range of interrogative devices ('Would you do X?' 'Could you do X?' 'Would you

mind doing X?' 'How about doing X?' 'Why don't you do X?' 'Why not do X?',
and so on).

But these weren't just changes in the patterns of communication. There were
also changes in my personality. I was becoming a different person, at least when
I was speaking English. Students' course assessment questionnaires have often
thrown light on my cultural dilemmas. Thus, while often very positive and praising
my 'enthusiasm', for a long time they also often included critical accents referring
to my 'intensity', 'passion' and 'lack of detachment'. Clearly, in Thomas
Kochman's (1981) terms, I tended to give my lectures as an 'advocate', not as a
'spokesman' – or at any rate, I was too much of an 'advocate', not enough of
a 'spokesman'. I was coming from a language-and-culture system (Polish) where
the very word *beznamiętny* (lit. 'dispassionate') has negative connotations, but I
was lecturing in a language (English) where the word 'emotional' has negative
connotations, while the word 'dispassionate' implies praise. I had to learn, then,
to lecture more like a 'spokesman' and less like an 'advocate'. I had to learn to
become less 'emotional' and more 'dispassionate' (at least in public speaking and
in academic writing).

There were, however, limits to my malleability as a 'culturally constituted self'.
There were English modes of interaction that I never learnt to use – because I
couldn't and because I wouldn't: they went too much against the grain of that
'culturally constituted self'. For example, there was the 'How are you' game:
'How are you? – I'm fine, how are you?'; there were weather-related conversational openings ('Lovely day isn't it? – Isn't it beautiful?'). There were also
'white lies' and 'small talk' (the latter celebrated in a poem by the Polish poet and
professor of Slavic literatures at Harvard University, Stanisław Barańczak).

The acute discomfort that such conversational routines were causing me led me
to understand the value attached by Polish culture to 'spontaneity', to saying what
one really thinks, to talking about what one is really interested in, to showing what
one really feels. It also led me to contemplate the function of such linguistic
lubricants in Anglo social interaction. Why was it that Polish has no words or
expressions corresponding to 'white lies' or 'small talk'? Why was it that English
had no words or expressions corresponding to basic Polish particles and
'conversational signposts' such as *przecież, ależ* ('but can't you see?'), *ależ skądże*
(lit. 'but where from?' i.e. where did you get that idea?), *skądże znowu* ('but where
from again?'), all expressions indicating vigorous disagreement, but quite
acceptable in friendly interaction in Polish?

Clearly, the rules for 'friendly' and socially acceptable interaction in Polish and
in English were different. Consequently, I could never believe in the 'universal
maxims of politeness', in the universal 'logic of conversation', and the 'cooperative principle' promulgated by scholars such as Grice (1975), Leech (1983)
or Brown and Levinson (1978). I knew from personal experience, and from two
decades of meditating on that experience, that the Polish 'maxims of politeness'
and the Polish rules of 'conversational logic' were different from the Anglo ones.
I also knew that the differences between the Anglo 'rules', 'maxims' and
'principles' (presented in the literature as 'universal') and, for example, Polish

ones were not superficial, but reflected differences in deep-seated, subconscious attitudes – attitudes which were fused with the core of a person's personality. Thus, I came to feel that by learning the Anglo ways I could enrich myself immeasurably, but I could also 'lose myself'.

To function in the Anglo society, I had to learn to be a new person; but I didn't want to 'betray' the old person. So living in an Anglo society, working at an Anglo university, and yet speaking Polish domestically, travelling almost every year to Poland, reading in Polish, writing letters in Polish, thinking to a very large extent in Polish, meant constantly shifting between two personalities. I had to constantly stretch myself; but there were limits beyond which I didn't want to go. And these limits needed to be constantly explored and negotiated.

For example, I have never brought myself to use formulaic expressions such as 'Pleased to meet you', 'It was nice meeting you', or 'How are you?', and not just because they are formulaic (Polish, too, has formulaic expressions), but because they are not fully formulaic, and, unlike, for example, Japanese politeness formulae, 'pretend' to be spontaneous and individualised. To use such expressions would have gone too much against the grain. On the other hand, I *have* learnt to use, and even to savour, Anglo conversational strategies such as 'I agree, but on the other hand . . .' (instead of simply saying 'No!').

I felt, then, that 'cultural psychology' was definitely a field for me. It resonated with my experience, and it seemed to be dealing with something very real, very important, and endlessly fascinating. I could not, however, see 'cultural psychology' as an alternative to a search for the 'psychic unity of humankind'. The 'psychic unity', too, seemed to me real, important, and fascinating. It, too, resonated with my experience. I didn't want to choose between the two. I wanted to pursue both.

MY PURSUIT OF UNIVERSALS

Although my university studies and early academic career were focused on Polish language and literature, several years before moving to Australia my attention had shifted to universals. One could say that this shift was due to chance (although personally I always felt it was a kind of a miracle rather than just chance). I had already completed, and published, my PhD dissertation (on Polish Renaissance prose), and was looking for direction in my further life and work, when a linguist at Warsaw University, Andrzej Bogusławski, gave a lecture in 1965 which precipitated me towards a pursuit of universal conceptual primitives, in the spirit of Leibniz's search for 'the alphabet of human thoughts'.

Leibniz's 'alphabet of human thoughts' (1903 [1704], p. 435) could be dismissed as utopian because he never proposed anything as concrete as a list of hypothetical primitives (although in his unpublished work he left several partial drafts). As one modern commentator wrote, 'The approach would be more convincing if one could at least gain some clue as to what the table of fundamental concepts might look like' (Martin 1964, p. 25). Bogusławski suggested that the best clues as to what the table of fundamental concepts might look like can come from the study of languages and that for this reason modern linguistics has a chance of succeeding where philosophical speculation had failed. The 'golden dream' of the seventeenth-century thinkers, which couldn't be realised within the framework of philosophy and which was therefore generally abandoned as Utopian, could now be realised, Bogusławski maintained, if it were approached from a linguistic and empirical rather than from a purely philosophical point of view.

I was immensely impressed by the programme that Bogusławski set for linguistics, and I decided to devote myself to its pursuit – a decision which was strengthened by a year spent in America at MIT, a stronghold of non-semantic generative grammar, which by comparison seemed to me sterile and uninspiring. Thus I embarked on a pursuit of universals, which soon resulted (while I was still living in Poland) in the publication of my *Semantic explorations* (1969) and *Semantic primitives* (1972).

Meanwhile, my husband's stay in Poland came to an end, and, as we had previously agreed, though in my case with considerable misgivings, we set out for Australia. I resigned from my position in the Polish Academy of Sciences and prepared, psychologically, for a period of great difficulties in pursuing my goal: a linguistically based search for universals of human cognition. Unexpectedly, Canberra, which had seemed the end of the world, proved to be a paradise for research in universals. I landed in a thriving academic milieu, engaged in the study of a wide range of languages: the languages of Australia, New Guinea, numerous Pacific Islands, South-East Asia. . . I found students and colleagues deeply familiar with a wide range of languages who were willing to join me in my search for universals and in the process of testing, revising and validating hypotheses about the range of possible diversity and the reality of universals. This resulted, in particular, in a collective volume where substantive hypotheses about conceptual universals were tested in a systematic way across a wide range of languages from different families and different continents (see Goddard and Wierzbicka, 1994); and a second collective volume, focused on universal syntactic patterns, is under way (see Goddard and Wierzbicka, forthcoming).

UNIVERSALS – GENUINE OR SPURIOUS?

With my imagination fired by the Leibnizian 'golden dream', I was eager to pursue the search for the 'psychic unity of humankind'; but I wanted to discover its contours on an empirical basis (with the help of students and colleagues). At the same time, my own cross-cultural life had made me deeply suspicious of many alleged universals proclaimed in the literature.

For example, when I came to read about the alleged 'basic colour terms' and 'universals of colour', I was sceptical: I knew that the Polish word *niebieski* (from *niebo* 'sky') didn't mean the same, and didn't even have the same focus, as the English word *blue*, and that, for example, 'blue jeans' could not be described in Polish as *niebieskie* (plural). I also knew that the Polish word *granatowy* ('navy-blue') did not designate in Polish 'a kind of blue' but was seen as a different kind of colour (as different as grey or green).

When the theory of speech acts came into vogue, and when I read that different kinds of speech acts such as 'warning', 'request' or 'promise' were to be seen as 'natural conceptual kinds' (cf. Searle 1979, p. ix), rather than as artefacts of the English language, I knew that this could not be right either, for I was aware of the language-specific character of such putative 'philosophical categories'. I knew, for example, that characteristic Polish speech act verbs like *częstować* (roughly speaking, verbally press food upon guests), *namawiać* (roughly, a combination of *urge* and *persuade*), or *przyrzekać* (roughly speaking, an act half-way between promise and oath) had no exact equivalents in English, just as English speech act verbs like *suggest, offer*, or *hint* had no exact equivalents in Polish. It seemed clear to me that had the philosophers of speech acts such as Searle been native speakers of Polish rather than English, the philosophical charts of 'different speech acts' proposed by them would have looked decidedly different (despite the authors' claims that they were interested not in English speech act verbs but in 'natural kinds of illocutionary acts').

The same applied to emotions. In particular, the theory of 'basic human emotions', advanced by Paul Ekman and others and widely accepted as a 'scientific truth', was at variance with my own cross-cultural experience. I knew that emotion concepts linked with English words such as *happy, angry*, or *disgusted* were different from emotion concepts encoded in the Polish lexicon. For example (as mentioned earlier), the Polish reflexive verb *cieszyć się* was closer in meaning to the archaic English verb *rejoice* than to the adjective *happy*; and the noun *złość* (from *zły* 'bad') described an emotion which could be seen, from a Polish cultural point of view, as more basic than *anger*. Given that English emotion terms did not correspond in meaning to Polish ones, why should the concepts embodied in these terms identify emotions more 'basic' than those singled out by the Polish terms? The theory of 'basic human emotions' identified through English emotion terms gave the emotions singled out by the English lexicon a privileged position over those encoded in any other language; and the ethnocentrism of such a standpoint seemed to me quite astonishing, as did the attempts to play down the significance of such lexical differences between languages and to hold on, *coûte que coûte*, to the English terms, and the Anglo emotions.

I did not doubt that there could be some 'universal human emotions' or that different cultures could have independently developed some universal conceptual categories to interpret human emotional experience. But it seemed clear to me that to search for genuine universals of human experience, and human conceptualisation of experience, it was necessary first to debunk the false universals, which had arisen from the unwitting absolutisation of the conceptual distinctions embodied in the English language, and which were held on to with great tenacity by scholars unwilling to acknowledge the relevance of languages to any search for human universals (cf. Wierzbicka, 1992b; in press).

CONCLUSION

Academic life in a cross-cultural setting is a blessing, for it provides both fascinating questions and ample opportunities for trying to search for answers and for sharing this search with others. The questions it poses are not 'academic', but very closely linked with the dilemmas and the challenges of daily life, of daily encounters with other people and daily encounters with myself. For example, in what language should I write my lecture notes today? My shopping list? The entries in my desk calendar? In what language should I pray? Write notes to my daughters? Speak to my husband in the presence of other people? Speak to my Polish friends in mixed company? And should I try to change the parameters of my non-verbal behaviour, depending on which language I use? Or regulate the loudness of my voice, the animation of my face, the degree of emotional 'demonstrativeness', the 'directness' of my requests, my invitations, my disagreements?

Just as two mirrors provide endless opportunities for reflections so too do two languages and two cultures reflected in one psyche, in which the daily confrontation of cultures can be turned into the subject of theoretical reflection, discussion, and investigation.

I try to respond to these challenges by investigating and writing about topics such as emotions (diversity and universals), cultural 'key words' (and how they can be explained to cultural outsiders), culture-specific 'cultural scripts' (and their recurring, universal components), semantic universals (and their occurrence in culture-specific configurations), and so on – different themes but always the same double focus: cultural diversity and conceptual universals (see, e.g., Wierzbicka, 1972, 1991, 1992a and b, 1996a, 1997 and in press).

In this fashion, I and my cross-cultural life constantly question, challenge, define and redefine each other.

REFERENCES

Brown, P. and Levinson, S. (1978). *Politeness: Some universals in language usage.* Cambridge: Cambridge University Press.

Goddard, C. and Wierzbicka, A. (eds) (1994). *Semantic and lexical universals: Theory and empirical findings.* Amsterdam: John Benjamins.

Goddard, C. and Wierzbicka, A. (eds) (forthcoming). *Meaning and universal grammar.* New York: Oxford University Press.

Grice, H.P. (1975). Logic and conversation. In P. Cole and J. Morgan (eds), *Syntax and semantics: Speech acts* (pp. 41–58). New York: Academic Press.

Hall, E.T. (1976). *Beyond culture.* New York: Anchor Books.

Hoffman, E. (1989). *Lost in translation: A life in a new language.* New York: Dutton.

Kochman, T. (1981). *Black and white styles in conflict.* Chicago, IL: University of Chicago Press.

Leech, G. (1983). *Principles of pragmatics.* London: Longman.

Leibniz, G.W. (1903 [1704]). Table de définitions. In L. Couturat (ed.), *Opuscules et fragments inédits de Leibniz.* (pp. 437–510). Paris: Presses Universitaires de France. Repr. (1961) Hildesheim: Georg Olms.

Martin, G. (1964). *Leibniz: Logic and metaphysics*. Trans. K.J. Northcott and P.G. Lucas. Manchester: Manchester University Press.
Searle, J.R. (1979). *Expression and meaning: Studies in the theory of speech acts*. Cambridge: Cambridge University Press.
The shorter Oxford English dictionary (1964). Oxford: Clarendon Press.
Shweder, R.A. (1990). Cultural psychology. What is it? In J.W. Stigler, R.A. Shweder and G. Herdt (eds), *Cultural psychology: Essays on comparative human development* (pp. 1–43). Cambridge: Cambridge University Press.
Wierzbicka, A. (1969). *Dociekania semantyczne* [Semantic explorations]. Wrocław: Ossolineum.
Wierzbicka, A. (1972). *Semantic primitives*. Frankfurt: Athenäum.
Wierzbicka, A. (1986). Does language reflect culture? Evidence from Australian English. *Language in Society 15*, 349–374.
Wierzbicka, A. (1991). *Cross-cultural pragmatics: The semantics of human interaction*. Berlin: Mouton de Gruyter.
Wierzbicka, A. (1992a). *Semantics, culture and cognition: Universal human concepts in culture-specific configurations*. New York: Oxford University Press.
Wierzbicka, A. (1992b). Talking about emotions: Semantics, culture, and cognition. *Cognition and Emotion 6*, 289–319.
Wierzbicka, A. (1994a). Cultural scripts: A semantic approach to cultural analysis and cross-cultural communication. *Pragmatics and Language Learning*, Monograph Series, vol. 5 (pp. 1–24). Urbana-Champaign, IL: DEIL University of Illinois.
Wierzbicka, A. (1994b). Cultural scripts: A new approach to the study of cross-cultural communication. In M. Pütz (ed.), *Language contact language conflict* (pp. 69–87). Amsterdam/Philadelphia: John Benjamins.
Wierzbicka, A. (1994c). Emotion, language, and 'cultural scripts'. In S. Kitayama and H. Markus (eds), *Emotion and culture: Empirical studies of mutual influence* (pp. 133–196). Washington, DC: American Psychological Association.
Wierzbicka, A. (1996a). *Semantics: Primes and universals*. Oxford: Oxford University Press.
Wierzbicka, A. (1996b). Między modlitwą a przekleństwem [Between praying and swearing]. *Ethnolingwistyka 8*: 25–39.
Wierzbicka, A. (1996c). Japanese cultural scripts: Cultural psychology and 'cultural grammar'. *Ethos 24* (3): 527–555.
Wierzbicka, A. (1997). *Understanding cultures through their key words: English, Russian, Polish, German, Japanese*. New York: Oxford University Press.
Wierzbicka, A. (in press). *Emotions across languages and cultures: Diversity and universals*. Cambridge: Cambridge University Press.

11 Crossing the Bosphorus
Toward a socially relevant and culturally sensitive career in psychology

Çiğdem Kağitçibaşi

When Michael Bond asked me to write this chapter, I found myself asking the questions: What was the main identifying characteristic of my work? What made my orientation somewhat different from that of my colleagues? And when did I assume this orientation? More specifically, I thought of my recently published book *Family and human development across cultures: A view from the other side* (1996a), and wondered what had prompted me to write that book and what made that book different from other books in psychology with which I was familiar; indeed, what was 'the view from the other side'?

Many answers flooded my consciousness. In fact I had already written two chapters involving personal accounts of how I became who I am today academically. One of these is the Preface to my above mentioned book and the other is a chapter 'A personal account of my involvement in cross-cultural developmental psychology' (1996b) in a book entitled, *A History of Developmental Psychology in Autobiography*, edited by Dennis Thompson and John D. Hogan. However, this time I was thinking rather differently and was preoccupied with when and how my academic orientation to psychological phenomena, and in particular to familial and interpersonal relations, had changed. This will be the main focus of this chapter.

To reflect upon my orientation to psychology, however, I need to delve into my personal history in search of the meaning and reasons underlying my work. This history also carries the seeds of my emphasis on the 'social relevance' of psychology and my wider social scientific and cultural perspective. It revolves around moving between cultures, which took the form of 'crossing waters' first within my native Turkey and afterwards going much further 'West'.

CROSSING THE BOSPHORUS

The Bosphorus is the natural strait between Europe and Asia beside which Istanbul is located. For me, crossing the Bosphorus meant literally and symbolically moving from Asia to Europe – a landmark in my life. When I was thirteen years old, I left my family and my provincial home town to study at the American College for Girls (ACG) in cosmopolitan Istanbul as a boarding student. ACG was an exclusive private high school with a high academic standard at the level of an American junior college.[1]

ACG provided me with a profound early culture learning experience. Some advanced courses I took, especially those in British and American literature and philosophy, conveyed Western culture – its values and truths. I remember being intrigued by Emerson and Thoreau and their American transcendentalism, and being impressed with European phenomenology and existentialism in reading the scholarly works of Kierkegaard, Jaspers, Husserl, Heidegger, and Sartre. A common theme running through my readings was the primacy and the importance of the individual. The emphasis on individual liberties, taking different forms, was paramount from *Hamlet* to the American Constitution. It reached its logical extremes in the ending words of Sartre's play *No exit*: 'Hell is other people'.

This was a secondary socialisation for me into a value system – a worldview representing the developed Western world, which I accepted at an intellectual level. It was reinforced further by the psychology courses I took, first at ACG and then especially at Wellesley. In my last year at ACG, I applied to Wellesley College (in Massachusetts, USA) and was accepted.

Wellesley was my real entry into the American culture after ACG. What I studied in my courses at ACG at the abstract level I started to live in the concrete at Wellesley. As I had taken some advanced courses at ACG, I entered Wellesley as a junior, skipping two years. My secondary socialisation into Western thought had prepared me intellectually for Wellesley. However, *living* another culture was an altogether different task! At the root of my difficulty was the fact that even though I had intellectually accepted Western individualism as ideology, I was not prepared to *live* it.

Despite my culture learning at ACG, I was the product of a 'culture of relatedness' (Kağitçibaşi, 1985), and I found out that individualism and its independence also often implied competition, friendly though shallow inter-personal relations, and 'separated selves' with clearly defined boundaries pro-tected by 'privacy'. I longed for the closely knit, 'enmeshed' relationships which I had grown up with, and most of all for my family. In retrospect and with much scholarship since that time, I am using these terms to characterise the contrasts I then experienced in my first sojourn.

At that time, I only experienced conflicted feelings: appreciation and gratitude toward Wellesley for providing me with a full scholarship which made it possible for me to study in the USA; again the same feelings for a Fulbright travel grant which had helped me get there; more of the same feelings toward my American family who hosted me[2] upon arrival and during some short periods; admiration for American achievements, both intellectual and material, and its high standards of living. In contrast, however, was the strong feeling that something was missing or wrong, though I could not put my finger on it; it had to do with self–other relations. I admired the beauty of the yards with trees and flowers and spacious homes in suburban America (Newton Center, Massachusetts) where my American family lived. But there was no one around, no neighbourly visiting; each house was an island unto itself.

EARLY YEARS

In the last section I wrote about my symbolic and literal crossing of the Bosphorus, from Asia to Europe, from East to West, all the way to the New World America. To explain the contrasts and conflicted feelings and indeed to explain *why* I did cross the Bosphorus, I need to go back even further to my early years.

I was brought up with the ideal of 'doing something worthwhile' (for society), an ideal especially nourished by my mother. She was an extraordinary person, whom I loved and admired all my life. She was a respected public figure in a provincial town, Bursa, and a role model for me; I could not imagine a life that was not devoted to public service, just like my mother's. Both my parents were teachers; they were fully committed to the modernising Ataturk reforms of the Republican Era, starting in the 1920s, and felt that as teachers they had a mission to build up a modern secular society out of the ashes of an old one based on tradition and religion.[3] They established a private kindergarten with very limited means, which slowly grew into a primary and secondary school. I was the first pupil in the school at the age of two, and grew with the school.

The ideal of social commitment, which I internalised in my early socialisation, has been a guiding principle for me; it has influenced my world view and academic perspective. It was coupled with an achievement motivation not for self-enhancement but for self-transcendence; it involved a commitment to entities transcending myself (family, school, society). Modernisation was the national goal, and at the time societal development meant Westernisation.

I was always given the responsibility of representing my parents and our family school. As my parents and our school were known in the educational community in Bursa, my performance would reflect upon them. As young as ten years of age, I was responsible for maintaining a 'good name' for our family school. This was especially stressed during the oral examinations for graduation from the fifth grade which were attended by outside examiners from other schools and during the subsequent years when I attended the public secondary school for girls, since at that time our family school was only a primary school.

This was a 'social achievement motivation' (Phalet and Claeys, 1993; Yang, 1986; Yu and Yang, 1994) which I readily accepted, though feeling its heavy weight. It was a combined sense of responsibility and commitment to those for whom I felt a deep sense of attachment and loyalty. As early as I can remember, my mother had high educational/professional aspirations for me. She wanted me to study abroad, to come back and to administer our family school. It was simply inconceivable to me not to work hard and not to achieve. Thus, growing up in a (collectivistic) culture of relatedness with ideals of social progress and loyalty toward family, school, society, paved the way toward my developing a strong social consciousness and a sense of social commitment.

It was against this background that I applied to ACG when I finished the secondary public school in Bursa. I was aspiring to something better than the high school in Bursa. My parents thought that I deserved to get the best education in Turkey, and ACG was probably the best school then available (still is!). The decision was for me to go away, though it was emotionally and materially costly for me and my parents. I took the entrance examinations and was accepted with a partial scholarship.

ACG widened my horizons, but it did not change my ideals of social commitment to a modern society. It added new components to them, and in particular the concept of individual liberties. However, at that time I did not yet see any conflicts among these components; they were to emerge with the next crossing of larger waters – the Atlantic Ocean.

Thus, for me, the cross-cultural encounter had two steps, the first one in the American school in Istanbul, the second one in the USA, Wellesley and Berkeley. My reactions to American interpersonal styles were indeed reinforcements of my already established characteristics which I took with me to the States. My early life was filled with ideals, love, loyalty, and heroes. I was clearly myself by the time of my second cross-cultural encounter; America just threw my shadow into sharp relief.

A SOCIAL SCIENCE PERSPECTIVE

Throughout my academic career I have been as much a social scientist as a psychologist. This is with respect to the scope of my topical interests, and the units of analysis and the methodology I use. Together with this wider scope goes an orientation to psychology as a science which can and should be socially relevant. This is also an academic reflection of my deep-seated sense of social commitment.

After Wellesley, I went to the University of California, Berkeley, for graduate work. Berkeley was a haven of multiculturalism. I stayed at the International House and made friends with American and foreign students, especially from Europe. This experience brought 'culture' into even sharper relief for me, which became reflected in my work. I questioned the explanation of a political outlook (fascism) by deep-lying personality dynamics in *The authoritarian personality* (Adorno *et al.*, 1950). I recognised that some of the so-called *personality* characteristics were in fact *social norms* in Turkey and proceeded to test the universality of the authoritarian personality theory through a cross-cultural comparison for my PhD dissertation work (Kağitçibaşi, 1970). This was the first manifestation in my academic work of a social normative and cross-cultural perspective. Since then, I have always been sensitive in my thinking and research to the larger social structural and cultural context and have objected to the rather narrow 'psychologising' by psychologists in explaining human phenomena.

This perspective was integrated in my mind with my sense of social commitment, arising out of my early socialisation. I originally started my graduate studies at Berkeley in the clinical psychology programme. However, after the first year I shifted to social psychology. This was mainly because I came to reject the exclusively individualistic orientation in clinical psychology, dealing with the problems of the privileged few and ignoring those of the underprivileged majority. I was thinking at the time of the large numbers of 'normal' children in Turkey growing up in impoverished environments who needed attention.

Two mentors, Dr Brewster Smith at Berkeley and the late Dr Rebekah Shuey from ACG had something to do with my development at that time. Dr Smith was not an experimental social psychologist but a scholar with a wide vision who was very supportive and who appreciated my cross-cultural questioning. Dr Shuey, who was my teacher at ACG, continued to stay in Turkey for many years as a consultant to the Ministry of Education, and in contacts over the years alerted me to the pervasive human problems in my country, mainly educational ones, which needed solutions.

It was against this background and as a 'natural' course of action that I went back to Turkey rather than staying on in the USA. The deep-seated sense of commitment to my country, as well as to my family and family school, pulled me back. By this time I was married, to a Turkish man, and had a baby. My father died of a heart attack at the age of fifty-three; to help my mother with the management of our school, we returned to Bursa. I had just analysed my cross-cultural data; I wrote up the dissertation in Bursa, while busy running our family school. With Dr Smith's help through the mail (no fax or e-mail at that time!), I finished the dissertation within one year and received my PhD degree from Berkeley *in absentia*.

We established the high school part of our family school and improved the school greatly. However, it soon became clear to me that I didn't like administration very much and wanted to pursue an academic career. As there was no university in Bursa at the time, three years later we moved to Ankara.

I started out in academia at the Middle East Technical University in Ankara. I was in the Department of Social Sciences, which comprised psychology and sociology majors with several common courses. Through interactions with the sociologists in my department, I came to appreciate even more the importance of social structural variables, such as social class, in understanding behaviour. This was a valuable experience that helped me to conceptualise events in a social context and to recognise the existence of other approaches than purely psychological ones in studying human behaviour.

I was also a member of the active and politically involved community of social scientists in Ankara. Issues accompanying social change and development, migration, population, women's roles were topics of concern and research. This was my first exposure to socially relevant research, and I became intrigued with the psychological aspects of social change and modernisation.

I carried out research with final-year high school students, examining their attitudes and relating these to their familial and social structural characteristics. This study was conceptualised within the 'modernisation paradigm' and supported its assumptions. This is in the sense that I found youth from urban middle/high socio-economic backgrounds and families which had undergone mobility (rural to urban or upward) to have more 'modern' attitudes, compared with youth from more traditional (rural, non-mobile, low SES) families. Family affection was associated with the more modern pattern, and family control with the more traditional one (Kağitçibaşi, 1973). Family thus mediated between the social structural factors and individual outlooks.

My next major research was the value of children study, a nine-country study into motivations for childbearing. This was a collaborative study, initiated by James Fawcett of East–West Population Institute. Jim and I had been graduate students of Brewster Smith at Berkeley. Jim knew about my work, and we were in touch. He asked me to join the project, and I agreed enthusiastically. This was to be a turning point in my academic career. An interdisciplinary team of researchers, psychologists, sociologists and demographers studied values attributed to children and fertility behaviour through a survey conducted with more than 20,000 people. I carried out the Turkish survey of more than 2,300 married respondents in a nationally representative sample.

We found that even when social structural and economic variables were controlled, values attributed by parents to children helped explain some of the variance in fertility behaviour. We also found that psychological variables mediated between the background socio-economic factors and the resultant fertility (Bulatao, 1979; Fawcett, 1983; Kağitçibaşi, 1982a, b). This was another instance of relating psychological variables to social variables. The main finding was that in low levels of socio-economic development the economic/utilitarian value of children is important, and as this value is cumulative with child numbers (more children providing more economic benefits and old-age security to their parents), high fertility is the result. With urbanisation and socio-economic development, however, children's psychological value comes to the fore, since children now entail economic costs rather than economic benefits. As the psychological value of children is not number-based (even few children providing adequate love, pride, etc., to their parents), fertility decreases.

The decreased economic value of children was striking both within countries (among urban, educated groups living in more developed areas, compared with less affluent, less educated groups) and across countries (much less important in the USA and Germany than in Turkey, the Philippines, Indonesia, Thailand, etc.). This was apparent in responses to questions inquiring about expected dependency on adult offspring in old age. Much dependency was expected in less-developed contexts in the form of future financial assistance from adult offspring, whereas such dependency was rejected in the more-developed contexts. The dependency on adult offspring appeared to be a part of a general pattern of interdependent family relationships, first comprising the dependency of the child on the parents and later its reversal. With socio-economic development, this interdependent pattern seemed to give way to a pattern of independence, with old-age security value of children losing importance (Kağitçibaşi, 1982a, b).

This is a functional analysis which looks into the underlying social/economic causes for behaviour, linking the psychological and the sociological levels of analysis. This interpretation of the value of children study results was also again within a general modernisation paradigm in the sense that with increased urbanisation, education and economic development, interdependent family relationships were to be replaced with independent patterns and nucleation, and interdependent interpersonal patterns with individuation. I made this interpretation rather readily, given my general acceptance of the modernisation paradigm which assumed a convergence toward the Western pattern of nucleation/individuation with socio-economic development, urbanisation and industrialisation (Inkeles, 1969; Inkeles and Smith, 1974).

PARADIGM SHIFT

While working on the analyses of the value of children study, I edited a book, entitled *Sex roles, family and community in Turkey* (1982c), within my 'social scientist' role, in which research by sociologists and anthropologists, as well as psychologists, was presented. In his chapter Alan Duben (1982), an anthropologist doing research in Turkey, discussed his finding that even among the most educated urban families, the significance of interdependent family and kinship relationships was not decreasing. Another study from an urban centre in Turkey by a sociologist (Kongar, 1972) had also reported *continuing* close relations among family and kin.

During the 1983–4 academic year I was a Fulbright scholar at Harvard and a fellow at the Bunting Institute of Radcliffe College. There I started working on a theoretical paper on the family and family interaction patterns and how these change with socio-economic development, based on my own research results and others. I was trying to come to terms with the apparent conflict between my own findings supporting the 'convergence' hypothesis of modernisation theory (toward Western individuation) and others which pointed to continuing cultural diversity.

Reexamining the value of children study results, I realised that all our questions referring to intergenerational interdependencies had concerned financial/economic/utilitarian matters. And when the answers clearly pointed to a decrease in these dependencies with socio-economic development, I had interpreted this decrease as a general move toward independence and individuation. In other words, I had drawn a conclusion regarding *general* familial interdependencies from a finding on *material* interdependencies, focusing on the decreasing economic value of children with socio-economic development, without paying sufficient attention to the fact that the psychological value of children *increased* through socio-economic development.

This led to a conceptual breakthrough. I came to see that we can differentiate both conceptually and empirically two different dimensions of interdependencies – material and emotional. Though these may relate to one another, they are independent. Indeed, the value of children study findings pointed to decreasing material interdependencies but continuing, even increasing, emotional (psychological) interdependencies with socio-economic development. Given this distinction, the convergence hypothesis of modernisation theory was *not* supported regarding decreasing psychological interpersonal interdependencies, though it was supported regarding decreasing material interdependencies. As the former is the key, in psychological terms, to the modernity theory claims of individuation/nucleation with development, the data in fact questioned such claims.

Afterwards I encountered research from other parts of the world which also pointed to continuing closely knit collectivistic relationships (interdependencies) even among the developed sectors in non-Western countries (see Kağitçibaşi, 1990, 1994, 1996a, and 1997 for reviews), while material dependencies become negligible. At the time however, my initial 'awakening' and 'paradigm shift' found expression in a rather unlikely outlet. While still at Harvard in 1984, I was invited to a symposium held at Ohio State University on George Orwell's *Nineteen Eighty-four*. An interesting group of philosophers, literary critics, psychologists and other social scientists were going to be there, so I accepted the invitation and started to read *Nineteen Eighty-four* again after many years.

Orwell's vision is often regarded as a critique of totalitarian forces crushing individualism. However, by this second reading of the novel, I had developed an entirely different mind set, for it occured to me that Orwell's nightmarish London could be seen as a portrait of an extremely individualistic society rendering the human being vulnerable. So I wrote a rather unusual interpretive essay (Kağitçibaşi, 1985), which caused quite a bit of debate at the symposium:

> Winston Smith [the main character in *Nineteen Eighty-four*] is an individual separated from everyone else. Everyone is alone in *Nineteen Eighty-four*, a society where the Party has correctly perceived that relatedness and close emotional ties among humans are dangerous sources of strength and moral support. *Nineteen Eighty-four* is the world of radical individualism taken to its logical conclusion – a culture of separateness in extreme form. ... Big brother ... triumphs in breaking down all human care and loyalty – 'All you care about is yourself', Winston echoes. After this final individuation and separation, Winston is completely vanquished.
>
> (pp. 93–94)

Then I proceeded to propose

> a new synthesis of the individual self with the relational self. Such a synthesis must be achieved if the individual is not to be isolated and vulnerable ..., not driven to denounce others for self-preservation as Winston Smith was, but able instead to form and protect close interpersonal and familial relationships for mutual growth. ... This synthesis would assure human dignity and strength; it would provide for the coexistence of individual autonomy with closeness and loyalty to others; it would form the modern familial–communal culture of relatedness which allows full individual growth; it would assure that *Nineteen Eighty-four* never materialises.
>
> (p. 98)

Obviously *Nineteen Eighty-four* is a fantasy and bears no resemblance to any known society. Nevertheless, reinterpreting it helped me question the value base of much of my Western training, particularly in psychology. When I recognised that there may also be problems with individualism, I was freed, so to speak, to accept that there may be alternative paths to social change and to oppose the modernisation theory assumption of a unidirectional *progression* toward a *better* model (individualism) through socio-economic development. This recognition helped me integrate various research results, mentioned above, into a theory of family change and the development of the self (Kağitçibaşi, 1990), incorporating the 'synthesis' I called for in my interpretive essay (quoted above). What I was questioning was the Western value system which I had embraced earlier.

Another major research project, which I directed, provided the opportunity to test the feasibility of such a synthesis in applications and to realise some of my social commitment goals. This was the ten-year Turkish Early Enrichment Project (TEEP). Using an experimental design, this intervention project used before–after and experimental–control group comparisons and examined the short- and long-term effects of a training programme on mothers, children, and families. Mothers with low income and education levels were given a support/training programme to promote their young children's cognitive development as well as their overall development. Their own needs as women were also targeted through an empowerment approach focusing on better communication skills and an increased sense of competency. Both the fourth-year (short-term) and the long-term effects (seven years after the end of intervention) showed significant gains in children's overall development and school success, as well as in women's intrafamily status and family harmony in general (Kağitçibaşi, Sunar and Bekman, 1988; Kağitçibaşi,1996a). Of particular relevance for my synthetic theory of the family and of the autonomous-related self, mothers who went through training developed more positive attitudes toward their children's autonomy while staying as closely linked to them as the control group.

With such positive results that were sustained over time, this project was well received, and initiatives were taken to apply the programme as public service. We established the Mother–Child Education Foundation (MOCEF) for this purpose. MOCEF, in collaboration with UNICEF, the Turkish Ministry of Education and the World Bank, has been expanding the applications, with more than 20,000 families having benefited from the programme up to now. It has also helped change educational policies in Turkey to include family-based, non-formal models of preschool education. This is an example of how scientifically sound and socially relevant research can inform policies and lead to applications.

TEEP has been most gratifying to me personally in terms of serving 'the underprivileged majority', a deep-seated ideal. There have been other opportunities for me to realise this ideal in my work as consultant with the Turkish Ministry of Education, and several non-profit volunteer organisations. Of particular importance was my involvement as academic advisor for the Turkish 'Sesame Street' TV programme, which was shown in research conducted with socially disadvantaged children to be highly beneficial for their cognitive and social development (Sahin, 1990).

PUTTING IT ALL TOGETHER

Michael Bond told me that our goal in this book is to examine the impact of the cross-cultural encounter. I have been pursuing that goal, looking into the effects of my two-step culture contact on me as a person and on my work as a psychologist. The person and the psychologist are so intermingled that I can not differentiate them. The encounter with another culture stimulated, provoked and engaged a personal and scientific response at the same time. Putting it all together and reiterating, I discern some threads of influence running through this adventure.

Awakening to Culture and Self

As a fish out of water, I came to 'see' culture when I left my own. Though the beginning of this awakening was at the young age of thirteen, it was a continuous process. It started out as personal experience and, by the time I was a graduate student, it began to influence my scientific work. It was because I was using a cultural filter in my observations, as well as in my reading of the literature, that I wondered about the universal validity of the authoritarian personality theory, that in fact I asked the question, 'Is it personality or social norms?', and I undertook laborious cross-cultural research for my dissertation work.

The most significant effect of my cultural encounter occured at the point of intercept between culture and self. It was in the definition of the self and of self–other relations that my cultural filter was sharpened. Based on my own experiences, as well as benefiting from cross-cultural research findings, I came to recognise basic distinctions between related selves and separated selves and their familial backgrounds. Looking into the functional underpinnings in family dynamics and the values attributed to children in different socio-cultural-economic contexts, I realised that the modernisation theory expectation of convergence toward the Western individualistic model was *not* occurring. A third, synthetic model of family function emerged, almost naturally out of this culture-sensitive searching, which was again based on my own experience. My current views about individualism–collectivism (Kağitçibaşi, 1994, 1997), and my model of the autonomous-related self (Kağitçibaşi, 1996c) are products of this work. The latter has also informed my applied work.

Social commitment and the role of psychology

Social commitment, which dates back to my early socialisation, has found expression in my work. This has been particularly gratifying to me. Though the roots of this sense of social commitment go back to my childhood, encountering another culture intensified it. The sheer contrasts in standards of living and the recognition of what is missing in the early lives of a great number of children were precipitating factors in my involvement in applied research in Turkey. My wide social science perspective in approaching human issues has been helpful in situating problems in a social context and in working with multidisciplinary teams.

I recognise and stress more and more the compatibility of scientific rigour and socially relevant research. This position has emerged out of my early questioning of the role of psychology and out of my growing need to do psychology which contributes to human wellbeing. Indeed, I have come to identify myself with my definition of the role of psychology. I have in the past, and continue in the present, to aspire to a scientifically sound, culturally sensitive and socially responsible career in psychology.

NOTES

1   ACG was the girls' school associated with the Robert College, the oldest American educational institution abroad. Later on it was merged with the Robert College, forming a coeducational school.

2   This was the family of my AFS sister, who had visited my family earlier for a summer through the AFS International Student Exchange Program.

3   A short historical background may be in order. The Turkish Republic was established in 1923. Its predecessor, the Ottoman Empire, after six centuries of sovereignty, was destroyed at the end of World War 1. Istanbul and Anatolia, its central heartland, was occupied. A war for independence was then fought against the occupying forces under the leadership of Ataturk. When it was won, against all odds, the Turkish Republic was founded. Ataturk was elected the first president, and a series of reforms were undertaken which covered all spheres of civil society, entailing secularisation and modernisation.

REFERENCES

Adorno, T.W., Frenkel-Brunswik, E., Levinson, D.J. and Sanford, R.N. (1950). *The authoritarian personality*. New York: Harper.

Bulatao, R.A. (1979). *On the nature of the transition in the value of children*. Hawaii: East–West Population Institute.

Duben, A. (1982). The significance of family and kinship in urban Turkey. In Ç. Kağitçibaşi (ed.), *Sex roles, family and community in Turkey* (pp. 73–99). Bloomington, IN: Indiana University Press.

Fawcett, J.T. (1983). Perceptions of the value of children: Satisfactions and costs. In R. Bulatao, R.D. Lee, P.E. Hollerbach, and J. Bongaarts, (eds), *Determinants of fertility in developing countries, 1*. Washington, DC: National Academy Press.

Inkeles, A. (1969). Making men modern: On the causes and consequences of individual change in six developing countries. *American Journal of Sociology, 75*, 208–225.

Inkeles, A. and Smith, D.H. (1974). *Becoming modern: Individual changes in six developing countries*. Cambridge, MA: Harvard University Press.

Kağitçibaşi, Ç. (1970). Social norms and authoritarianism: A Turkish–American comparison. *Journal of Personality and Social Psychology, 16*, 444–451.

Kağitçibaşi, Ç. (1973). Psychological aspects of modernisation in Turkey, *Journal of Cross-Cultural Psychology, 4*, 157–174.

Kağitçibaşi, Ç. (1982a). *The changing value of children in Turkey*. Publ. No. 60-E. Honolulu: East–West Center.

Kağitçibaşi, Ç. (1982b). Old-age security value of children: Cross-national socio-economic evidence. *Journal of Cross-cultural Psychology, 13*, 29–42.

Kağitçibaşi, Ç. (ed.) (1982c). *Sex roles, family and community in Turkey*. Bloomington, IN: Indiana University Press.

Kağitçibaşi, Ç. (1985). Culture of separateness–culture of relatedness. *1984 Vision and Reality. Papers in Comparative Studies*. vol. 4, 91–99. Ohio State University.

Kağitçibaşi, Ç. (1990). Family and socialisation in cross-cultural perspective: A model of change. In J. Berman (ed.), *Cross-cultural perspectives: Nebraska symposium on motivation, 1989*, 37, Lincoln, NB: Nebraska University Press.

Kağitçibaşi, Ç. (1994). A critical appraisal of individualism–collectivism: Toward a new formulation. In U. Kim, H. Triandis, Ç. Kağitçibaşi, S.-C. Choi and G. Yoon (eds),

Individualism and collectivism: Theory, method and applications (pp. 52–65). Beverly Hills, CA: Sage.

Kağitçibaşi, Ç. (1996a). *Family and human development across cultures: A view from the other side*. Hillsdale, NJ: Lawrence Erlbaum.

Kağitçibaşi, Ç. (1996b). A personal account of my involvement in cross-cultural development psychology. In D. Thompson, and J.D. Hogan, (eds), *A history of developmental psychology in autobiography* (pp. 121–136). Boulder, CO.: Westview Press.

Kağitçibaşi, Ç. (1996c). The autonomous-relational self: A new synthesis. *European Psychologist, 1,* 3.

Kağitçibaşi, Ç. (1997). Individualism and collectivism. In J. Berry, M. Segall and Ç. Kağitçibaşi (eds), *Handbook of cross-cultural psychology*, vol. 3. Boston, MA: Allyn & Bacon.

Kağitçibaşi, Ç., Sunar, D. and Bekman, S. (1988). *Comprehensive preschool education project: Final report*. Ottawa: International Development Research Center.

Kongar, E. (1972). *Izmir'de kentsel aile* (The urban family in Izmir). Ankara: Turkish Social Science Association.

Phalet, K. and Claeys, W. (1993). A comparative study of Turkish and Belgian youth. *Journal of Cross-cultural Psychology, 24,* 319–343.

Sahin, N. (1990). Research on the Turkish co-production of Sesame Street. In P.B. Mann (ed.) *Sesame Street research: A 20th anniversary symposium* (pp. 239–250). Educational Testing Service – Children's Television Workshop, New York.

Yang, K.-S. (1986). Chinese personality and its change. In M.H. Bond (ed.), *The psychology of the Chinese people* (pp. 106–170). New York: Oxford University Press.

Yu, A.-B. and Yang, K.-S. (1994). The nature of achievement motivation in collectivistic societies. In U. Kim, H.C. Triandis, Ç. Kağitçibaşi, S.-C. Choi and G. Yoon (eds), *Individualism and collectivism: Theory, method, and applications* (pp. 239–250). Newbury Park, CA: Sage.

12 Cruising the world
A nomad in Academe

J. W. Berry

INTRODUCTION: GETTING IN

Diversity is a fact of life; whether it is the 'spice' or the 'irritant' to people is the fundamental psychological, social, cultural and political issue of our times. The study of diversity both at home and abroad has been the focus of my academic life. It is not at all clear to me whether this was a conscious choice; perhaps it just allowed me to pursue my two core values of hedonism and social activism simultaneously, in the guise of a respectable academic career. This chapter provides an opportunity to search for answers, and possibly a justification.

At the 1988 congress of the International Association for Cross-cultural Psychology Symposium 'From ideas to research ventures', many participants observed that early personal experiences of intercultural relations set them on a cross-cultural career course. In my own case, I grew up in an English-speaking family, in a French-speaking village, adjacent to a Mohawk Indian reservation, dealing daily with these 'others'. In adolescence, this exposure to diversity was extended by working as a merchant seaman, with periods coasting in Africa, the Indian Ocean, and the Canadian Arctic. Virtually all my subsequent national and international research has been rooted in these initial intercultural encounters. How they have shaped my orientation to various issues in cross-cultural psychology constitutes the focus of this chapter.

My first exposure to the world of WASP (Western academic scientific psychology) was as an undergraduate at Sir George Williams University in Montreal. Like most students there in the early 1960s, I was a part-time student, working during the day (at various real-life jobs, such as assistant production manager in a furniture factory and stock control for beer, wine and whiskey bottles in a glass factory). But unlike most of my fellow students and workmates, I was not an immigrant to Canada. In both the factory and the classroom my exposure to cultural diversity continued to escalate.

Most important, though, was that virtually all my psychology courses were taught by Professor J.W. Bridges (born in Prince Edward Island in 1885, PhD from Harvard in 1913, under the supervision of Hugo Munsterberg; see Bridges, 1966). Both psychologist and anthropologist and long-time colleague of Otto Klineberg, Bridges taught all his psychology courses with a concern for the cultural limitations of the ideas and findings he was presenting, and, where possible, he attempted to put his lecture materials into their cultural context. Given this concern for culture in my psychology courses, on top of my earlier and continuing experiential exposure to diversity, it is probably the case that I never really had a choice: a cross-cultural psychologist I must become.

I applied to the University of Edinburgh for graduate work, in part because of their long history of involvement with the two areas of the world that most interested me (Africa and the Arctic). With great good fortune, I was accepted by James Drever as his PhD student there. I have never understood why he took a chance on such an atypical applicant, but he provided me with an opportunity, and his full academic support, to carry out a comparative study of sensory and perceptual skills among two groups of people (one in Sierra Leone, the Temne; the other in the Canadian Arctic, the Inuit, formerly called Eskimo), in addition to the Scots of the north-east coastal region.

With all this background, I was well on my way to meshing my personal and academic interests in human diversity. I now considered myself a cross-cultural psychologist.

AN ECOLOGICAL PERSPECTIVE: CONTEXT IS ALL

Where does diversity come from? As a result of working in Africa, the Arctic and with immigrants from various parts of the world, I became sure that 'culture' (whatever that might mean) had its own diversity, and that it had an impact on individual psychology. But where did cultural diversity come from? Sitting in the upper library at Edinburgh (in an alcove previously occupied by Charles Darwin), I began to read more widely in cultural anthropology, and was struck by the work of Daryll Forde (1934) and Alfred Kroeber (1939) on cultural ecology. Simply put, they had found that *cultural areas* of Africa and aboriginal North America mapped onto *ecological areas*, so that major features of a group's culture coincided with major features of that group's habitat. In 1964 I was seized by the idea that there might be a reciprocal chain of influence: ecology – culture – behaviour. But how did the relationships work? These researchers in the field of cultural ecology had shown that cultures are *adaptive* to context; and the work by Herb Barry and colleagues (e.g., Barry, Child and Bacon, 1959) was beginning to show that child rearing is *adaptive* to ecology, and that adult personality should be *adaptive* to culture. Thus the process of *adaptation to context* (culture to ecology; human behaviour to culture) became central to my thinking (Berry, 1975, 1994a). It has also become central to some versions of cross-cultural psychology (see textbooks by Berry *et al.*, 1992; Segall *et al.*, 1990).

As Jahoda (1995) points out, this kind of thinking was not new: these concepts and linkages had been part of Western thought for over 2,000 years. And in the twentieth century, others (notably Kardiner, 1939, and Whiting and Whiting, 1975) were thinking in similar terms. My view (1995b) is that the ecological perspective is a continuing and evolving theme in thinking about the origins and functions of human diversity, and that a periodic attempt to synthesise and organise such thought into frameworks is a useful exercise.

My current version of the ecocultural framework is presented in Figure 12.1. The framework distinguishes between the *population* level and the *individual* levels of analysis. The flow of the framework is from left to right, with population-level variables (on the left) conceived of as influencing individual outcomes (on the right). This general flow is intended to correspond to the interests of cross-cultural psychology; we wish to account for individual and group differences in psychological characteristics as a function of population-level factors. However, it is obvious that a full model, one that attempts to completely specify relationships in the real world, would have many more components and numerous feedback arrows, representing reciprocal influences between components and by individuals on other variables in the framework.

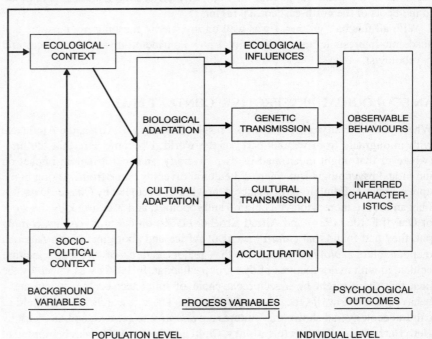

Figure 12.1 An ecocultural framework linking ecology, culture and behaviour

The notion of feedback recognises the individual as an actor and avoids viewing the developing and behaving individual as a mere pawn. For ease of presenting the framework, the two feedback relationships illustrated in Figure 12.1 (individuals influencing their *ecological* and *socio-political* contexts) are used to signal feedback in the framework more generally.

At the extreme left are two major classes of influence (background variables of ecological and socio-political context), while at the extreme right are the psychological characteristics that are usually the focus of psychological research (including both observable behaviours and inferred characteristics such as motives, abilities, traits, and attitudes). The two middle sets of variables (the process variables) represent the various forms of transmission or influence from population variables to individuals. For completeness, both biological and cultural factors are included, although the usual emphasis in cross-cultural psychology is on cultural influences.

The ecological context is the setting in which human organisms and the physical environment interact. It is best understood as a set of relationships that provide a range of life possibilities for a population. Such an interactive point of view is the essence of an ecological approach and avoids the pitfalls of earlier approaches, such as that of environmental determinism. Since the organism interacts with its habitat primarily to exploit resources in order to sustain individual and collective life, the basic feature of this ecological context is economic activity. This variable involves cultural groups that are rated with respect to their degree of reliance on five kinds of economic activity: hunting, gathering, fishing, pastoralism, and agriculture. Recent work has extended this kind of analysis to urban–industrial societies in which other dimensions of economic activity have emerged, the most common being increased occupational specialisation (Berry, 1994b). Each form of economic activity implies a different kind of relationship between the local human population, their resources, and their habitat. These relationships in turn imply varying cultural, biological, and psychological outcomes.

With respect to adaptation at the population level, individual behaviour can be understood across cultures only when both cultural and biological features are taken into account. This joint interest in cultural and biological influences on behaviour appears necessary because the exclusion of either as a factor in the explanation of human psychological variation makes little sense. However, as noted above, culture and cultural transmission are the focal interest. Culture is transmitted by the processes of *enculturation* and *socialisation*, which are the central concepts used to describe this cultural transmission.

Not all outcomes are necessarily the result of ecological relationships. Also depicted in Figure 12.1 is the view that culture and individual behaviour are affected by influences stemming from cultural contact in the socio-political context that impinges on one's group. These influences form the basis for *acculturation*, resulting from such historical and contemporary experiences as colonial expansion, international trade, invasion, and migration.

Not all relationships between the two major background variables and psychological outcome are mediated by cultural or biological adaptation. Some influences are direct and rather immediate, such as environmental learning in a particular ecology (leading to a new performance), or a new experience with another culture (leading to new attitudes or values). Since individuals can recognise, screen, appraise, and alter all of these influences, whether they are direct or mediated, there are likely to be wide individual differences in the psychological outcomes.

The first comprehensive use of this framework was in a volume (Berry, 1976) that assembled my work on perception, cognition and acculturation in Africa, Australia and the Canadian Arctic. Earlier, less-elaborated versions were presented in two papers (Berry, 1966 and 1971) reporting on specific studies. The term *ecocultural* was first introduced (as far as I can tell) by me in 1979 (Berry, 1979, p. 186) to signal the joint influences of ecology and culture on human development and behaviour. Others have also employed the term, particularly in relation to the concept of *niche* (e.g. Weisner, 1984; Super and Harkness, 1986).

THEORY AND METHOD: WHAT AND HOW?

'Culture first, psychology second' has been a catch phrase in my work from the beginning: understanding the cultural (and ecological) context is the essential basis for any psychological research (Berry, 1985). In practical terms, one should spend half one's time on the context, the other half with the individual. These ideals are hardly ever met, of course, but a concern for them has driven me to confront theoretical and methodological issues from the beginning, including comparability (Berry, 1969a; 1989), equivalence (Berry 1980a) and field methods (both ethnographic and psychological; Lonner and Berry, 1986).

The *emic–etic* distinction (Pike, 1967) has now been widely adopted in the field. I saw in this distinction a useful way to move away from the ethnocentrism of Western academic scientific psychology (particularly in domains such as intelligence and social behaviour). However, to make use of the contrast, it became clear that there are 'good' etics and 'bad' etics. So I had to distinguish *imposed etics* from *derived etics*. The former are the psychological concepts and procedures that are brought to the research enterprise, often with the assumption that they are valid, even universal; the latter may emerge from comparative research as valid psychological knowledge in more than one culture. The full methodological sequence interposes *emic* analyses and empirical studies between the two *etics*. This sequence was then taken (Berry and Dasen, 1974) as a series of goals for the field. First, *transport and test* one's concepts and presumed knowledge gained from work in one's own culture; this is an *emic* investigation for your own, but an *imposed etic* when taken to other cultures. Second, *explore* the other culture(s) to discover differences or variations in meaning that are not available in your own culture; this is an *emic* investigation. Finally, *compare* knowledge gained in these first two activities in order to produce a more universal understanding; this is the *derived etic* goal for the field.

It is plausible to see the sequence (*imposed etic – emic – derived etic*) and the associated goals (transport and test, explore new cultural meanings, and attempt a broader integration) as an historical unfolding of the field: initial work focused on psychological differences across cultural groups using existing concepts and instruments, but guided by the constraints of comparative theory and methodology; then there was an increasing concern for local, culturally specific phenomena ('indigenous' or 'cultural' perspectives); and now increasingly there is interest in putting it all together in a pan-human psychology that is both comparative and sensitive to context (the 'universalist' perspective; see Berry, 1996). This is an *inclusive* view of the field, one that guided the editing of the second edition of the *Handbook of cross-cultural psychology* (see Berry, 1997a). In my view, we are simultaneously *cultural* and *comparative*; taken together, we create the field of cross-cultural psychology.

COGNITION: WHAT IS SMART?

On first learning in a psychology course about intelligence tests and supposed population differences my immediate reaction was, 'That can't be right!' Anyone who has worked with people from other cultures knows that virtually all aspects of cognitive competence can differ from one group to another. It was clear to me then, simply on the basis of personal experience, that across cultures people value different abilities, think about competence in different ways, and understand the development and organisation of abilities in different terms. For example, learning by observing and doing (rather than by verbal instructing and responding) was highly valued among the Cree (Indians) with whom I worked one summer as a wood cutter. Since then, much research has shown that this intuitive reaction was valid (see, e.g., Berry, 1984a; Berry and Bennett, 1992; Dasen, 1984).

However, in 1963 there was very little literature to guide a beginning researcher. Ferguson (1956, p. 121) had proposed that 'Cultural factors prescribe what shall be learned and at what age; consequently different cultural environments will lead to the development of different patterns of ability.' And Biesheuvel (1959, p. 12) considered that 'Through the medium of educational practices and other social pressures, a culture produces the kind of personalities that are adapted to its requirements.' These early insights directed me toward an examination of 'different cultural environments' and 'educational practices' as factors in the development of 'different patterns of abilities' that are 'adaptive to the require-ments' of different cultures. Thus was born my study of 'Temne and Eskimo perceptual skills' (Berry 1966), in which 'ecological demands' and 'cultural aids' were predicted (and shown) to lead to the development of differential 'perceptual skills'.

Specifically, an 'ecological analysis' (Berry, 1980b) of what hunting- and farming-based peoples need to do (and do well) in order to survive and thrive led first to the prediction that hunters (in contrast to farmers) need to develop fine sensory acuity, visual analytic and disembedding skills, and a spatial orientation. Second, the ecological engagement of hunters should produce adaptive cultural practices that promote the development of these perceptual and cognitive abilities. Most important were socialisation practices (following Barry *et al.*, 1959), arts and crafts training and production, and linguistic distinctions that emphasise visual and spatial features of one's environment. Third, Ferguson's (1956) notion of 'patterns of abilities', combined with an interest in 'disembedding skills', led me to the work of Hy Witkin on cognitive styles as a way of linking socialisation to cognitive development (e.g., Witkin and Berry, 1975).

Following this initial study (Berry, 1966), I emigrated to Australia to work with Aboriginal (hunters) and New Guinea (farmers) as a way of replicating and extending my work. As expected, results showed that Australian Aboriginal hunters were similar to Arctic Inuit, and New Guinean farmers were similar to the Temne in their profile of abilities (Berry, 1971).

Unfortunately, I was unable to stay in Australia because of the hedonism and social activism mentioned at the beginning of this chapter; too much of both was interfering with the development of an academic career. With respect to the first, the quality of the sailing, swimming and wine seriously distracted me from working; for the other, research involvement in anti-war (Berry, 1968; 1969b) and Aboriginal rights (Berry, 1970) issues were being judged as not suitable for a proper academic career. Moreover, skirmishes with the Australian Security Intelligence Organisation led to questions being raised publicly (even in Parliament) about the wisdom of allowing foreign agitators to teach innocent Australian youth in their universities. On the move again in 1969, I settled at Queen's University, where I have stayed (more or less) since.

Work on perceptual–cognitive abilities continued among the Cree hunting peoples of Northern Québec and Ontario, as well as among the Dene and Tsimshian of British Columbia. This work contrasted (within aboriginal North America) hunting with non-hunting peoples in an attempt to obtain a more controlled comparison. Results of this work (along with all my previous studies) were assembled into a book, *Human ecology and cognitive style* (Berry, 1976) which made a case for differential abilities as adaptive to ecocultural context. Further evidence was sought in another controlled comparative study in Central Africa (1976–8) among hunting-based Biaka Pygmy, and more agricultural Bagandu and Gbanu peoples (Berry *et al.*, 1986), and among Adivasi in India (Mishra, Sinha and Berry, 1996).

Taken together, these further studies confirmed the predictions stemming from the ecocultural framework, and support the early insights of Ferguson and Biesheuvel: people develop those abilities that are useful (adaptive) in their cultures, that allow them as a group to meet their ecological demands, and for which they are specifically socialised. This view contrasts sharply with the *imposed etic* of general intelligence as a single invariant *a priori* package of competences valued in WASP.

ACCULTURATION: WHAT'S NEW?

In the ecocultural framework (Figure 12.1), the lower line takes the influence of other cultures into account, simultaneously and with an importance equal to that of the ecological context. Human behaviour cannot be accounted for solely on the basis of ecological adaptation; external cultural influences are an essential (and possibly increasingly important) source of influence. Initially, acculturation served as a variable that needed to be controlled, as a factor whose influence could alter the development and assessment of perceptual–cognitive abilities. By 1970, it became clear to me that many psychological phenomena associated with culture contact were going to be of increasing importance to society. Hence, I turned to acculturation as an object of study in its own right.

While acculturation is a neutral term in principle (that is, change may take place in either or both groups), in practice acculturation tends to induce more change in one of the groups (usually termed the *acculturating group*). Acculturation is essentially a form of culture change that results from contact between two independent cultures. It is important to note that *assimilation* is not the only kind of acculturation; it can also be *reactive* (triggering resistance to change in both groups), *creative* (stimulating new cultural forms, not found in either of the cultures in contact), and *delayed* (initiating changes that appear more fully years later).

An important distinction has been made by Graves (1967) between acculturation as a collective or group-level phenomenon and *psychological acculturation*. In the former acculturation is a change in the *culture* of the group; in the latter, acculturation is a change in the *psychology* of the individual. This distinction between levels struck me as being important for two reasons: first, it allows us to examine the systematic relationships between culture and behaviour; and second, because not all individuals participate to the same extent in the general acculturation being experienced by their group, we can examine individual differences in the way they arrange their new lives.

My first excursion into acculturation research was stimulated by the announcement of a policy change by the Australian government in 1967: henceforth Aborigines would no longer be segregated; they would be assimilated, and become like all other Australians. My letter to the then Prime Minister suggested that this was a matter of importance to those affected, and that Aborigines should be consulted about their own preferences. A reply stated that this was a complex matter, and that Aborigines would not have sufficient understanding of it to render an informed opinion! This arrogance and ethnocentrism was a clear challenge and prompted the first studies on orientations to acculturation (Berry, 1970; Sommerlad and Berry, 1970).

In order to work with this issue, we introduced the concept of *acculturation attitudes*. It has since become clear that, in all plural societies, cultural groups and their individual members, in both the dominant and non-dominant situations, must deal with the issue of *how* to acculturate. Strategies with respect to two major issues are usually worked out by groups and individuals in their daily encounters with each other. These issues are: *cultural maintenance* (to what extent cultural identity and characteristics are considered to be important, and their maintenance strived for); and *contact and participation* (to what extent should they become involved in other cultural groups, or remain primarily among themselves).

Because of the importance of viewing acculturation as a two-dimensional (rather than a unidimensional, 'either/or') process, I believe that the following exposition of the framework is essential. When these two underlying issues are considered simultaneously, a conceptual framework (see Figure 12.2) is generated which posits four acculturation strategies. These two issues can be responded to on attitudinal dimensions, represented by bipolar arrows. For purposes of presentation, generally positive or negative ('yes' or 'no') responses to these issues intersect to define four acculturation strategies. These strategies carry different names, depending on which group (the dominant or non-dominant) is being

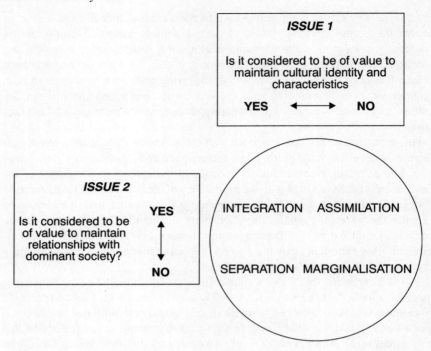

Figure 12.2 Four acculturation strategies based upon two underlying issues

considered. From the point of view of non-dominant groups, when individuals do not wish to maintain their cultural identity and seek daily interaction with other cultures, the *Assimilation* strategy is defined. In contrast, when individuals place a value on holding onto their original culture, and at the same time wish to avoid interaction with others, then the *Separation* alternative is defined. When there is an interest in both maintaining and developing one's original culture, while also having daily interactions with other groups, *Integration* is the option; here, there is some degree of cultural integrity maintained, while at the same time seeking to participate as an integral part of the larger social network. Finally, when there is little possibility or interest in cultural maintenance (often for reasons of enforced cultural loss), and little interest in having relations with others (often for reasons of exclusion or discrimination), then *Marginalisation* is defined.

This presentation is based on the assumption that non-dominant groups and their individual members have the freedom to choose how they want to acculturate. This, of course, is not always the case (Berry, 1974). When the dominant group enforces certain forms of acculturation, or constrains the choices of non-dominant groups or individuals, then other terms need to be used. Most clearly, people may sometimes choose the Separation option; but when it is required of them by the dominant society, the situation is one of *Segregation*. Similarly, when people choose to Assimilate, the notion of the *Melting Pot* may be appropriate; but when forced to do so, it becomes more like a *Pressure Cooker*. In the case of Marginalisation, people rarely choose such an option; rather they usually become marginalised as a result of attempts at forced assimilation (Pressure Cooker) combined with forced exclusion (Segregation); thus no other term seems to be required beyond the single notion of Marginalisation.

Integration can only be 'freely' chosen and successfully pursued by non-dominant groups when the dominant society is open and inclusive in its orientation toward cultural diversity (Berry, 1991b). Thus, a *mutual accommodation* is required for integration to be attained, involving the acceptance by both groups of the right of all groups to live as culturally different peoples. This strategy requires non-dominant groups to adopt the basic values of the larger society, while at the same time the dominant group must be prepared to adapt national institutions (e.g. education, health, labour) to better meet the needs of all groups now living together in the plural society.

Obviously, the integration strategy can only be pursued in societies that are explicitly *multicultural*, in which certain psychological preconditions are established (see below). Just as obviously, integration (and separation) can only be pursued when other members of one's ethnocultural group share in the wish to maintain the group's cultural heritage.

Individuals and groups may hold varying *attitudes* toward these four ways of acculturating, and their actual *behaviours* may vary correspondingly. Together, these attitudes and behaviours comprise what we have called *acculturation strategies* (Berry, 1990a). Attitudes towards (preferences for) these four alternatives have been measured in numerous studies (reviewed in Berry *et al.*, 1989).

A second essential concept has been that of *acculturative stress*. One of the most obvious and frequently reported consequences of acculturation is societal disintegration accompanied by personal crisis. The old social order and cultural norms often disappear, and individuals may be lost in the change. At the group level, previous patterns of authority, civility, and welfare no longer operate; and at the individual level, hostility, uncertainty, identity confusion, anxiety and depression may set in. Taken together these changes constitute the negative side of acculturation, changes that are frequently, but not inevitably, present. The opposite, successful adaptation may also take place; the outcome appears to vary as a function of a number of variables.

The concept of *acculturative stress* was introduced by Berry and Annis (1974) and refers to one kind of stress, in which the stressors are identified as having their source in the process of acculturation; in addition, there is often a particular set of stress behaviours that occur during acculturation, such as lowered mental health status (especially confusion, anxiety, depression), feelings of marginality and alienation, heightened psychosomatic symptoms, and identity confusion. Acculturative stress thus may underlie a reduction in the health status of individuals (including physical, psychological, and social aspects). To qualify as *acculturative* stress, these changes should be related in a systematic way to known features of the acculturation process as experienced by the individual.

Recent reviews and integration of the literature (Berry, 1997b; Berry and Sam,

1997) have attempted to identify the cultural and psychological factors that govern the relationship between acculturation and mental health. These reviews show that mental health problems clearly often do arise during acculturation; however, these problems are not inevitable and seem to depend on a variety of group and individual characteristics that enter into the acculturation process. That is, acculturation sometimes enhances one's life chances and mental health and sometimes virtually destroys one's ability to carry on; the eventual outcome for any particular individual is affected by numerous variables that govern the relationship between acculturation and stress.

MULTICULTURALISM: WHAT'S ALLOWED?

When individuals and groups come to live together, while retaining some of their heritage cultures, we have a society that is *culturally plural*: in some such societies, governments and citizens enjoy and appreciate this diversity in their daily lives and seek to maintain it; in others it is considered to be a source of difficulty, and attempts are made to eliminate it.

A continuing research interest has been how to conceptualise these national and individual policies and attitudes with respect to multiculturalism. The four acculturation strategies (outlined above) provide a convenient conceptualisation. National policies and programmes may be analysed in terms of these four approaches (Berry, 1990b): some societies seek *assimilation*, expecting all ethnocultural groups to become like those in the dominant society (a theme in contemporary France and Germany); others seek *integration*, willing (even pleased) to accept and incorporate all groups to a large extent on their own cultural terms (this is the official position taken by Canada); yet others have pursued *segregation* policies (such as in South Africa until recently); and others have sought the *marginalisation* of unwanted groups (e.g., Indigenous Peoples in the Western Hemisphere). Thus, the framework in Figure 12.2 can be used to analyse and categorise orientations toward cultural group relations of both individuals and groups in both the dominant and non-dominant sections of society, and at three levels: national policies, cultural groups, and individual attitudes.

To illustrate, in Canada while numerous attempts were made historically to assimilate Canada's diverse population to British cultural norms, by 1956 the Government's view was that assimilation had not worked anywhere in the contemporary world, and that it was impracticable as a general policy. In 1971, a policy of multiculturalism was announced, the key elements of which were designed to achieve harmonious intercultural relations by promoting simultaneously *cultural maintenance* and *intergroup contact and participation* in the larger society. This is clearly an *integration* policy, in the terms used in Figure 12.2. (See Berry, 1984b, and Berry and Laponce, 1994, for a more detailed description and analysis of the policy.)

For most *cultural groups* in Canada, their articulated goals express some version of this integrationist policy. For example, Aboriginal Canadians generally seek cultural self-determination within the larger Canadian society, and most French-

Canadians (particularly those outside Quebec) generally espouse the same goal. More recent immigrant-derived cultural groups all express this preference for some degree of cultural maintenance, combined with full rights to participation in the larger society.

At the individual level, a number of psychological preconditions are essential if we are to live successfully in a multicultural society. As proposed by Berry and Kalin (1995, p. 302):

First, there needs to be general support for multiculturalism, including acceptance of various aspects and consequences of the policy, and of cultural diversity as a valuable resource for a society. Second, there should be overall low levels of intolerance or prejudice in the population. Third, there should be generally positive mutual attitudes among the various ethnocultural groups that constitute the society. And fourth, there needs to be a degree of attachment to the larger Canadian society, but without derogation of its constituent ethnocultural groups.

A number of these conditions have been studied in two national surveys in Canada (1974 and 1991). Results of this work suggest a number of conclusions: first, diversity appears to be alive and well in Canada, indicated by a broad general acceptance of this social fact, and moderately high level of tolerance; second, ethnic attitudes are generally positive; and third identity as 'Canadian' and attachment to Canada are generally widespread and strong. These findings suggest that this one plural society may actually be working!

APPLICATIONS: WHAT'S THE USE?

Knowledge is good to have, but useful knowledge is even better! So, how can cross-cultural (including acculturational and multicultural) research make a difference to people's lives? By itself, of course, it cannot; research-based knowledge needs to meet a number of conditions if it is to be useful.

First (ideally, but perhaps not necessarily), the research question needs to be driven by, and formulated in terms of, an important human issue. I believe that clarifying the nature of cognitive competence, understanding the roots of stress during acculturation, or promoting positive intergroup relations in plural societies all meet this criterion. But second, their understanding needs to be situated in the cultural contexts in which they occur; it is this second feature that distinguishes applied cross-cultural psychology from applied psychology in general. Third, there needs to be a framework for action that includes both communicating clearly and directly from the researcher to the intended audience (policy maker, community group, institutions, etc.), and a readiness and ability to act by the recipient. Unfortunately, there is large variability among cross-cultural researchers to deliver their findings in an appropriate way, and an equally large variability among intended recipients (often government officials) to accept information and advice.

In my own work across the various topics (as outlined in this chapter), the common and constant theme has been the *value of pluralism*. Diverse societies (indeed our diverse world) are in need of understanding if the 'spice' rather than the 'irritant' is to carry the day. Concern for this core human issue has driven my research and applied work for over thirty years.

Second, my view (that we should study culture first, psychology second) has served to establish the cultural context; this exploration has often been in collaboration with anthropologist colleagues, and also sometimes by working closely with members of the cultural communities concerned.

Third, I have tried my hand at communicating my findings and their implications outside academia, through my consulting corporation (Cross-Cultural/ Multicultural Associates). Sometimes this has been to governments (e.g. Canadian Ministry of Multiculturalism: Berry, Kalin and Taylor, 1977), sometimes to agencies, (e.g. Economic Council of Canada: Berry, 1991b), sometimes to international agencies (e.g. CIDA: Berry and Dalal, 1996; and WHO: Dasen *et al.*, 1988), sometimes to Royal Commissions (e.g., Aboriginal Peoples: Berry 1995a) and sometimes to institutions (e.g. Queen's University: Berry, 1991a). My goal throughout has been to influence policy and programme changes with respect to diversity. It is difficult to judge the effects of these attempts; perhaps their success will depend more on the readiness to change than on the quality or persuasiveness of the research and their implications. In all of these attempts, the core message has been that advocated by G.B. Shaw: 'Don't do unto others what you would they should do unto you; they may be different from you'!

ACKNOWLEDGEMENTS

Even nomads need a home, or at least a series of homes. My primary home has always been my family, extended or nuclear, depending on where I have found myself. But institutional homes have also been central to my identity and my work. Foremost among these has been the International Association for Cross-cultural Psychology, within which I have found like-minded colleagues, who have often become close personal friends. Other homes have harboured me, and even paid me, much to my amazement, for doing exactly what I love to do. These include Sir George Williams University (which first took me in), the University of Edinburgh (which tried to polish me), the University of Sydney (which more or less tolerated me), and Queen's University (which tolerated me somewhat more than less). A number of temporary homes also helped along the way, including the Netherlands Institute for Advanced Study in the Humanities and Social Sciences, Institut d'Etudes Interethniques et Interculturelles (Université de Nice), Faculté de Psychologie et Sciences de l'Education (Université de Genève), Mental Health Division (World Health Organization), Centre for Health Promotion (University of Bergen) and Refugee Studies Programme (University of Oxford). Short stays at other universities (Åbo, Helsinki, Münster, Stockholm, Tilburg) have stimulated me at various stages. And real money has come from many sources, most consistently from the Social Sciences and Humanities Research Council of Canada, the Canadian Ethnic Studies Committee, and the Canadian International Development Agency. I thank them all.

REFERENCES

Barry, H., Child, I. and Bacon, M. (1959). Relation of child training to subsistence economy. *American Anthropologist*, *23*, 337–350.

Berry, J.W. (1966). Temne and Eskimo perceptual skills. *International Journal of Psychology*, *1*, 207–229.

Berry, J.W. (1968). Who are the marchers? A socio-psychological study of peace demonstrators. *Politics*, *3*, 163–175.

Berry, J.W. (1969a). On cross-cultural comparability. *International Journal of Psychology*, *4*, 119–128.

Berry, J.W. (1969b). The Vietnam marchers. In H. Mayer (ed.), *Australian Politics* (pp. 70–81). Melbourne: Cheshire.

Berry, J.W. (1970). Marginality, stress and ethnic identification in an acculturated Aboriginal community. *Journal of Cross-cultural Psychology*, *1*, 239–252.

Berry, J.W. (1971). Ecological and cultural factors in spatial perceptual development. *Canadian Journal of Behavioural Science*, *3*, 324–336.

Berry, J.W. (1974). Psychological aspects of cultural pluralism, *Topics in Culture Learning*, *2*, 17–22.

Berry, J.W. (1975). An ecological approach to cross-cultural psychology. *Nederlands Tijdschrift voor de Psychologie*, *30*, 51–84.

Berry, J.W. (1976). *Human ecology and cognitive style: comparative studies in cultural and psychological adaptation.* New York: Sage/Halsted.

Berry, J.W. (1979). A cultural ecology of social behaviour. In L. Berkowitz (ed.), *Advances in experimental social psychology* (vol. 12, pp. 177–206). New York: Academic Press.

Berry, J.W. (1980a). Introduction to methodology. In H.C. Triandis, and J.W. Berry (eds), *Handbook of cross-cultural psychology*, vol. 2: *Methodology* (pp. 1–28). Boston, MA: Allyn & Bacon.

Berry, J.W. (1980b). Ecological analyses for cross-cultural psychology. In N. Warren (ed.), *Studies in cross-cultural psychology* (vol. 2, pp. 157–189). London: Academic Press.

Berry, J.W. (1984a). Toward a universal psychology of cognitive competence. *International Journal of Psychology*, *19*, 335–361.

Berry, J.W. (1984b). Multicultural policy in Canada: A social psychological analysis. *Canadian Journal of Behavioural Science*, *16*, 353–370.

Berry, J.W. (1985). Cultural psychology and ethnic psychology: A comparative analysis. In I. Reyes-Lagunes and Y. Poortinga (eds), *From a different perspective* (pp. 3–15). Lisse: Swets & Zeitlinger.

Berry, J.W. (1989). Imposed etics, emics, derived etics: The operationalisation of a compelling idea. *International Journal of Psychology*, *24*, 721–735.

Berry, J.W. (1990a). Psychology of acculturation. In J. Berman (ed.), *Cross-cultural perspectives: Nebraska symposium on motivation* (vol. 37, pp. 201–234). Lincoln, NB: University of Nebraska Press.

Berry, J.W. (1990b). The role of psychology in ethnic studies. *Canadian Ethnic Studies*, *22*, 8–21.

Berry, J.W. (1991a). Towards diversity and equity at Queen's: A strategy for change. *Queen's Gazette*, *23*, Supplement, 8 April (with Committee Members).

Berry, J.W. (1991b). Understanding and managing multiculturalism: Some possible implications of research in Canada for developing societies. *Journal of Psychology and Developing Societies*, *3*, 17–49.

Berry, J.W. (1993). An ecological approach to understanding cognition across cultures. In J. Altarriba (ed.), *Cognition and culture* (pp. 361–375). Amsterdam: North-Holland.

Berry, J.W. (1994a). An ecological perspective on cultural and ethnic psychology. In E. Trickett (ed.), *Human diversity: Perspectives on people in context* (pp. 115–141). San Francisco, CA: Jossey-Bass.

Berry, J.W. (1994b). Ecology of individualism and collectivism. In U. Kim *et al.* (eds), *Individualism and collectivism* (pp. 77–84). Newbury Park, CA: Sage.

Berry, J.W. (1995a). *Aboriginal cultural identity.* Ottawa: Royal Commission on Aboriginal Peoples.

Berry, J.W. (1995b). The descendents of a model. *Culture and Psychology, 1*, 373–380.

Berry, J.W. (1996). On the unity of the field: Variations and communalities in understanding human behaviour in cultural context. *Interamerican Journal of Psychology, 30*, 89–98.

Berry, J.W. (1997a). Preface. In *Handbook of Cross-cultural Psychology*, 2nd edn (pp. x–xv). Boston, MA: Allyn & Bacon.

Berry, J.W. (1997b). Immigration, acculturation and adaptation. *Applied Psychology: An International Review, 46* (1), 5–68.

Berry, J.W. and Annis, R.C. (1974). Acculturative stress: the role of ecology, culture and differentiation. *Journal of Cross-cultural Psychology, 5*, 382–406.

Berry, J.W. and Bennett, J.A. (1992). Cree conceptions of cognitive competence. *International Journal of Psychology, 27*, 73-88.

Berry, J.W. and Dalal, A. (1996). 'Disability attitudes, beliefs and behaviours'. Unpublished report, International Centre for the Advancement of Community Based Rehabilitation.

Berry, J.W. and Dasen, P. (eds) (1974). *Culture and cognition.* London: Methuen.

Berry, J.W. and Kalin, R. (1995). Multicultural and ethnic attitudes in Canada. *Canadian Journal of Behavioural Science, 27*, 301–320.

Berry, J.W. and Laponce, J.A. (eds) (1994). *Ethnicity and culture in Canada: The research landscape.* Toronto: University of Toronto Press.

Berry, J.W. and Sam, D.L. (1997). Acculturation and adaptation. In J.W. Berry, M.H. Segall and Ç. Kağitçibaşi (eds), *Handbook of Cross-cultural Psychology*, vol. 3: *Social behavior and applications* (pp. 291–326), Boston, MA: Allyn & Bacon (in press).

Berry, J.W., Kalin, R. and Taylor, D. (1977). *Multiculturalism and ethnic attitudes in Canada.* Ottawa: Ministry of Supply and Services.

Berry, J.W., Kim, U., Minde, T. and Mok, D. (1987). Comparative studies of acculturative stress. *International Migration Review, 21*, 491–511.

Berry, J.W., Kim, U., Power, S., Young, M. and Bujaki, M. (1989). Acculturation attitudes in plural societies. *Applied Psychology, 38*, 185–206.

Berry, J.W., Poortinga, Y.H., Segall, M.H. and Dasen, P.R. (1992) *Cross-cultural psychology: Research and applications*, New York: Cambridge University Press.

Berry, J.W., van de Koppel, J.M.H., Sénéchal, C., Annis, R.C., Bahuchet, S., Cavalli-Sforza, L.L. and Witkin, H.A. (1986). *On the edge of the forest: Cultural adaptation and cognitive development in Central Africa*, Lisse: Swets & Zeitlinger.

Biesheuvel, S. (1959). *Race, culture and personality.* Johannesburg: South African Institute of Race Relations.

Bridges, J.W. (1966). A professional autobiography, with comments on teachers and associates. *Canadian Psychologist, 7*, 399–406.

Dasen, P.R. (1984). The cross-cultural study of intelligence: Piaget and the Baoulé. *International Journal of Psychology, 19*, 407–434.

Dasen, P.R., Berry, J.W. and Sartorius, N. (eds) (1988). *Health and cross-cultural psychology: Towards applications.* London: Sage.

Ferguson, G. (1956). On transfer and the abilities of man. *Canadian Journal of Psychology, 10*, 121–131.

Forde, D. (1934). *Habitat, economy and society.* New York: Dutton.

Graves, T.D. (1967). Psychological acculturation in a tri-ethnic community. *Southwestern Journal of Anthropology, 23*, 337–350.

Jahoda, G. (1995). The ancestry of a model, *Culture and Psychology, 1*, 11–14.

Kardiner, A. (1939). *The individual and his society.* New York: Columbia University Press.

Kroeber, A. (1939). *Cultural and natural areas of Native North America.* Berkeley, CA: University of California Press.

Lonner, W.J. and Berry, J.W. (eds) (1986). *Field methods in cross-cultural research.* London: Sage.

Mishra, R.C., Sinha, D., and Berry, J.W. (1996). *Ecology, acculturation and psychological adaptation: A study of Adivasis in Bihar.* New Delhi: Sage.

Pike, K.L. (1967). *Language in relation to a unified theory of the structure of human behaviour.* The Hague: Mouton.

Segall, M.H., Dasen, P.R., Berry, J.W. and Poortinga, Y.H. (1990). *Human behavior in global perspective: An introduction to cross-cultural psychology.* New York: Pergamon.

Sommerlad, E. and Berry, J.W. (1970). The role of ethnic identification in distinguishing between attitudes towards assimilation and integration of a minority racial group. *Human Relations, 23,* 23–29.

Super, C. and Harkness, S. (1986). The developmental niche: A conceptualization at the interface of child and culture. *International Journal of Behavioral Development, 9,* 545–569.

Weisner, T. (1984). Ecocultural niches of middle childhood: A cross-cultural perspective. In W.A. Collins (ed.), *Development during middle childhood* (pp. 335–369). Washington, DC: National Academy Press.

Whiting, B.B. and Whiting, J.W.M. (1975). *Children of six cultures: A psycho-cultural analysis.* Cambridge, MA: Harvard University Press.

Witkin, H. and Berry, J.W. (1975). Psychological differentiation in cross-cultural perspective. *Journal of Cross-cultural Psychology, 6,* 4–87.

13 Enculturation of a semi-alien

Journeyings in the construction and reconstruction of identity

Peter Weinreich

THE ONLY REALITY: CHILDHOOD ENCULTURATION

I do not know when I first noticed that I was different from my contemporaries. I do not mean just the ordinary uniqueness of being a person distinguishable from another, but a more telling difference in that I did not belong, in that as the offspring of refugees from Nazi Germany I was an alien in the cosy comfortable world of shared meanings that all others around me took happily for granted. As a refugee family, mine had become isolated from others of a German background: there is a complex story here of my parents' flight to what was then Czechoslovakia, then a fraught escape during the final moments before the outbreak of war, and my father's internment in Britain as a 'friendly enemy alien' during the war.

I was born in England and that was the only country I knew as a child; hence it was 'my country'. But I had a problem in that I was quite a problem to others. My parents were of peasant stock on my mother's side and of working class on my father's. As refugees living in extreme poverty and depending initially entirely on charity, they had no access to the middle-class accessories of books and tutors. Not wanting to speak the enemy's language, German, but not having a word of English, they resorted to picking up fragments of English vocabulary, generally mispronounced, to form essential communications heavily influenced by German semantics and grammar. This was the linguistic environment within which I was brought up.

The problem I posed to others was that they found communication with me awkward as I did not possess a comprehensible linguistic medium, only the sketchy elements of a very fractured English. That made me dumb from their standpoint. This was especially so as far as the teachers at my early schools were concerned, when, in those far-off unenlightened days, to be dumb was to be a dunce. For my part, as an infant and a child at my first schools, the world was fraught with all manner of linguistic terrors: even speaking my name – with uncertain child diction – a name that had the wrong syllables for the English ear, drew the adult retort, 'Doesn't even know his name'!

Later, one summer at another school, in despair at trying to find some occupation for me, teachers would send me out of class to the modest grounds of the school with a paintbox and brushes. By this time my father was working and home was in an area of the then skilled working class and lower middle class. The school close by was basic, orderly, and commendable for its kind of pupils, being 100 per cent mainstream boys and girls, but insensitive to a pupil of foreign extraction. It must have been a trainee teacher who rescued me. She kept me back in the classroom during lunch-breaks, instructed me in how to write using a pen, and taught me to read. I must have been about nine or ten by then.

But, of course, I am describing these experiences in retrospect. At the time, for me this was totally 'normal' for I did not know any other way. Also, even though I was in many respects reduced to passivity in the face of the powerful institutional forces of the indigenous English culture, in other respects I was an active agent, picking up fragmentary skills, making sustained efforts towards a mastery of the language, and participating a little more in school activities. Teachers and to lesser extent peers provided models that I could in part identify with. Much, much later, when I was becoming a professional psychologist, I responded to writings (e.g., Harré, 1979; Erikson, 1963, 1968) emphasising the agentic qualities of people and their active identification with others, and incorporated their concerns into the conceptualisation of identity I began to develop.

Real migrants, who are old enough to know their world of origin, consciously experience the new 'host' culture as different and difficult to negotiate. They are aware of the disjunctions between the cultures, lifestyles and languages of the different worlds, and adapt with greater or lesser success. In contrast, the offspring of migrants know no other world than the one they are currently experiencing. This, for them, is the only reality; hence this is the 'normality' of their everyday being. In their early years they have only the vaguest notion that there is something a bit different about their experiences, their parents and families, and their backgrounds, compared with those of the indigenous boys and girls. Parents and offspring are fully occupied with the immediacy of making a go of things, and the disturbing past is best left unspoken.

Much later on, professionally I became aware of the dominant conceptualisation of 'acculturation' studies in cross-cultural psychology (Berry, 1988) as one providing a reasonable starting point for late adolescent and adult migrants. However, it was a misleading one for the offspring of migrants who, successively over an extensive time-span *enculturated* valued features of the indigenous culture alongside features of their own ethnic background, as part of the everyday normality of growing up. Thus, for Berry people of an 'acculturating group' have four distinctive options or strategies towards the 'dominant group'. If they are not concerned with maintaining their cultural identity but value maintaining relationships with the dominant group, the strategy and outcome is said to be 'assimilation'. 'Integration' is Berry's term for when they simultaneously endorse maintaining their cultural identity and value maintaining relationships with the dominant group. If they are concerned with maintaining their cultural identity but not relationships with the other group, then they are said to opt for 'separation'. When they neither value maintaining their cultural identity nor maintaining relationships with other groups, they are said to adopt the 'marginalisation' option (see Berry, Chapter 12 in this volume).

Options and strategies clearly presume choice and decision, with connotations of full, conscious awareness of what people are doing. However, the person, as infant growing into the child, moving through early adolescence and on towards young adulthood, is not aware of the social world in this fashion. As Erikson (1968) stresses, children make part-identifications with successive role models: they *enculturate* features that they value from representatives of whatever cultures have everyday significance to them, not *acculturate* towards the dominant culture. To be sure, some such features will be from the dominant culture, but others will be from one's own ancestry, and the person's resynthesis of the mix will be unique to that person. While subsequently incorporating features of the mainstream culture, the child uses them in conjunction with others derived from earlier identifications in the home with one's parental, hence ancestral, culture. What consequences then follow will in part depend on the ascriptions to self that others make. If these ascriptions bear the hallmarks of discrimination and victimisation, the individual is unlikely to feel much attraction to being part of the mainstream community. If on the other hand the mainstream ethos is benign, the individual is likely to appreciate being a fully active citizen. In either case a degree of ethnic distinctiveness will remain though in different manner – defensively when confronted with overwhelming victimisation and with easy equanimity when enjoying a benign environment.

ANOTHER REALITY: BEING ALIEN IN THE EYES OF OTHERS

Children are curious about everything around them and enjoy all manner of phenomena, solving cognitive puzzles by reasoning, and mastering numerous skills. My transition from primary to secondary education confounded my primary school teachers in that I succeeded, through the eleven-plus exam system then in operation, in obtaining a place at a grammar school. There I was presented with new subjects such as algebra, geometry, physics and chemistry, and did well in them. Also, in continuity with my earlier absorption with paintbox and brushes, I frequented the art room. Athletically I had the build, and managed to represent my school at athletics, and captained that quintessential English institution, the school rugby team. My teachers praised me.

However, I was beaten up in the playground too: whether for being a Jew or for being a German I do not know. But it was for being one, or perhaps even both. I was an intruder, an alien. In actuality, I was not Jewish – my refugee parents, as then Communists, were anti-Nazi on humane and ideological grounds – but people frequently assumed that I was: nor in my own mind was I German, but English. This victimisation stopped when, to my own surprise, I lashed out with a punch that sent my assailant reeling.

It was around this time that I became conscious of the full import of my position, though still with elements that I did not understand, perhaps due to protective denial. I was atypical, an alien. My English teacher made me aware of this 'status', when reading a passage in class from a novel I read out *alien* as *allein* (pronounced as in German, meaning 'alone'). My English teacher's retort was that I of all people in the class should know the word *alien*. If I had not been aware of being alien, others were, and I came to acknowledge my peculiarity in this respect even more. Until then, however, I did not know the term *alien*, let alone what it meant. As I said, my world was normal – the mundane experience of a mix of gratifying and disturbing events.

In reality, although I could not conceptualise it then, I was a *semi-alien*. I had been identifying with elements of mainstream middle-class English culture as represented by the teachers and curriculum of my grammar school, while also continuing to identify with core domestic aspects of my parental culture. I was not an alien, because I knew no other country than England and because of my daily participation in the mainstream institutions of British life, the schools, the broadcasts of the BBC, the shops and the cinemas. But part of my existence, at home, was alien and different from that of the mainstream: others would find great blanks when relating to me in what they took for granted in their shared childhood experiences of family relations (including having grandparents, uncles and aunts, and cousins), numerous incidental manners, party traditions, and children's stories. Later, I found that central European mannerisms, intellectualism, and food-tastes provided bonds with others I came across who shared them, namely secular Jewish friends whose ancestry was also central European. In due course, in my professional work (Weinreich, 1983a, 1989a), I made a point of highlighting the distinction between the view that others have of oneself (an *alter-ascribed social identity*, in my case that of an 'alien') and the view that one ascribes to oneself (an *ego-recognised social identity*, in my case that of a 'semi-alien' or 'semi-English').

My parents were anti-Nazi, but not anti-German. They were actually quite dismissive of many things British, most noticeably English food and the lax standards of British workmanship. A strong Germanic ethos prevailed at home, albeit without the German language which had early on been replaced by a butchered English. From the little modern history I read in the school history text-books, I became engrossed in the Allied activities which defeated the Nazis, but impressed with Germanic contributions to science and the arts. I had developed a core component of my identity that extolled Germanic concerns with *Wissenschaft*, a more inclusive range of activities than encompassed by the English word, *science*. From these heights I looked down my nose at certain things British, and achieved a kind of existential independence, such that if I were not fully English this was a strength, because I could be more independent of thought.

Derogatory images of ourselves and hostile comments were directed against the family ('go back to where you came from' and 'go home foreigners'). Rather than being demeaned by them, the family had forged a strong view of its superior moral status over the ignorant indigenous beings with their evident shortcomings. Being alone (*allein*) and being a semi-alien was frequently uncomfortable, but it was a habitual state and therefore 'normal'. Since conformity did not give rise to acceptance anyway, independence of thought became a virtue and a much valued orientation against both oppressive tendencies and received wisdoms. I developed a surreptitious anti-authority stance, but not having power or control over many matters, played along with existing authority. Science was the theory and method that I extolled, that both enabled one to pose different kinds of questions on theoretical grounds and find empirical evidence that frequently challenged accepted wisdoms. I worshipped a galaxy of independent thinkers in the development of science, and came to appreciate the virtues of the continental emphasis on theoretical thinking and the British emphasis on empiricism. In the meantime, a prized English teacher taught me that there was a skill in expressing scientific concepts in the language of everyday communication.

I was heading for Manchester University to study physics, having fantasised only briefly about a romantic life at art college. The high and varied intellectual life of university did not materialise in the way I expected, though I made a stab at finding and contributing to it. My first year room-mate was studying French and introduced me to the existentialist writers, Camus and Sartre, whom I read in English. After somewhat mixed fortunes at university in the varied activities I pursued, I graduated well enough in physics, and registered at Manchester for a doctorate in biophysics.

But something was wrong. I did not understand society and I became overwhelmed by an accumulated set of unresolved issues in which a sense of alienation featured strongly. As a semi-alien I found society itself increasingly problematic, and felt the idea of spending a lifetime in a physics laboratory to be detrimental to understanding society. What was it about the education tram-lines that induced a person to study at college the subjects he or she performed best at school, in my case physics? That was to be my next intellectual enquiry.

EXISTENTIAL BEING-IN-SOCIETY: ORIGINS OF IDENTITY STRUCTURE ANALYSIS

Instead, after training as a physics teacher, I short-cut the education route by enlisting for a doctorate in social psychology at the London School of Economics. At LSE I experienced the luxury of attending seminars in sociology, social anthropology, and the history of science. Academic psychology in the British tradition proved, however, as far as I was concerned, to be rather disappointing. Nevertheless, I could not afford to let go of my commitment to understand at least a little about society, and, without being fully aware of this need, to comprehend my own identity.

The area of psychology concerned with attitude organisation and change seemed to have something to do with what I felt I had to comprehend, but a lot was still missing. Where were one's attitudes located within one's sense of identity? How did one's identity develop? How could one incorporate people's existential sense of self as being centrally involved in the process of appraising the social world from their differing vantage points?

It was the height of the 1960s flower power era. The focus was on society, and all things seemed possible. So I (Weinreich, 1969) combined Festinger's theory of *cognitive dissonance* (Festinger, 1957, 1964; Brehm and Cohen, 1962) and other *cognitive-affective consistency* theories of attitude organisation and change (Rosenberg and Abelson, 1960; Osgood and Tannenbaum, 1955; Sherif, Sherif and Nebergall, 1965) with the existential theory of *construal* implicit in Kelly's (1955) personal construct psychology, set in the context of a modification of Erikson's (1963) and R. D. Laing's (1961) definitions of *identity*, and giving central place to the processes of *appraisal* and *reappraisal* (Arnold, 1960; Lazarus, 1967). I used algebra and graphical illustrations to demonstrate how the elements of these theoretical approaches could be integrated within a schematic notion of *identity structure*. Empirical evidence from experiments supported the deductions derived from the conceptualisation I had advanced (Weinreich, 1969).

A year's spell lecturing in the Academic Department of Psychiatry at a London teaching hospital introduced me to clinically depressed patients and activated my thinking about the significance of negative self-appraisals in depression and the *remote idealisation* of other people in one's identity structure. Following London, I worked in Bristol attempting to get to grips with the highly emotive and politicised arena of ethnic relations (generally referred to then as 'race relations'). My reading about prejudice and discrimination, stigma, culture-fair tests for IQ and other psychometrically conceived characteristics, cultural differences in world-views, culture and identity, institutionalisation of racism, mental illness and psychiatric disorders across cultural groups brought me into contact with an extraordinary range of literature in social and developmental psychology, social psychiatry, social anthropology, and symbolic interactionism. I learnt about the distinction in the cross-cultural literature between *etic* (cross-culturally universal) and *emic* (culturally specific) concepts (DeVos and Hippler, 1969).

I knew I had to understand identity diffusion (Erikson, 1963, 1968). This was evidently the key to many of the problematic issues in identity development and was likely to be a significant tool for comprehending the identity development of the offspring of migrants. Identity development could only be sensibly conceptualised if the emic world-views of individuals featured centrally, but etic concepts had to be used if the conceptualisation were to be used across different cultures.

Erikson (1963, 1968) had strongly emphasised that children make partial identifications with people and that the crucial process in identity development was the resynthesis of these partial identifications into some viable sense of identity. Erikson furthermore wrote of the resynthesis as a *task*: the individual strives to resynthesise these identifications and if unsuccessful in this task remains in a state of identity diffusion. But how was one to conceptualise *partial identifications*? What conceptually *in terms of identifications* did it mean to resynthesise them?

I became aware of two conceptual problems (Weinreich, 1979a, 1979b, 1983a, 1983b). First, two meanings of *identification* were conflated: *aspirational* identification and *de facto* identification. *Aspirational* signifies either wishing to emulate some other – as hero figure – (*idealistic-identification* with that person) or wishing to dissociate from some other – as despised figure (*contra-identification* with that person). *De facto* refers not to the desired wish, but to the actuality between self and the other, or the fact of the matter in the here and now, for which the term *empathetic identification* is used. Distinguishing between these two distinctive meanings or modes of identification advanced a solution to the second conceptual problem, which was that a resynthesis of identifications is more than an alignment of compatible identifications. A resynthesis involves dealing with incompatible or conflicted identifications, that is, not identity conflict in an amorphous sense, but specific incompatibilities at an elemental level. Now, if one *empathetically* identifies with another while simultaneously *contra-identifying* with that other, one has a *conflicted identification* with that person to an extent depending on the strengths of both empathetic and contra-identification.

Identity diffusion could therefore be conceptualised as an appropriate summation of the individual's conflicted identifications with others, whereby each conflicted identification with a particular person could be of varying strength. At a conceptual level, the concepts *aspirational* and *de facto identification* are etic, and so therefore are the derived concepts *conflicted identification* and *identity diffusion*. In addition, for the operationalisation of the identification concepts in empirical research, the emic content of identification elements has to be established. In this light, the etic and the emic characteristics of identification pose no dilemma or tension one with the other, because they are separated but integratable.

Another language has to be used in order to encompass faithfully the definitions of the concepts alluded to here. Algebra has the beauty of being able to symbolise precisely and efficiently variables across specified limits, and the operations applied to them. For the parameters of identification, elementary Boolean algebra is used (Weinreich, 1980).

From symbolic interactionism (Blumer, 1969; Weigert, 1983) is taken the important notion that self is situated as a process in differing social contexts from moment to moment. Empirically, the changing patterns of empathetic identifications with others from one context to another can be assessed, as they also can be following on from variations in identity state from, say, euphoria to despair. The conceptualisation of identity referred to here, which is an integration of key concepts from the aforementioned theorists, is known as Identity Structure Analysis (ISA) (Weinreich, 1980, 1986b, 1989a, 1991). ISA is an open-ended conceptual framework, depending crucially on the expert input of social science professionals, and has numerous applications from clinical to societal issues.

As for the practical operationalisation of these concepts, customised identity instruments using ethnographic information about emic discourses habitually used by a people are generated. Clients appraise themselves and their social worlds using the customised instruments, and from the resultant data the parameters of identity, such as a person's extents of empathetic identifications with others and overall identity diffusion, are assessed. The whole business of generating identity instruments, presenting them to clients for their appraisals of self and social world, and subsequent assessment of identity parameters, can be carried out on lap-top computers by using the Identity Exploration (IDEX) computer software (Weinreich *et al.*, 1989).

The foregoing is in essence a sketchy overview of the construction and redefinition of one person's identity, inspired by attempting to resolve the social and intellectual problems involved with comprehending the developmental and societal processes of identity development, in the context of issues of migration and ethnicity. I have omitted personal details of importance and the significance of intimate relationships and friendships, as I have sought to emphasise some of the intellectual journeyings that seemed to me most relevant for dealing with issues of ethnic identity arising in cross-cultural psychology.

UNIVERSALS AND PARTICULARS: IDENTITIES IN SOCIAL CONTEXT

In many respects my journeyings through the academic literature in psychology and other social science disciplines mirrored my quest to comprehend my own identity development, in the course of which I sought to integrate seminal concepts from different theoretical orientations. My resulting ISA conceptualisation made use of algebraic formulations of psychological concepts in order to represent the complexity of structures and processes involved in the intricate patterns of formation and redefinition of identity, but a further agenda was to work towards the efficient operationalisation of the conceptual framework so as to investigate empirically questions of identity in the community. I found myself drawing upon the notion of algebraic representation of concepts, with which I was familiar from my study of physics, in order that I could comprehend empirically the processes of identity development in the human world. To do this effectively I concluded that I would have to have recourse to the power and efficiency of computers, hence the development of the IDEX computer software.

In generating a conceptual framework that could in principle be applied to any culture, I made the resolution of the *etic–emic* conundrum an absolute priority: I defined psychological concepts presented in etic (cross-culturally universal) manner within an open-ended framework, such that emic (culturally specific) elements constitute the anchoring points for the etic concepts, thereby *integrating* the emic with the etic.

I discovered that this general conceptual framework, though formulated within mainstream social science traditions, when applied to issues of migration, ethnicity and cross-cultural psychology, continually surprised me by revealing the diversity of identity structures that went with the existential sense of being-in-the-world. A range of empirical findings queried certain established conceptions within cross-cultural psychology pertaining to such issues as acculturation and individualism–collectivism.

Thus, empirical work using ISA on Hong Kong Chinese university students (Weinreich, Luk and Bond, 1996) finds variations in enculturation of characteristics from differing cultural groupings, a finding which challenges 'ethnocentric' models of acculturation. In this study an important discovery was that Hong Kong Chinese ethnicity was expressed with differing emphases: a greater degree of identification with mainstream Hong Kong people correlated with both peer and parental identification and with self-esteem; greater identification with modern

East Asians (Taiwanese and Japanese) correlated again with peer and parental identification but also with identity diffusion; greater identification with the traditional Chinese correlated with maternal identification, but not with peer identification, and with identity diffusion; an increasing degree of identification with Western people (British, American, American-born Chinese) correlated with peer identification only, and with self-esteem; whereas greater identification with developing peoples (Mainland Chinese, Vietnamese boat people, and Filipinos) correlated with lower peer identification, and with lower self-esteem, and correlated with increasing identity diffusion.

Several ISA studies demonstrate the ramifications of self situated in different social contexts. In one study (Weinreich, Kelly and Maja, 1988) South African youth were found to have generally well-adjusted identities when describing themselves interacting with their own people, but quite a high proportion of the same individuals were found to have vulnerable identities (in crisis, diffusion, or negative) when interacting with English-speaking whites, and an extraordinarily high proportion of them with vulnerable identities when interacting with Afrikaners. In another on the expression of identity in bilingual Gujerati-English youth in Britain (Northover, 1988), those of orthodox orientation in relation to their ancestral culture modulated their empathetic identifications with others of both communities between English and Gujerati contexts very little compared to those of progressive orientation. Kelly (1989) found somewhat similar results in a comparative study on youth with Pakistani Muslim, Greek Cypriot or Anglo-Saxon British ancestry. In the latter study, the evidence queries the notion of collectivism–individualism being a continuum. Without losing their ethnic distinctiveness, the progressive Muslim girls had enculturated certain Anglo-Saxon 'individualist' characteristics, but held them alongside 'collectivist' notions, such that their appraisal of their social world was in terms of a hybrid of dimensions of both individualism and collectivism, where their usage of individualist discourses was of a modified form compared to Anglo-Saxon usage.

A SEMI-ALIEN'S PERSPECTIVE ON MAINSTREAMERS

Identity transitions, stressful social contexts, vulnerabilities in identity states, aspirational identifications with some people and empathetic identifications with others, hybrid mixtures of enculturated characteristics and views of the world, self situated in benign contexts and distressing ones, generation of identity diffusion, phases of defensive adaptation: all these and more reflect much of my own experience. With my perspective as the offspring of migrants, I found that I would be continually assessing what was being stated in the literature about people such as myself, and querying statements that purported to describe the experiences and reactions of people like me. Many of these writings suggested pathological outcomes. Of course, there are causalities among migrants, but there are many within the mainstream too.

Ethnocentric versions of what options and strategies are available to migrants can be patronising and there are many well-intentioned people who project the victim syndrome on to those who are not of the mainstream, who are discriminated against, and are seen to be caught between two cultures. Many migrants and offspring of migrants succeed in their endeavours within the larger community, just by grasping the opportunities available to them. Being between cultures, or suffering from culture conflict, is not generally an issue, because enculturating valued skills and characteristics does not undermine one's origins, but exercises one's thinking about how to resolve the various dilemmas that may arise in such a way as to maintain the integrity of one's origins. Ethnic distinctiveness continues, albeit updated and changed, for it reflects the biographical experiences integrated during one's life from the first day on, and the early identifications with parents and kin, and they with their parents and kin. And then forward to the new identifications, and identity transitions in a forever changing social and techno-logical world. . .

Migrants and their offspring can appear to mainstreamers to be challenging cosy local assumptions and comfortable shared meanings through their successes in business and the professions. Some mainstreamers may become reactively defensive of the status quo and aggressive towards the interlopers; others may enculturate aspects of the migrants' lifestyles and ways of doing things. Studies using ISA indicate that the intersection of biography, cultural values and traditions, changing historical contexts and relationships between ethnic groups, impact on the ongoing development and redefinitions of ethnicity, such that the explication is generally particular to the case in question. Generalisation across such varied circumstances is unlikely, except at the lowest common denominator. So I am indeed a semi-alien, but one with a distinctive identity despite my typicality.

REFERENCES

Arnold, M.B. (1960). *Emotion and personality*. New York: Columbia.

Berry, J.W. (1988). Acculturation and psychological adaptation: A conceptual overview. In J.W. Berry and R.C. Annis (eds), *Ethnic psychology: Research and practice with immigrants, refugees, native peoples, ethnic groups and sojourners* (pp. 41–52). Amsterdam/Lisse: Swets & Zeitlinger.

Blumer, H. (1969). *Symbolic interactionism*. Englewood Cliffs, NJ: Prentice-Hall.

Brehm, J.W. and Cohen, A.R. (1962). *Explorations in cognitive dissonance*. New York: John Wiley.

DeVos, G.A. and Hippler, A.A. (1969). Cultural psychology: Comparative studies of human behaviour. In G. Lindzey and E. Aronson (eds), *The handbook of social psychology*, vol. 4: *Group psychology and phenomena of interaction* (pp. 323–417). Reading, MA: Addison-Wesley.

Erikson, E.H. (1963). *Childhood and society*. New York: W.W. Norton.

Erikson, E.H. (1968). *Identity, youth and crisis*. New York: W.W. Norton.

Festinger, L. (1957). *A theory of cognitive dissonance*. Stanford, CA: Stanford University Press.

Festinger, L. (1964). *Conflict, decision and dissonance*. Stanford, CA: Stanford University Press.

Harré, R. (1979). *Social being: A theory for social psychology*. Oxford: Blackwell.

Kelly, A.J.D. (1989). Ethnic identification, association and redefinition: Muslim Pakistanis and Greek Cypriots in Britain. In K. Liebkind (ed.), *New identities in Europe: Immigrant ancestry and the ethnic identity of youth* (pp. 77–114). Aldershot, Hants: Gower.

Kelly, G.A. (1955). *The psychology of personal constructs*. New York: W.W. Norton.

Laing, R.D. (1961). *The self and others*. London: Tavistock.

Lazarus, R.S. (1967). Cognitive factors underlying stress and coping. In M.H. Appley and R. Trumbull (eds), *Psychological stress* (pp. 151–180). New York: Appleton-Century-Crofts.

Northover, M. (1988). Bilinguals or 'dual linguistic identities'? In J.W. Berry and R.C. Annis (eds), *Ethnic psychology: Research and practice with immigrants, refugees, native peoples, ethnic groups and sojourners* (pp. 207–216). Amsterdam/Lisse: Swets & Zeitlinger.

Osgood, C.E. and Tannenbaum, P.H. (1955). The principle of congruity in the prediction of attitude change. *Psychological Review, 61*, 270–276.

Rosenberg, M.J. and Abelson, R.P. (1960). An analysis of cognitive balancing. In M.J. Rosenberg, C.I. Hovland, W.J. McGuire, R.P. Abelson and J.W. Brehm, *Attitude organisation and change* (pp. 112–163). New Haven, CN: Yale University Press.

Sherif, C.W., Sherif, M. and Nebergall, R.W. (1965). *Attitude and attitude change*. Philadelphia, PA: Saunders.

Weigert, A.J. (1983). Identity: Its emergence within sociological psychology. *Symbolic Interaction, 6*, 183–206.

Weinreich, P. (1969). 'Theoretical and experimental evaluation of dissonance processes'. Unpublished PhD thesis. London: University of London.

Weinreich, P. (1979a). Cross-ethnic identification and self-rejection in a black adolescent. In G. Verma and C. Bagley (eds), *Race, education and identity* (pp. 157–175). London: Macmillan.

Weinreich, P. (1979b). Ethnicity and adolescent identity conflicts. In V. Saifullah Khan (ed.), *Minority families in Britain* (pp. 89–107). London: Macmillan.

Weinreich, P. (1980). *Manual for identity exploration using personal constructs*. Coventry, Warwick: Centre for Research in Ethnic Relations, University of Warwick.

Weinreich, P. (1983a). Psychodynamics of personal and social identity: Theoretical concepts and their measurement in adolescents from Belfast sectarian and Bristol minority groups. In A. Jacobson-Widding (ed.), *Identity: Personal and socio-cultural* (pp. 159–186). Stockholm: Almqvist & Wiksell International; Atlantic Highlands: Humanities Press.

Weinreich, P. (1983b). Emerging from threatened identities: Ethnicity and gender in redefinitions of threatened identities. In G. Breakwell (ed.), *Threatened identities* (pp. 149–185). Chichester, West Sussex: John Wiley.

Weinreich, P. (1986a). Identity development in migrant offspring: Theory and practice. In L.H. Ekstrand (ed.), *Ethnic minorities and immigrants in a cross-cultural perspective* (pp. 230–239). Amsterdam/Lisse: Swets & Zeitlinger.

Weinreich, P. (1986b). The operationalisation of identity theory in racial and ethnic relations. In J. Rex and D. Mason (eds), *Theories of race and ethnic relations* (pp. 299–320). Cambridge: Cambridge University Press.

Weinreich, P. (1989a). Variations in ethnic identity: Identity Structure Analysis. In K. Liebkind (ed.), *New identities in Europe: Immigrant ancestry and the ethnic identity of youth* (pp. 41–76). Aldershot, Hants.: Gower.

Weinreich, P. (1989b). Conflicted identifications: A commentary on Identity Structure Analysis concepts. In K. Liebkind (ed.), *New identities in Europe: Immigrant ancestry and the ethnic identity of youth* (pp. 219–236). Aldershot, Hants.: Gower.

Weinreich, P. (1991). National and ethnic identities: Theoretical concepts in practice. *Innovation in Social Science Research, 4(1)*, 9–29.

Weinreich, P., Asquith, L., Lui, W. and Northover, M. (1989). *IDEXPC – Identity Exploration using Identity Structure Analysis: Software for personal computers* and *Userguide*. Jordanstown: University of Ulster.

Weinreich, P., Kelly, A.J.D. and Maja, C. (1988). Black youth in South Africa: Situated identities and patterns of ethnic identification. In D. Canter, C. Jesuino, L. Soczka and G. Stephenson (eds), *Environmental social psychology* (pp. 231–245). Dordrecht, The Netherlands: Kluwer Academic.

Weinreich, P., Luk, C.L. and Bond M.H. (1996). Ethnic stereotyping and identification in a multicultural context: 'Acculturation', self-esteem and identity diffusion in Hong Kong Chinese university students. *Psychology and Developing Societies, 8(1)*, 107–169.

14 Bridging spiritual sojourns and social science research in native communities

Joseph E. Trimble

You have noticed that everything an Indian does is in a circle, and that is because the Power of the World always works in circles, and everything tries to be round ... the life of a man is a circle from childhood to childhood, and so it is in everything where power moves.

(Black Elk, *Black Elk speaks*, quoted in Neihardt, 1961, pp. 198–199)

THE BEGINNING OF THE JOURNEY

My journey to the academic sphere of life probably began at the age of eight, and although I didn't know it then, it marked the beginning of my interest in becoming an educator and a researcher. I remember the day now as a spiritual experience. It was an unusually hot and dry early August day, so, to seek refuge from the blistering noonday heat, I hiked several miles to a grove of cottonwood trees that grew along the bank of a small, shallow, slow-moving creek. Once there, I sat and nestled myself beneath my favourite old tree and began whittling and carving faces in a piece of pine wood. My grandfather taught me to carve, so I was careful to remember all of the little tricks he thoughtfully and patiently introduced to one of his many grandsons.

I wasn't alone in my little forested private refuge. A nest of red-tail hawks was nearby. Mockingbirds flew in and out of the trees and across the tall grass, sounding out garbled warnings to intruders. And an occasional rabbit bounded out of nowhere to quench its thirst. The gentle wind occasionally whistled across the tall grass and through the quaking leaves. In time, the soothing melodies helped me nod off. I don't know what awakened me but when I did I quickly noticed that a horse was standing on a small knoll not far from the creek's edge. Seated high on the mare was a man wearing nothing more than beaded moccasins, a breechcloth and an eagle-feathered warbonnet; the reins were in his left hand and in the other he was holding a long staff decorated with coloured ribbons and spotted tail feathers from an eagle. A red painted line ran down the centre of his face and separated his natural colouring from white paint that covered the other side. I blinked and rubbed my eyes. I turned my head in another direction. Then I closed my eyes for a few seconds. But the rider and his friend remained. The rider gazed directly at me for a while then slowly turned his head to focus on something off on the horizon. I turned to pick up my carvings and when I returned my gaze to the knoll the rider and friend were gone.

I ran home and told my father about the vision and he said I should tell the story to my grandfather. Grandfather Sage listened attentively and told me that someday the vision would influence my future and that the rider and his friend would return and provide me with more guidance. I returned to my refuge day after day hoping and praying that the mysterious pair would be there. But they never returned or, if they did, I wasn't then able to see them.

Grandfather said that they probably were there and just because I couldn't see them didn't mean they didn't exist. From these words, Grandfather helped me to understand the nature of spirituality and that life exists in all forms. 'All life is sacred,' he said many times as we walked the many trails of my youth.

Through my father and grandfather I learned many other valuable lessons that remain with me to this day. Lessons were always taught through stories while we did things together such as cleaning out the barn, pulling weeds from the small garden, shovelling snow, or walking the many trails around our homes. Although many lessons were learned, three stand out: (a) it isn't enough to depend on yourself as all life shares in your growth; (b) strive to be independent but never at the expense of those who contribute to your growth. Acknowledge that others, however remote they may be, contribute to your growth and your accomplishments; and (c) value and express generosity, kindness, empathy, and loyalty in all that you do. Unfortunately, many of the lessons were challenged and even compromised as I made my way through stages of my life, especially in the course of my formal education and career.

STUDENT EXPERIENCES AND THE SEARCH FOR CULTURE

Perhaps because I was interested in the differences among people, I made the decision to study psychology while in high school. 'I'm going to college, Grandfather, and I'm going to study psychology,' I said later when I opened my first and only acceptance letter. He and my father were proud but didn't say so; proud because I was the first of eighty-four children and grandchildren to go to college, but reluctant to say anything because they weren't sure what it meant. 'And so what is psychology and what will you do with it?' inquired my parents. My grandfather said that I had to tell him what it was all about after I finished my studies; that conversation occurred some fifteen years later.

As a student I quickly learned that in order to be a researcher in psychology I had to divorce myself from subjective impressions and focus on the units of analysis as objects. My professors insisted that the human was a 'black box' and the study of the human condition had to occur by manipulating variables and carefully measuring and recording outcomes; some even forcefully argued that the best way to understand behaviour was to study psychologically driven hypotheses among lower order species. I jumped into the rhetoric with a passion and at the same time put my early childhood lessons and experiences on the shelf; culture, I was told, belonged with anthropology and had no place in psychology's laboratories. Also, I soon learned that most of my colleagues and professors did not share some of the values that were ingrained in me as a child.

My family taught me to share my thoughts, ideas, and experiences with others. In time I discovered that some of my ideas became the themes for other students' term papers and theses and, in a few instances, the subject of faculty-sponsored research which found its way into publication in journals. In all instances, I was not referenced or consulted. Perhaps I was naive about the vicious and competitive world of academic research and student scholarship. Yet, in my innocence, I truly believed that knowledge was advanced by sharing ideas and carrying them out in a collaborative and collegiate manner. Few seemed to share that value as they thought only of their egocentric and ambitious needs to 'succeed'. Maybe such experiences were limited to those few bulwarks of higher education. Nonetheless, my early experiences left me confused, bitter and wondering if the life and career of an academic had to be built on the backs of naive contributors. These experiences continued to haunt and follow me in my professional career. Sadly, I continued to encounter the self-centred, scientist-educator in other professional spheres.

Grandfather constantly reminded me that one's destiny was in the hands of the Creator although one's path could be altered slightly by chance, curiosity, and self-determination. Therefore, I tacitly believed that my future was already laid out but I had a small say in the direction it took. Whether or not it was destiny, a seemingly innocent question posed to one of my mentors during a graduate seminar in 1964 changed the course of my studies and my career. Simply put, I asked him, 'Where are the group and cultural influences in the science of the individual?' He responded rather softly, 'Well, the way we divide up the world affects our reasoning about it. And our ability to understand a situation is a function of the understanding we bring to the situation.' 'So,' I responded, 'if we have no understanding about culture's effects on individual behaviour, then one is not likely to raise the question. And if psychology's unit of analysis is solely the individual, then one also is not likely to seek answers about group influences.' He responded by restating his two points again and inviting me to walk him home on that very cold and snowy but unforgettable New England evening. The talks and walks continued for the remainder of the semester and along with it the revelation that individual thought and behaviour was far more complicated than I had ever imagined when contextual, group, and cultural factors were entered into the equation.

This revelation renewed my then waning interest in psychology. I knew I had to expand my perspective along with abandoning a narrow theoretical orientation that only emphasised behaviour; something inexplicable seemed to be gnawing at me, urging me to seek alternatives. As chance would have it, the opportunity came sooner than I expected, if, indeed, I had expected it to occur at all. In a Boston restaurant, a colleague introduced me to an old acquaintance of his. After a brief conversation, my new acquaintance invited me to enrol at the Institute of Group Relations at the University of Oklahoma located on the south central plains of the United States. 'You will fit in nicely and I believe you'll find our programme accommodating and stimulating,' he stated candidly, 'and you know there are numerous American Indian tribes in the state that may serve as a valuable asset for your studies and interests.' His invitation and enthusiasm revitalised my interest in psychology. This revitalisation led me to a more satisfying orientation within the field and back to a way of life with which I was more familiar. A few months after this chance encounter, I loaded up my car and headed for the southern plains of the United States for an experience that would change the course of my life completely.

The long drive from New England to the southern plains gave me the opportunity to reflect on where I had been and where I was headed. Somewhere toward the end of the long road trip I concluded that my undergraduate experience had provided me with a vocabulary to understand and write about basic psychological principles, while my early graduate experiences provided me with the tools to critique psychology's methods and theories. Along the way, I also gained confidence in my intellectual abilities. For me, long drives are like long walks or fishing alone on a lake as they usually provide me with valuable, uninterrupted, and uncluttered time to reflect on the past, present, and future. The time on the road engendered a new-found confidence, excitement, and anticipation that my forthcoming educational experiences would provide some closure and also expand my intellectual curiosity. In fact, the experiences of the next few years far exceeded my expectations, as they set the course for my career in cross-cultural psychology.

SPIRITUAL RENEWAL AND INTELLECTUAL DISCOVERY ON THE SOUTHERN PLAINS

The social psychology graduate programme in the 1950s and 1960s at the University of Oklahoma's Institute of Group Relations emphasised an inter-disciplinary course of study where students were required to pursue courses outside of psychology; and, as a result, one's doctoral advisory committee typically consisted of at least two faculty from other disciplines. The founder of the programme, Muzafer Sherif, maintained that 'social psychology is the scientific study of the experience and behaviour of individuals in relation to social stimulus situations' and that 'social stimulus situations are composed of people (individuals and groups) and items of the sociocultural setting' (Sherif and Sherif, 1956, p. 4). Sherif and his close followers argued that to understand the influence of social stimuli such as 'other people' and 'cultural products' one must explore and examine theoretical and scientific contributions generated from social science disciplines other than psychology. My doctoral studies were set against this theoretical framework and fitted quite naturally with my world-view. Indeed, investigating and studying 'cultural products' consumed much of my curricular and extra-curricular activities at Oklahoma, and I truly came to believe that the course of study and the geocultural setting were tailored to my interests and concerns.

Along with learning about Sherifian perspectives on intergroup relations, attitude change and measurement, reference groups, and the deep meaning of social judgement theory, I was subtly indoctrinated to the notion that for theory to have value it must be applicable to one's daily experiences. 'Time and again, psychologists have displayed a tendency to be so absorbed in their own abstractions', urged Muzafer Sherif, 'that they have lost sight of vitally important factors in real life' (Sherif, 1951, p. 112).

As I interacted with my American Indian friends and spent valuable time in their home communities, I couldn't help but notice the presence of many individual and social problems deriving I believed from prejudice, lower economic status, and alcohol abuse. These experiences and observations kept me from becoming too absorbed with social psychological abstractions; also, they posed new and unsettling questions about the applicability of theory and science in solving fundamental social problems, especially those of a culture that was of great concern to me. I knew I had to maintain a balance between theory and practice, yet it was difficult as, at times, I became too passionately involved in real-life problems. I have never achieved that 'ideal balance' as I continue to be drawn to the 'vitally important factors in real life', especially those that suppress or deny human rights and encourage and endorse incivilities.

As I became more deeply immersed in my studies, it rapidly became clear to me that there was a paucity of information in the psychological literature about culture and even less on America's ethnic-minority groups. The little that was available typically was found under the headings of 'prejudice' and 'intelligence testing' and most of that centred on African-Americans. There were only a few articles that centred on American Indians. The more I scoured the literature, the more miffed I became about psychology's blithe lack of concern about America's indigenous population. Out of frustration, coupled with my burning desire to learn anything substantive, I sought out the anthropological literature and, to a lesser extent, readings about the history of the state of Oklahoma.

As I pored over the accounts of historians and cultural anthropologists, I would often reflect on the psychological meaning of those topics that lent themselves to such speculation. My musings and reflections filled the pages of a growing stack of spiral-bound notebooks; and, as the stack grew, it became clear to me that it would require several lifetimes to respond to all of my queries. I also sensed that my interests wouldn't fit in with any conventional programme in psychology. Furthermore, I knew that the chances of landing a position in the academy would be difficult, if not impossible, if I focused my psychological research solely on American Indians. Most of my fellow graduate students and the faculty constantly reminded me that I was a misfit and that I actually belonged in an anthropology programme; there were fleeting moments when I considered transferring to another programme, not because of the pressure and sometimes subtle criticism, but more because I wouldn't have to constantly justify my interests to those with seemingly intolerant enquiries.

Support for staying in the programme came from my Advisory Committee, friends from various American Indian communities, and my extended family. My five-person Advisory Committee represented four academic disciplines and two of my advisers were of ethnic-minority background. Collectively, they were totally supportive of my curricular and academic interests, although they insisted on stringent academic standards about my course of study, the comprehensive exams, the foreign language requirement, and the quality of my dissertation research. For example, they encouraged me to take independent studies in multivariate statistics at a time when the area was just emerging as a viable field of inquiry. To earn my rite of passage in this area, I had to calculate a few factor analyses manually, calculations which were considerably more demanding than performing simple one- or two-way analyses of variance. Also, they actively supported my dissertation research, which involved samples of male American Indians from several tribes in Western Oklahoma. At the time, it was the first graduate-level psychological research project conducted on Indians at the University of Oklahoma (Trimble, 1969).

As my studies intensified, support for my academic interests from my American Indian friends and colleagues swelled as they showered me with personal and cultural advice. Practically every weekend I was whisked off to someone's home community to visit family, participate in ceremonies and traditional dances, and talk in depth with a few traditional shaman and healers. With each passing visit, I returned to my tiny office at the Institute of Group Relations overflowing with new knowledge and a desire to complete my studies and put my skills to work. Most importantly, though, these experiences brought on a spiritual awakening, making me realise that a spiritual and mystical essence transcended everything I was learning. That essence was especially embodied in the elders and healers who openly shared their knowledge and life's experiences with me. On a few occasions, I experienced what I thought was the spiritual core through participation in ceremonials and dances – a transcendent embracement of my physical and spiritual self with nature's souls.

In one class meeting of a graduate seminar I foolishly attempted to share these spiritual experiences with my classmates. The presentation went nowhere as I was challenged about my commitment to the scientific method and the possibility that the subject belonged in religious studies. I argued vigorously that a spiritual essence transcended all of life's experiences and to ignore it in studies of culturally unique populations was myopic and unpardonable. 'How can you possibly measure or objectify spiritual experiences?' asked one outspoken and often argumentative student. Another commented, 'If you can't perceive "this essence" then you can't possibly quantify it.' The next day I found a copy of William James's text, *Varieties of religious experiences*, in my mailbox with a short typed anonymous note that said, 'I want you to know that I share your convictions and so does one of the most prominent American figures in psychology. I trust that you will enjoy this book as much as I do. I was reluctant to enter into the debate yesterday for fear that I might further compound the debate and I apologize.' It was signed, 'A friend who shares your convictions.' Many years later I learned that the anonymous author had been the seminar's instructor.

Although the arguments beat me down on that memorable occasion, I knew from my early childhood and successive experiences in later life that spirituality was omniscient and omnipresent and it couldn't be ignored; however, I recognised then, as I do now, that I must choose my audience wisely when the subject comes up in academic surroundings.

I defended my dissertation in 1969 and accepted my first major academic appointment in Oklahoma City. After discussing the meaning of my degree with my father and Grandfather Sage, I was offered two pieces of pungent but soft advice: (a) never forget where you came from and the lessons you learned as a child; and (b) you now have a responsibility to pass along your knowledge and skills in a way that is non-threatening yet informative. Several of the elders who befriended me also quietly urged me to use my knowledge to help them understand many of their problems such as alcoholism, racism, and related social and psychological problems. One very old and wise elder from Buffalo, Oklahoma, gently said, 'The American Indian is a frozen image in the minds of many. You can draw attention to the way we live now and the many things that affect our daily lives, particularly the bad ones.' I made a commitment to all of them that I would honour their advice. In the course of my career, despite many criticisms, frustrations, and setbacks, I have diligently and fervently struggled to honour their wishes and my pledge.

FROM GROUNDED THEORY TO APPLICATION: PROFESSIONAL GROWTH AND DEVELOPMENT

Buoyed with the confidence engendered by my mentors and friends, I set forth on yet another leg of my journey. My journey into the academy, though, was tempered with cautionary words from my departmental chair and a few of my former professors. In a succinct and blunt manner they cautioned me to go slow on my interest in the fledgling and emerging field of cross-cultural psychology: 'Build a career on "acceptable social psychological research" and slowly move into research with American Indians,' formed the heart of their advice. With reluctance and apprehension I initiated a series of attitude measurement and change research studies following Muzafer Sherif's (1967) perspectives on social judgement theory and attitude measurement (Trimble, 1972; Trimble and Chance, 1974). Another fortuitous and propitious event, however, changed my conventional research agenda and set me on a track that I have followed for the past twenty-five years.

In 1971, a well-known social psychologist and I submitted a symposium proposal for consideration at the annual meeting of the Eastern Psychological Association entitled 'Developmental issues of American Indian youth'. The panel consisted of a multidisciplinary team that was framed around what we thought was a well-written proposal. The proposal was rejected for the following reasons: (a) 'Psychologists generally are not interested in American Indians, so try the American Anthropological Association where your topic would most likely be viewed more favorably'; (b) 'There are very few American Indians in the eastern part of the United States, so why don't you submit your interesting proposal to a psychological association in the West'; and (c) 'Your panel was too interdisciplinary and must have more psychologists represented for it to fit with a more balanced psychological orientation.' We were aghast at the comments and fired back a rejoinder countering the criticisms; we never received a reply. The experience was a turning point in my career and served to firm up my conviction to devote my energies fully to bringing recognition and legitimacy to the inclusion of American Indians in the fabric of psychological inquiry. Also, it was a jolting reminder of the bigotry, rigidity, provincialism, and ignorance of many of those in my chosen profession about cultural and ethnic topics; I continued to encounter these elements in ensuing years and, to a large extent, they still persist although they are not as blatantly and overtly expressed as they were in the early 1970s.

The circle of my career became more defined in 1972 because of yet another chance encounter. A member of the Council of the Society for the Psychological Study of Social Issues (SPSSI), one of the more prominent divisions of the American Psychological Association, stopped me at a regional convention of psychologists and urged me to form a SPSSI-sponsored interest group. A small interest group was formed and led to my becoming extremely active in SPSSI, largely because many of the members, especially the more vocal and noted ones, rallied around the importance of ethnic-minority issues and seemingly advocated the psychological study of culture and ethnicity. In rapid succession, I served terms on SPSSI's Council, chaired their programme committee for the 1976 annual meeting of the American Psychological Association (APA), and served as one of their representatives to the Council of Representatives of the APA. Because of my involvement and support, SPSSI served to reinforce and validate my commitment to the psychological study of culture, ethnicity, and the application of psychological principles.

In 1978, I accepted a position at Western Washington University (WWU) which had a solid reputation for supporting and advancing cross-cultural psychology through its Center for Cross-Cultural Research and the seminal work of Walter J. Lonner. Before moving to WWU, I had conducted research and subsequently published a number of articles and chapters dealing with a diverse array of American Indian topics including: measurement of self-image, values, alienation, philosophy of life, and locus of control (Trimble, 1987; Trimble and Richardson, 1982); cross-cultural counselling (Dinges *et al.*, 1981; LaFromboise, Trimble, and Mohatt, 1990; Trimble, 1976; Trimble and Fleming, 1989; Trimble *et al.*, 1995; Trimble and Hayes, 1984; Trimble and LaFromboise, 1985); mental health models (Manson and Trimble, 1982; Trimble, 1982; Trimble, 1991; Trimble *et al.*, 1984; Trimble and Medicine, 1976); adolescent socialisation (Dinges, Trimble and Hollenbeck, 1979); elderly and their adaptation to life-threatening events (Trimble, Richardson, and Tatum, 1981–2); and methodological and measurement directions (Trimble, 1977; Trimble, Lonner, and Boucher, 1984). In accepting my position at WWU, I felt a sense of urgency to focus more directly on fundamental American Indian problems that could be addressed from a psychological perspective.

I was always aware that alcoholism was a major problem among American Indians. Many of my American Indian friends had severe alcohol problems and seemed hopeless in being able to cope with them. For a few friends, alcohol abuse was directly involved in their tragic deaths. Members of my own extended family, too, had serious alcohol problems; one of many uncles died of exposure following alcohol intoxication. Prior to moving to WWU, I had worked with a number of community agencies in Oklahoma and elsewhere on alcohol education and prevention activities but backed off because I was reminded yet again that the field 'was not academic enough'.

Upon settling into the Pacific Northwest I made new friends from several American Indian communities. In time, a few asked if I could assist them in developing programmes to deal with their alcohol and drug use problems. After some serious consultation with a few trusted colleagues, I decided to ignore the criticisms I had received in Oklahoma and plunged into working with a few community leaders to design and implement prevention programmes from a culturally resonant perspective. In one article, I referred to it as 'putting the etic to work' (Trimble, 1988). We examined a series of psychological theories that offered a blend of behavioural and cognitive strategies that could be adapted to fit the culturally unique lifeways and thoughtways of the communities. After much discussion, planning, and testing we implemented a series of prevention efforts that were somewhat successful in changing the alcohol and drug-related thoughts and behaviours of Indian youth (Beauvais and Trimble, 1992; Cvetkovich *et al.*, 1987; Gilchrist *et al.*, 1987; Schinke *et al.*, 1988; Trimble, 1992, 1993, 1995a; Trimble, Bolek, and Niemcryk, 1992). I continue to work in the field, as alcoholism and drug use remain one of the major problems in many Indian and Native communities.

I have always valued collaboration, especially in ventures that require a blend of social psychological principles with cultural lifeways. Part of the orientation can be attributed to the wisdom of Grandfather Sage and my interdisciplinary training at the University of Oklahoma. Also, I am constantly reminded of the words of Lone Man, a late nineteenth-century Teton Sioux, who reportedly said that 'I have seen that in any great undertaking it is not enough for a man to depend simply upon himself' (*Native American wisdom*, 1993). In the past ten or so years all of my 'undertakings' have occurred in collaboration with valued colleagues and friends, especially those at the Tri-Ethnic Center for Prevention Research at Colorado State University and the National Center for American Indian and Alaska Native Mental Health Research at the University of Colorado Health Sciences Center. There are others with whom I have worked closely who are located at various colleges, universities, and communities around the country. Regrettably the list is so lengthy that space prevents me from listing them. Nonetheless, they know who they are.

In recent years I have turned some of my research energies toward exploring the correlates of ethnic identification (Trimble, 1990–1, 1995b). Perhaps the struggles of my many multiethnic friends and acquaintances with their own sense of identity may account for part of my interest in ethnic identification. Additionally, there appears to be a growing interest in the construct at a number of other levels. Social and behavioural scientists are exploring the correlates of identity with a variety of outcome variables such as alcohol and drug use, depression, academic achievement, and quality of life. But at another level, there appears to be a growing tendency for collective factions and controlling powers of certain countries to view ethnicity as a threat to national stability and world order (Moynihan, 1993). Many of us are deeply concerned about the direction that national policies are taking to erode, if not eliminate, ethnic identification from their national character; some commentators have labelled it 'ethnic cleansing'. Research undoubtedly will shed light on the fundamental psychological principle that identity is located in the self or core of the individual, and one's communal culture, self-esteem, and sense of affiliation and belongingness are deeply affected by the process (Moynihan, 1993). At another level is the assertion that all of us have an inalienable right to state who and what we are and 'we must come to recognize that one of the fundamental human rights of individuals and of groups includes the right to self-identification and self-definition, so long as one does not adopt an identity which has the effect of denying the same rights to others' (Forbes, 1990, pp. 48–49).

Advances in cross-cultural psychology can assist in establishing the significance of identity at the individual and group level. Upon reflection it is disturbing to contemplate the possibility that cross-cultural psychology and all that it has contributed to the understanding of culture and ethnicity might not be with us today. Fortunately, the tireless and persistent efforts of those who saw the wisdom of expanding the notion of individual and group differences to include culture generated a force that can no longer be ignored and labelled as the sole province of single academic fiefdoms.

My spiritual journey is not over, and the circle, instead of narrowing, is expanding. In the course of my journey, I have closely adhered to the wisdom of my elders, especially in passing along my experiences and knowledge and closely collaborating with trusted and valued colleagues. Along the way there have been some modest successes in bringing about awareness and sensitivity to the salience and significance of cultural and ethnic variables. For example, we have been involved in advancing a research agenda for several US government research institutes that emphasises substantial studies of America's ethnic-minority populations. This involvement has led to the result that most researchers are required to include ethnic samples in their study designs.

Nationally, in the late 1960s, there were about four or five psychologists who were of American Indian heritage; now there are close to 100. In the same time frame, the number of published articles, books, and chapters has increased from a mere handful to over 2,000. In 1995, thanks to the efforts of the American Psychological Association (APA), we edited an annotated bibliography of the abstracts of the psychological and behavioural literature on North American Indians and Alaska Natives (Trimble and Bagwell, 1995). The publication and commitment of the APA confirmed for me that our efforts far exceeded our earlier expectations. It is comforting to know that over sixty presentations dealing with ethnic and cultural topics were included as part of the American Psychological Association's programme in their 1996 convention in Toronto, Ontario, Canada; thirty years earlier there were maybe one or two.

As I look back over the past quarter of a century, I view the spiritual journey as one over which I had little personal control. At times, especially when all efforts looked bleak, I sensed a soft hand nudging me forward and the presence of a spiritual source encouraging me to continue. Maybe some of the more significant influences were due to chance, but I don't think so. Perhaps the elders are right when they say that our life journeys are already laid out for us when we take our first step.

Every once in a while I am reminded of my journey's beginnings. In the early morning of certain summer days, if I relax and let go of the burden of everyday hassles and problems, I think I can see a horse grazing on our small acreage nestled in a mountainous basin beside a lake. Next to him stands his friend holding the reins, glancing over at me with a smile and a raised eyebrow. Quite possibly they have been there all along and I have just been too absorbed to notice. And when I sense their presence, I wonder if others are experiencing similar spiritual episodes and whether or not they are being nudged along, too.

ACKNOWLEDGEMENTS

I wish to express my sincere gratitude to Marcia Bastian and Fred Beauvais of the Tri-Ethnic Center for Prevention Research at Colorado State University for reviewing and providing me with thoughtful comments on the flow and content of the manuscript. Support for writing this chapter was provided through grants from the National Institute on Drug Abuse (P50 DA07074) and the National Institute on Alcohol Abuse and Alcoholism (AA 083020) awarded to the Tri-Ethnic Center for Prevention Research at Colorado State University.

REFERENCES

Beauvais, F. and Trimble, J. (1992). The role of the researcher in evaluating American Indian alcohol and other drug abuse prevention programmes. In M. Orlandi (ed.), *Cultural competence for evaluators working with ethnic minority communities: A guide for alcohol and other drug abuse prevention practitioners* (pp. 99–110). Rockville, MD: Office of Substance Abuse Prevention, Cultural Competence Series 1.

Cvetkovich, G., Schinke, S., Gilchrist, L. and Trimble, J. (1987). Child and adolescent drug use: A judgement and information processing perspective to health behavior interventions. *Journal of Drug Education, 17*(4), 295–313.

Dinges, N., Trimble, J. and Hollenbeck, A. (1979). American Indian adolescent socialization: Review and critique of research. *Journal of Adolescence, 2*, 259–296.

Dinges, N., Trimble, J., Manson, S. and Pasquale, F. (1981). The social ecology of counseling American Indians. In A. Marsella and P. Pedersen (eds), *Cross-cultural counseling and psychotherapy: Foundations, evaluation, cultural considerations* (pp. 243–276). Elmsford, NY: Pergamon.

Forbes, J. D. (1990). The manipulation of race, caste, and identity: Classifying Afro-americans. *Journal of Ethnic Studies, 17*(4), 1–51.

Gilchrist, L., Schinke, S., Trimble, J. and Cvetkovich, G. (1987). Skills enhancement to prevent substance abuse among American Indian adolescents. *International Journal of the Addictions, 22*(9), 869–879.

LaFromboise, T., Trimble, J. and Mohatt, G. (1990). Counseling intervention and the

American Indian tradition: An integrative approach. *Counseling Psychologist, 18*(4), 628–654.

Manson, S. M. and Trimble, J. E. (1982). American Indian and Alaska Native communities: Past efforts, future inquiries. In L. Snowden (ed.), *Reaching the underserved: Mental health needs of neglected populations* (pp. 143–163). Beverly Hills, CA: Sage.

Moynihan, D. P. (1993). *Pandaemonium: Ethnicity in international politics*. New York: Oxford University Press.

Native American wisdom (1993). Philadelphia, PA: Running Press.

Neihardt, J. (1961). *Black Elk speaks*. Lincoln, NE: University of Nebraska.

Schinke, S., Botvin, G., Trimble, J., Orlandi, M., Gilchrist, L. and Locklear, H. (1988). Preventing substance abuse among American Indian adolescents: A bicultural competence skills approach. *Journal of Counseling Psychology, 35*(1), 87–90.

Sherif, M. (1951). Light from psychology on intercultural relations. In K. W. Bigelow (ed.), *Cultural groups and human relations* (pp. 110–126). New York: Columbia University, Teachers College.

Sherif, M. (1967). *Social interaction: Process and products*. Chicago, IL: Aldine.

Sherif, M. and Sherif, C. (1956). *An outline of social psychology* (Rev. edn). New York: Harper.

Trimble, J. E. (1969). 'Psychosocial characteristics of employed and unemployed western Oklahoma male American Indians'. Unpublished doctoral dissertation, University of Oklahoma, Norman.

Trimble, J. E. (1972, April). *Experimental design extension and its effects on a mixed-mode communication in attitude research*. Paper presented at the meeting of the Southwestern Psychological Association, Oklahoma City, OK.

Trimble, J. E. (1976). Value differences of the American Indian: Concerns for the concerned counselor. In P. Pedersen, J. Draguns and W. Lonner (eds), *Counseling across cultures* (pp. 65–81). Honolulu, HI: University Press of Hawaii.

Trimble, J. E. (1977). Research in American Indian communities: Methodological issues and concerns. *Journal of Social Issues, 33*(4), 159–174.

Trimble, J. E. (1982). American Indian mental health and the role of training for prevention. In S.E. Manson (ed.), *New directions in prevention among American Indian and Alaska Native communities* (pp. 147–168). Portland, OR: Oregon Health Sciences University Press.

Trimble, J. E. (1987). Self-understanding and perceived alienation among American Indians. *Journal of Community Psychology, 15*(July), 316–333.

Trimble, J. E. (1988). Putting the etic to work: Applying social psychological principles in cross-cultural settings. In M. H. Bond (ed.), *The cross-cultural challenge to social psychology* (pp. 109–121). Newbury Park, CA: Sage.

Trimble, J. E. (1990–1). Ethnic specification, validation prospects and the future of drug abuse research. *International Journal of the Addictions, 25*(2), 149–169.

Trimble, J. E. (1991). American Indian perspectives on mental health: Implications for training psychologists. In H. Myers, P. Wohlford, R. Echemendia, and P. Guzman (eds), *Minority mental health perspectives on clinical training and services in psychology* (pp. 43–48). Washington, DC: American Psychological Association.

Trimble, J. E. (1992). Drug abuse preventive intervention perspectives for American Indian adolescents. In L. Vargas and J. Koss (eds), *Working with culture: Psychotherapeutic interventions with ethnic minority children and adolescents* (pp. 246–275). San Francisco, CA: Jossey-Bass.

Trimble, J. E. (1993). Cultural variations in the use of alcohol and drugs. In W. Lonner and R. Malpass (eds), *Readings in psychology and culture* (pp. 79–84). Boston, MA: Allyn & Bacon.

Trimble, J. E. (1995a). Ethnic minorities. In R. Coombs and D. Ziedonis (eds), *Handbook on drug abuse prevention: A comprehensive strategy to prevent the abuse of alcohol and other drugs* (pp. 379–410). Needham Heights, MA: Allyn & Bacon.

Trimble, J. E. (1995b). Toward an understanding of ethnicity and ethnic identification and their relationship with drug use research. In G. Botvin, S. Schinke and M. Orlandi (eds), *Drug abuse prevention with multi-ethnic youth* (pp. 3–27). Thousand Oaks, CA: Sage.

Trimble, J. E. and Bagwell, W. M. (eds) (1995). *North American Indians and Alaska Natives: Abstracts of the psychological and behavioral literature, 1967–1994.* Washington, DC: American Psychological Association.

Trimble, J. E., Bolek, C. and Niemcryk, S. (eds) (1992). *Ethnic and multicultural drug abuse: Perspectives on current research.* New York: Haworth.

Trimble, J. E. and Chance, D. C. (1974). *A modification of the ordered alternative scale and its effects on the sensitivity of attitude change measurement.* Paper presented at the meeting of the Southwestern Psychological Association, El Paso, TX.

Trimble, J. E. and Fleming, C. (1989). Providing counseling services for Native American Indians: Client, counselor, and community characteristics. In P. Pedersen, J. Draguns, W. Lonner and J. Trimble (eds), *Counseling across cultures* (3rd edn) (pp. 177–204). Honolulu, HI: University Press of Hawaii.

Trimble, J., Fleming, C., Beauvais, F. and Thurman, P. (1995). Essential cultural and social strategies for counseling Native American Indians. In P. Pedersen, J. Draguns, W. Lonner and J. Trimble (eds), *Counseling across cultures* (4th edn) (pp. 177–209). Thousand Oaks, CA: Sage.

Trimble, J. E. and Hayes, S. (1984). Mental health intervention in the psychosocial contexts of American Indian communities. In W. O'Conner and B. Lubin (eds), *Ecological models: Applications to clinical and community mental health* (pp. 293–321). New York: John Wiley.

Trimble, J. E. and LaFromboise, T. (1985). American Indians and the counseling process: Culture, adaptation, and style. In P. Pedersen (eds), *Handbook of cross-cultural counseling and therapy* (pp. 127–146). Westport, CT: Greenwood.

Trimble, J. E., Lonner, W. and Boucher, J. (1984). Stalking the wily emic: Alternatives in cross-cultural measurement. In S. Irvine and J. Berry (eds), *Human assessment and cultural factors* (pp. 259–273). New York: Plenum.

Trimble, J. E., Manson, S., Dinges, N. and Medicine, B. (1984). Towards an understanding of American Indian concepts of mental health: Reflections and directions. In A. Marsella, N. Sartorius and P. Pedersen (eds), *Mental health services: The cross-cultural context* (pp. 199–220). Beverly Hills, CA: Sage.

Trimble, J. E. and Medicine, B. (1976). Development of theoretical models and levels of interpretation in mental health. In J. Westermeyer (ed.), *Anthropology and mental health* (pp. 161–200). The Hague, Netherlands: Moltune.

Trimble, J. E. and Richardson, S. (1982). Cluster structure analytic characteristics of locus of control measures among American Indians. *Journal of Cross-cultural Psychology, 13*(2), 228–238.

Trimble, J. E., Richardson, S. and Tatum, E. (1981–2). Minority elderly adaptation to life-threatening events: An overview with methodological considerations. *Journal of Ethnic Minority Aging, 7*(1,2), 12–24.

15 Two decades of chasing the dragon
A Canadian psychologist assesses his career in Hong Kong

Michael Harris Bond

As they gain experience, scientists reach a stage when they look back upon their own beginnings in research and wonder how they had the temerity to embark upon it, considering how ignorant and ill-equipped they were.

Peter Medawar, *Advice to a Young Scientist*

INTRODUCTION

I am fifty and well into the second half of my professional career as a cross-cultural psychologist. With less of a future and more of a past, I have lately been musing about my work much more than before. How did I get into this peculiar business? What have I discovered about my self and the world, really? What possibilities does my remaining career hold?

This exercise seems particularly relevant for those among us who deal with manifestations of culture. For culture presents itself in the shape, the sound, the feel, the taste – the shock, of difference. This difference challenges the structure of our taken-for-granted world. The confrontation can disturb us deeply, as terror management theorists have argued (Solomon, Greenberg and Pyszezynski, 1991); our ontological security gets shaken (Laing, 1962). Part of my response to such disturbance is to reflect often on what I am doing in this career of mine.

Despite my natural exuberance, I have lived long enough to be a little self-conscious about exposing these private reflections. Surely a decent modesty dictates silence! Furthermore, we are guests in the august halls of objective science. How dare I be personal?

My response is Korzbinski's aphorism that 'The map is not the territory'. I understand these words to mean that the content of our social science, the map, is not the process of creating that social science, the territory. An appreciation of that territory may help us to produce better maps, or at least give cartographers a sense of structure as they go about their business of making maps. I offer this essay/reflection in such a hope.

My map is the psychology of the Chinese people, more particularly their social functioning. I have lived and worked in Hong Kong for the last twenty years helping to produce our discipline's latest version of that map (Bond, 1996). So, I will illustrate my mapping of that territory by referring to various land-falls I have made.

THE CALL TO ADVENTURE

> There lies the port; the vessel puffs her sail;
> There gloom the dark, broad seas.
>
> Tennyson, *Ulysses*

In his synthesis of the mythical aspects to a person's life, *The hero with a thousand faces*, Joseph Campbell (1949, p. 58) divides the process into various thematic stages:

> This first stage of the mythological journey – which we have designated the 'call to adventure' – signifies that destiny has summoned the hero and transferred his spiritual center of gravity from within the pale of his society to a zone unknown. This fateful region of both treasure and danger may be variously represented: as a distant land, a forest, a kingdom underground, beneath the waves, or above the sky, a secret island, lofty mountaintop, or profound dream state; but it is always a place of strangely fluid and polymorphous beings, unimaginable torments, superhuman deeds, and impossible delight.

As Campbell points out, a distant land may issue this call to the potential adventurer and pull him or her 'from within the pale of his society to a zone unknown' (p. 49). Indeed, foreign cultures present us with the unknown, the alien, the magical, mysterious, mystifying other *par excellence*, challenging our familiar boundaries with 'strangely fluid and polymorphous beings, unimaginable torments, superhuman deeds, and impossible delight' (p. 49). Of course, for many of us, it is just this kaleidoscope of exotic promise that draws us into a love affair with different cultures.

For me that culture is the Chinese. It could have been some other culture, but perhaps for chance events (Bandura, 1982), it was not. In any case I can trace my fascination with things Chinese to a dinner celebration in Toronto. I was sixteen and my father took us to a restaurant in Toronto's Chinatown to welcome in the Western new year. At that time in high school, our class had been reading Coleridge's poem, *Kubla Khan*. Its opening quatrain had wormed itself into my mind:

> In Xanadu did Kubla Khan
> A stately pleasure-dome decree:
> Where Alph, the sacred river ran
> Through caverns measureless to man
> Down to a sunless sea.

I knew that Kubla Khan was a famous Chinese emperor, a foreigner I later discovered, but where was Xanadu? And how could a river be sacred, or pleasure domes stately, or caverns measureless? Could sunless seas hold life, too?

All these questions flooded over me when we entered the Jade Lotus restaurant to behold a garish, pulsating dragon standing guard. 'Symbol of Chinese culture,' my father announced. This electric image combined with the cacophony of the steamy, boisterous restaurant, the fragrance of crushed ginger, the slipperiness of plastic chopsticks, and the high-pitched laughter of the waiter when my father complained that our fried rice was burnt. I was hooked. My life's work of chasing the dragon, of exploring the riddle of Chinese culture, had begun.

To be effective, any call must first be heard. I believe that the call of different cultures is more likely to be heard by those high in the personality disposition of openness to experience, also studied as tolerance for ambiguity, intuition, sensation seeking, and so forth (McCrae and Costa, 1985). Such a disposition transforms a different culture from an affront to an affordance. High levels of openness may be a prerequisite for any intellectual to find the study of another culture attractive, and worth the inevitable hassles that come with the territory.

Intellectual reverberation

Most exploration begins with the annoyance of being lost.

Edward Hall, *Beyond Culture*

Do I imply a split between my life and my work if I create a separate heading for the intellectual 'call to adventure'? I think rather that my work provided a particularly acute call, since I needed publications in order to be tenured at the Chinese University and I was discovering some difficult-to-explain results. In a recently completed experiment, Hong Kong Chinese had indicated that they were more attracted to a future opponent than to a neutral target (Bond, 1979). This finding was the reverse of that derived from Heider's theorising about unit-sentiment balance, however, and all articles require a discussion section before they are publishable.

It seemed that my Chinese subjects responded differently than the Everyman of most social psychology theories I had read. Of course, I may have mis-understood these theories, or I may have used unreliable measures, or I may have inadvertently reversed my Chinese trait scales when coding the data. The possibilities were endless.

It was also possible, however, that the Chinese were different than our putative Everyman. The very week I was struggling with the discussion section, I tuned into the video sportscast of an international track meet in Beijing. There, across the top of the stadium stretched a long banner proclaiming in English: 'Friendship first, competition second!'. Could this Chinese adage be the answer to my conundrum, the key to unlocking my discussion section? Did the Chinese deploy the integrative force of friendship to counterbalance the divisive power of competition? If so, why? And where could I find the answers? I was hooked again!

SUPERNATURAL AID

Upon this gifted age, in its dark hour,
Rains from the sky a meteoric shower
Of facts . . . they lie unquestioned, uncombined.
Wisdom enough to leech us of our ill
Is daily spun; but there exists no loom

To weave it into fabric . . .
    Edna St. Vincent Millay[1]

Again, Campbell (1949, p. 69) speaks to the issue I was then facing:

> For those who have not refused the call, the first encounter of the hero-journey
> is with a protective figure (often a little old crone or old man) who provides the
> adventurer with amulets against the dragon forces he is about to pass.

How coincidental that Campbell would label my obstacles 'dragon forces', given
that I was wrestling with the problem of how to conceptualise Chinese culture in
a psychologically usable way. The touchstone was close at hand.

That year I met Hofstede in India and he introduced me to his four-dimensional
mapping of culture (Hofstede, 1980). I was agog at the range and the clarity of
his scholarship in that tome. Although it has taken me fifteen years to understand
his achievement, I sensed then that it was a struggle worth undertaking. For he
provided a theory, a framework within which culture's consequences could be
anticipated *a priori*, rather than explained *ex post facto*.

My colleagues and I went to work at once. According to Hofstede's (1980)
country scores, Hong Kong Chinese were higher than Westerners in both power
distance and collectivism. So, we argued, insults from a subordinate and from an
in-group member should be more strongly sanctioned by Chinese in order to
protect the social order (Bond, Leung, Wan and Giacalone, 1985). Or Chinese
should divide resources more equally among in-group compared to out-group
members (Leung and Bond, 1984). Or Hong Kongese would give greater weight
to a target's conscientiousness and agreeableness in guiding their behavioural
choices towards that target (Bond and Forgas, 1984). Ideas were tumbling out; I
felt like an arrow released from a bow, long held taut.

Personal reverberations

Mankind hath been created to carry forward an ever-advancing civilisation.
    Baha'u'llah, *Gleanings*

Amidst this heady effusion of intellectual output, I was still living in a foreign
culture. I had humidity to endure, exotic diseases to avoid, children to educate, a
promotion to secure, a house to buy (surely!), and a future to think about. Hong
Kong was a great place to visit for a few years, but where was I going to live my
life? Perhaps it was time to get serious.

My wife and I spent a lot of time consulting about our future. It was very hard
for me to cast adrift the received wisdom of pursuing a career at a solid Canadian
university, owning a house of our own in some leafy suburbia, becoming a local
guru on things Chinese, overhearing the comforting sounds of English at every
turn, and living among human beings who generally made sense. The temptation
to return was exquisite.

What held me in place was the Baha'i faith. I will be brief here, so as not to offend any sceptics. Basically, however, Baha'u'llah maintains that the world order is inexorably changing and advancing. We are all moving towards an appreciation of humanity's oneness and of our need for international forms of organisation to preserve peace and promote prosperity (Baha'i International Community, 1995). Each of us has a role to play in this possible future and I felt maximally useful promoting this possible future in Hong Kong.

There are of course other forms of 'supernatural aid' in Campbell's (1949) larger sense. I believe that some such aid is necessary, however, since those of us who freely choose to stand 'amid the alien corn' will be sorely tested. One's culture of origin is a comfort and its predictable scripting not lightly cast aside. Living overseas we need hope (Snyder, 1994) to dispel the Siren song of familiar sounds, faces, forms and dreams calling us back to our original culture.

CROSSING THE THRESHOLD

So convenient a thing it is to be a reasonable creature, since it enables one to find or make a reason for everything one has a mind to do.

Benjamin Franklin, *The Autobiography of Benjamin Franklin*

Armed with the amulet of Hofstede's (1980) theory, I sallied forth energetically, applying his dimensions to Chinese concepts like 'face' (Bond and Lee, 1981; Hu, 1944), 'connections' (Bond and Hwang, 1986; King, 1991), and 'modesty' (Bond, Leung and Wan, 1982). Concepts are fuzzy sets and creativity forges easy alliances.

But disquiet was being voiced. Some colleagues were telling me that I wasn't 'completely understanding' these indigenous Chinese terms. I had read enough about cultural imperialism in the social sciences (Berry, 1969; Featherman, 1993; Triandis, 1976) to feel shaken by these gentle challenges. My recent writing on the Chinese experience with Western colonialism (Bond and King, 1985) had left me feeling vaguely guilty and unsure of my intellectual footing when considering things Chinese.

At the same time Taiwanese psychologists under the leadership of Kuo-Shu Yang were launching a spirited exploration of Chinese social reality. Hwang (1977) examined Chinese modes of coping; King (1991) of Chinese 'relation-shipology', Yu (1996) of Chinese achievement motivation, and Yang himself (1986) of Chinese patterns of modernising. The tide of indigenous cultural enthusiasm was surging; and I was an outsider.

In Campbell's (1949, p. 77) sequence, I had reached the threshold:

With the personifications of his destiny to guide and aid him, the hero goes forward in his adventure until he comes to the 'threshold guardian' at the entrance to the zone of magnified power. Such custodians bound the world in the four directions – also up and down – standing for the limits of the hero's present sphere, of life horizon. Beyond them is darkness, the unknown, and danger.

The intellectual danger was embodied in the Chinese proverb, 'Cut toes, fit shoe'. Was I cutting the toes of Chinese culture to fit the shoe of my Western conceptions? If reality was as malleable as our post-modernists would have us believe (e.g. Gergen, 1985), then I could simply be engaging in an academic form of 'gunboat diplomacy' (Spence, 1990). How then to appease the custodians at the threshold of Chinese culture?

Personal reverberations

> I believe that ... someone who is a writer is not simply doing his work in his books.
>
> Michel Foucault

At this same time, I was well into my life in Hong Kong – children at school, a wife working as an English teacher, me doing some management training to supplement my income and coaching the University swim team. I was also facing promotion to Senior Lecturer, an exalted rank in the British system. Its attainment signals a careful vote of confidence by the university authorities that one has 'the right stuff' for an academic career in Hong Kong. When my promotion was finally granted in 1980, I realised that I had crossed the threshold despite my doubts.

INTO THE BELLY OF THE WHALE

> The East and the West must unite to provide one another with what is lacking.
>
> Abdu'l-Baha, *Paris Talks*

Campbell (1949, pp. 90, 91) describes this next stage as an engulfment which liberates:

> The idea that the passage of the magical threshold is a transit into a sphere of rebirth is symbolized in the worldwide womb image of the belly of the whale. The hero ... is swallowed into the unknown, and would appear to have died ... But here, instead of passing outward, beyond the confines of the visible world, the hero goes inward, to be born again.

I passed the magical threshold by vowing to engage in *Chinese* cultural imperialism. I promised to develop a distinctively Chinese survey of values, export it around the globe, and discover how it defined reality. Furthermore, I would then compare its reality with Hofstede's (1980) to determine if and where they intersected. Perhaps 'two wrongs could make a right', i.e. two culturally emic surveys could point to the same dimensions of values regardless of their origins. If so, then I for one would heave a sigh of relief and return to my psychological business as usual.

The results of this exercise were dramatically equivocal (Chinese Culture Connection, 1987). At the cultural level, the Chinese Value Survey yielded results which overlapped with three of Hofstede's; one dimension, Confucian work dynamism, was unique to the emic Chinese survey and generated considerable excitement because it mapped cultures in close correspondence to their level of economic growth over the last twenty-five years. One dimension from the Hofstede quartet, uncertainty avoidance, was unique to his Western values measure.

Eureka! The marriage of two important cultural traditions had brought forth offspring that only such a union could have produced. We now had evidence about which dimensions of value were available to the legatees of both traditions and which were distinctively available to legatees of each. The range of scientific constructs had been extended beyond their Western origins and cultural synergy had been empirically demonstrated. By making appropriate obeisance to 'the threshold guardian to the zone of magnified power' (Campbell, 1949, p. 77), I had been rewarded with a token of possible riches.

Personal reverberations

He that findeth his life shall lose it; and he that loseth his life for my sake shall find it.

Matthew 10: 39 (King James Bible)

At this time, and perhaps buoyed by the results from my exploration of Chinese values, I began to immerse myself more fully in Chinese cultural waters. I read Chinese history (Hookham, 1969; Spence, 1990); listened to Chinese music (but not Chinese opera!); bought Chinese pictorial scrolls for my office, pondered the philosophical classics of Taoism (e.g. Lau, 1989), began lecturing to management classes on *The art of war* (Giles, 1910), and widely sampled Chinese vegetarian cooking. I no longer felt threatened while chasing the dragon; instead, I now had hope that he would lead me in important directions. The dice were cast when I turned down a job approach from one of those solid Canadian universities.

THE ROAD OF TRIALS

The way that is bright seems dull;
The way that leads forward seems to lead backward;
The way that is even seems rough.

Tao Te Ching, *Poem 41*
(trans. D.C. Lau)

At this stage I become unsure of my bearings. Where am I now in the sequence of Campbell's journey? Perhaps I am on the road of trials:

Once having traversed the threshold, the hero moves in a dream landscape of curiously fluid, ambiguous forms, where he must survive a succession of trials.

(Campbell, 1949, p. 97)

Professionally, these trials have arisen out of the legacy of studying Chinese values cross-culturally. From that exercise I developed the strategy of combining emics in order to discover etics. That is, when investigating a given domain, say lay conceptions of cures for psychological problems, I take an established Western instrument designed for this purpose (e.g. Furnham and Henley, 1988). Then, this instrument is supplemented after consulting Chinese cultural informants. We ask what are Chinese psychological problems, and especially whether there are problems we might include that some have argued are uniquely Chinese cultural syndromes. In this case we included gambling, going through the backdoor (i.e. gaining advantage by using one's contacts), and 'koro' (i.e. fear of penis shrinkage). The instrument is also supplemented in respect of cures by including indigenous strategies, gleaned from our interviews (e.g. the body's power to recover, participation in religious rites, reduction in work load, etc.).

This expanded instrument is then given to a group of Chinese respondents. Our goal is to analyse the resulting data to determine whether the Chinese cultural additions enlarge Western conceptual space: is there a unique constellation of Chinese problems; indeed, is there a different set of such problem constellations? Is there a unique constellation of Chinese cures; indeed; is there a different set of such cure constellations? Or does the added material merely map on to previous constructs?

My collaborators and I have tried this approach with perceptions of causes and cures of psychological problems (Luk and Bond, 1992), with implicit personality perceptions (Yang and Bond, 1990; Yik and Bond, 1993), with dimensions of personality (Ho, 1994; Zhang and Bond, 1995). Typically the answer is an Oriental yes and no. In the case of personality perceptions, for example, Western measures of the Big Five (actually six!) are similarly grouped by Hong Kong Chinese; indigenous Chinese measures likewise yield six factors, but these six parcellate perceptual space differently from the Western six. When the Western and Chinese instruments are combined, they yield eight rather than six dimensions – some of these eight appear very similar to some of the six Western dimensions and some of the eight appear very similar to some of the six Chinese dimensions. And some are unique blends as well. 'Curiouser and curiouser', as Alice allowed while adventuring in Wonderland.

So, by widening our cultural sourcing, we appear to increase our psychological yield, at least sometimes (see also Kagitbak, Church, and Akamine, 1996). We find a different reality depending on which realities we include in trying to find that overarching reality. One might call this approach the multicultural construction of social science.

This is unsettling work; it leaves me worried about the arbitrariness of some decisions which affect my conclusions (e.g., How many factors or clusters shall I extract from this analysis? Suppose I use a more stringent alpha level? What if I had used a less well educated sample or even a different cultural sample?). It is difficult to feel on solid ground when the possibilities are so extensive.

My present answer is to tolerate this openness and discover where it leads. The informing strategy is to use cultural diversity as a resource and to discover how it extends our reach as social scientists. So, for example, does an eight-factor model of personality perception yield useful insights about Chinese friendship formation (Lee and Bond, 1996)? What new relationships does it offer in promoting our understanding of how member personalities contribute to group functioning (Bond and Shiu, in press)? Does its use broaden our conceptualisation of gender differences (Cheung, 1994)?

My colleagues and I are also taking this line of approach to the study of self-conceptions, social beliefs, and personality structure just as we had earlier adopted it to study values. Our underlying motive, if you will pardon the pun, is to reorient psychology. That is, we hope to infuse mainstream Western psychology with Oriental, in this case Chinese, cultural input. Our basic interest is in whether such concerted and sustained enterprise will help limn a more comprehensive mapping of the psychological world. For, as Gardner Murphy (1969, p. 529) so aptly put it, 'a human race speaking many tongues, regarding many values, and holding different convictions about the meaning of life sooner or later will have to consult all that is human'.

Personal reverberations

> Stability and prosperity.
> Hong Kong political
> incantation

Amidst this high-sounding intellectual rhetoric, I am constantly reminded that Hong Kong, our home for the last twenty years and the last major British colony, will pass into Chinese sovereignty on 30 June 1997. So my daily life, as well as my professional output, will soon be shaped by a new political authority. In the run-up to the transition, social, economic, and legal changes are already afoot, along with the political. This ferment produces its own social psychological brew (Bond, 1993), as Hong Kongese anticipate the future – some with dread, some with enthusiasm, most with riveted interest.

Who will administer our pension fund at the Chinese University? Will we retain control over our admission policy? What will happen to the value of the Hong Kong currency? Will foreign travel continue to be easy to undertake? How will non-Chinese be regarded, especially in sensitive educational positions? We have been chasing the dragon; has it now turned to face us with its fire? Should we leave or stay on? Such are the questions that confront us now as citizens on the road of trials in Hong Kong.

MEETING WITH THE GODDESS

> By the blending of breath
> From the sun and the shade,
> Equilibrium comes to the world.
> Lao Tzu, *The Way of Life*
> (trans. R.B. Blakney)

A subsequent stage in Campbell's mythical journey promises the hero a meeting with the goddess. He describes the spiritual reality of the encounter in these terms:

Woman, in the picture language of mythology, represents the totality of what can be known. The hero is the one who comes to know. As he progresses in the slow initiation which is life, the form of the goddess undergoes for him a series of transfigurations: she can never be greater than himself, though she can always promise more than he is yet capable of comprehending. She lures, she guides, she bids him burst his fetters.

(Campbell, 1949, p. 116)

This is heady stuff, indeed, whether one considers the outcome in intellectual or in personal terms.

I do not believe that I am yet in the presence of the goddess, though she beckons me on. One of my favorite portrayals of the dragon has him sinuously moving through billowing clouds, alive with energy. Upon his back, in regal stillness, aglow with light, stands Kwan Sai Yum, the Chinese goddess of mercy. I have a scroll of this *yin-yang* marriage which I often hang in my office. It draws me forward like a promise as I embark on my third decade of chasing the dragon:

> for my purpose holds
> To sail beyond the sunset, and the baths
> Of all the western stars, until I die.
>
> Tennyson, *Ulysses*

NOTES

1   Excerpt from 'Upon this age, that never speaks its mind' by Edna St. Vincent Millay. From COLLECTED POEMS, HarperCollins. Copyright © 1939, 1967 by Edna St. Vincent Millay and Norma Millay Ellis. All rights reserved. Reprinted by permission of Elizabeth Barnett, literary executor.

REFERENCES

Baha'i International Community (1995). *The prosperity of humankind*. New York: Office of Public Information.

Bandura, A. (1982). The psychology of chance encounters and life paths. *American Psychologist, 37*, 747–755.

Berry, J. W. (1969). On cross-cultural comparability. *International Journal of Psychology, 4*, 119–128.

Bond, M. H. (1979). Winning either way: The effect of anticipating a competitive interaction on person perception. *Personality and Social Psychology Bulletin, 5*, 316–319.

Bond, M. H. (1993). Between the *Yin* and the *Yang*: The identity of the Hong Kong Chinese. Professorial inaugural lecture, Chinese University of Hong Kong, May.

Bond, M. H. (ed.) (1996). *The handbook of Chinese psychology*. Hong Kong: Oxford University Press.

Bond, M. H. and Forgas, J. P. (1984). Linking person perception to behavioral intention across cultures: The role of cultural collectivism. *Journal of Cross-Cultural Psychology, 15*, 337–352.

Bond, M. H. and Hwang, K. K. (1986). The social psychology of Chinese people. In M. H. Bond (ed.), *The psychology of Chinese people* (pp. 213–266). Hong Kong: Oxford University Press.

Bond, M. H. and King, A. Y. C. (1985). Coping with the threat of Westernization in Hong Kong. *International Journal of Intercultural Relations, 9*, 351–364.

Bond, M. H. and Lee, P. W. H. (1981). Face saving in Chinese culture: A discussion and experimental study of Hong Kong students. In A. Y. C. King and R. P. L. Lee (eds), *Social life and development in Hong Kong* (pp. 288–305). Hong Kong: Chinese University Press.

Bond, M. H. and Shiu, W. Y. F. (in press). The relationship between a group's personality resources and the two dimensions of its group process. *Small Group Research.*

Bond, M. H., Leung, K. and Wan, K. C. (1982). The social impact of self-effacing attributions: The Chinese case. *Journal of Social Psychology, 118*, 157–166.

Bond, M. H., Leung, K., Wan, K. C. and Giacalone, R. (1985). How are responses to verbal insult related to cultural collectivism and power distance? *Journal of Cross-Cultural Psychology, 16*, 111–127.

Campbell, J. (1949). *The hero with a thousand faces.* New York: Meridian.

Cheung, I. W. S. (1994). 'Exploring individual differences in self-perception of personality and perceptions of sex-stereotypes'. Unpublished bachelor's thesis, Chinese University of Hong Kong.

Chinese Culture Connection (1987). Chinese values and the search for culture-free dimensions of culture. *Journal of Cross-Cultural Psychology, 18*, 143–164.

Featherman, D. L. (1993). What does society need from higher education? *Items, 47* (2/3), 38–43.

Furnham, A. and Henley, S. (1988). Lay beliefs about overcoming psychological problems. *Journal of Social and Clinical Psychology, 6*, 423–438.

Gergen, K. J. (1985). The social constructionist movement in modern psychology. *American Psychologist, 40*, 266–275.

Giles, L. (1910). *Sun Tzu on the art of war.* London: Croom Helm.

Ho, E. K. F. (1994). 'Validating the five-factor model of personality'. Unpublished bachelor's thesis, Chinese University of Hong Kong.

Hofstede, G. (1980). *Culture's consequences: International differences in work-related values.* Beverly Hills, CA: Sage.

Hookham, H. (1969). *A short history of China.* New York: New American Library.

Hu, H. C. (1944). The Chinese concepts of 'face'. *American Anthropologist, 46*, 45–64.

Hwang, K. K. (1977). The patterns of coping in a Chinese society. *Acta Psychologica Taiwanica, 19*, 61–73 (in Chinese).

Kagitbak, M. S., Church, A. T. and Akamine, T. X. (1996). Cross-cultural generalizability of personality dimensions: Relating indigenous and imported dimensions in two cultures. *Journal of Personality and Social Psychology, 70*, 99–114.

King, A. Y. C. (1991). Kwan-hsi and network building: A sociological interpretation. *Daedalus, 120*, 63–84.

Laing, R. D. (1962). Ontological insecurity. In H. M. Ruitenbeek, *Psychoanalysis and existential philosophy* (pp. 41–69). New York: E. P. Dutton.

Lau, D. C. (1989). *Tao te ching.* Hong Kong: Chinese University Press.

Lee, R. and Bond, M. H. (1996). 'Personality and roommate friendship in Chinese culture.' Manuscript submitted for publication.

Leung, K. and Bond, M. H. (1984). The impact of cultural collectivism on reward allocation. *Journal of Personality and Social Psychology, 47*, 793–804.

Luk, C. L. and Bond, M. (1992). Chinese lay beliefs about the causes and cures of psychological problems. *Journal of Social and Clinical Psychology, 11*, 140–157.

McCrae, R. R. and Costa, P. T. Jr (1985). Openness to experience. In R. Hogan and W. H. Jones (eds), *Perspectives in personality* (vol. 1, pp. 145–172). Greenwich, CT: JAI Press.

Murphy, G. (1969). Psychology in the year 2000. *American Psychologist, 24*, 523–530.

Snyder, C. R. (1994). Hope and optimism. *Encyclopedia of human behavior* (vol. 2, pp. 535–542). New York: Academic Press.

Solomon, S., Greenberg, J. and Pyszezynski, T. (1991). Terror management theory of self-esteem. In C. R. Snyder and D. Forsyth (eds), *Handbook of social and clinical psychology* (pp. 21–40). New York: Pergamon.

Spence, J. D. (1990). *The search for modern China.* New York: W. W. Norton.

Triandis, H. C. (1976). On the value of cross-cultural research in social psychology: Reactions to Faucheux's paper. *European Journal of Social Psychology, 6,* 331–341.

Yang, K. S. (1986). Chinese personality and its change. In M. H. Bond (ed.), *The psychology of the Chinese people* (pp. 106–170). Hong Kong: Oxford University Press.

Yang, K. S. and Bond, M. H. (1990). Exploring implicit personality theories with indigenous or imported constructs: The Chinese case. *Journal of Personality and Social Psychology, 58,* 1087–1095.

Yik, M. S. M. and Bond, M. H. (1993). Exploring the dimensions of Chinese person perception with indigenous and imported constructs: Creating a culturally balanced scale. *International Journal of Psychology, 28,* 75–95.

Yu, A. B. (1996). Ultimate life concerns, self, and Chinese achievement motivation. In M. H. Bond (ed.), *The handbook of Chinese psychology* (pp. 227–246). Hong Kong: Oxford University Press.

Zhang, J. X. and Bond, M. H. (1995). 'Filial piety and the Big Five measures of personality: Emics into etics?' Unpublished manuscript, Chinese University of Hong Kong.

16   The Haji Baba of Georgetown

Fathali M. Moghaddam

Where is my ruined life, and where the fame of noble deeds?
Look on my long-drawn road, and whence it came, And where it leads!

Hafiz, The Divan

As I write these words, I am sitting in a traditional Persian garden in Tehran, Iran. It is a hot summer afternoon in 1996, and I can hear the Muslim faithful being called to prayer in a tradition that is part of Persia's recent history of about 1400 years. Only a few days ago, I was sitting in Georgetown, Washington, DC, watching the Catholic faithful proceed to morning mass in the Georgetown University chapel. How did I, an Iranian Muslim, come to move to Catholic Georgetown, via England, Canada, and various other countries? In answering this question, which may seem to concern my personal life, I will also address a second one, which seems more directly to do with my academic interests: How did I, an experimentally trained social psychologist come to be a cultural researcher who now positions himself at the opposite philosophical corner from traditional social scientists? By the time the two questions have been addressed, it should be clear that, for better or for worse, there is no clear distinction between my personal and academic interests.

I see my own journey as a pilgrimage. When Muslims complete the pilgrimage to Mecca, they are given the title 'Haji'. This has traditionally been an illustrious title, because until recently, for most people, going to Mecca not only required financial sacrifices, but it was also a physically arduous and often dangerous journey. I well remember one of the servants in my great-grandfather's house near the great bazaar in Tehran gaining enormous prestige and status after completing the pilgrimage and earning the illustrious title 'Haj Agha' (Agha, meaning 'Mr'). Even his brother, who had achieved the less prized pilgrimage to Mashad, was honoured since he now has the title of 'Mash' added to his name, making him 'Mash-Mirza'. But, since I am in a bold and presumptuous mood, let me describe my journey to Georgetown in the grandest of styles. Thus, it is as the Haji-Baba of Georgetown that I address you, and relate to you my adventures which, as you will see, also involve dangers, since grappling with traditional researchers can be even more hazardous than confronting bandits on the road to Mecca!

Since modern researchers like to think of the lives of individuals as progressing in stages, let me also describe my story as involving stages. However, just as the stages concocted by Jean Piaget, Lawrence Kohlberg, Abraham Maslow, and many others, are really arbitrary and dependent on culture, rather than universal as is often claimed, so you will recognise the stages of my life story as social constructions. I might have told this story in many different ways, but what follows is the version I and our book's editor came to prefer.

EARLY LIFE IN IRAN

Among my strongest memories of life as a toddler in Tehran in the 1950s are two that are symbolically important to me. The first is of me sitting on a Persian carpet and eating pomegranates, listening to my grandfather giving advice to a group of visitors. Much later, I came to see my grandfather as a living symbol of Aristotelian wisdom. One reads in books that the Islamic world preserved and nurtured Greek philosophy, and then returned this knowledge back to the West after the 'Dark Ages' (actually, I like to think that we Persians taught the Greeks much of their philosophy in the first place). Well, it must have been through thinkers like my grandfather that this safeguarding and transferring of Greek philosophy took place. Interwoven in his religious beliefs and practices were ideals of a golden mean, of always avoiding extremes, of appreciating human conduct within the larger context, but of insisting that individuals are agentic and enjoy some measure of free will in, and hence responsibility for, their actions.

A second image I retain is of myself in a candle-lit room, surrounded by my father and a group of Dervishes. My father was university-educated and knew the modern world well enough, but like many other Eastern intellectuals he was not willing to abandon ancient traditions. The Sufi way offers a promise that individuals can achieve wisdom and enlightenment through the right kind of intellectual and spiritual training. But, above all, the Sufi way gives great importance to contemplation – an activity alien to many modern psychologists.

As part of my heritage, I retain the tradition of viewing humans as agentic beings, with the ability to achieve insight and a higher culture through correct training. Thus, I am not a relativist, in the sense that I do believe certain things have universal value.

LIFE IN AN ENGLISH BOARDING SCHOOL: NOT DARING TO ASK FOR MORE

> Tell me, now, of your own trials and troubles. And tell me truly first, for I should know, who are you, and where do you hail from, and where's your home and family? What kind of ship was yours, and what course brought you here? Who are your sailors? I don't suppose you walked here on the sea.
>
> Homer, *The Odyssey*

The trip we took in 1960 by ship, train, and bus, from Tehran, Iran, to London, England, was a colourful adventure for me and my two sisters, although it must have been more stressful for my mother as she took care of three young children in so many strange places by herself. My father had travelled ahead and was waiting for us in London. On only the second day of my stay in England, I was enrolled and started at an English school. In modern terminology, one would say I had been placed in a language immersion programme – since I knew no English. Very soon after that, my father died and I was placed in a boarding school, thus making it a total cultural immersion.

I experienced most of the things one has come through Dickensian images to associate with traditional boarding school life in England. This was before the days when caning and other such physical punishments had become illegal, and well before anything like political correctness had been dreamt up. However, getting 'six of the best' or even far more elaborate punishments was nothing compared to what I always consider the main trauma of life in England – the terrible food! When my schoolfriends and I read about Oliver Twist daring to ask for more porridge, we felt for sure he must have had better food than was available at our school. Actually, we very seldom dared to ask for more food, simply because we might have been granted our wish and have had to eat more of the same.

Despite the fact that my interpretation of the role of terrible cooking in the decline and fall of the British Empire was not received with enthusiasm by the masters, I did manage to carve out a place for myself in the school. I made it into various school sports teams, playing two seasons for the all-important rugby First XV. But whatever social success I had at school came through 'playing cricket' according to the rules. That is, I learned to recognise and to follow the English way of doing things, the local norms and rules for correct behaviour. But, more than this, through the boys in the school, I gained some insight about different life-styles around the world.

Many of the friends I made at boarding school had parents who lived outside England. They were the sons of diplomats, business people, missionaries, or families with other interests who travelled a great deal around the world. They were knowledgeable about the languages, religions, music, theatre and, in short, cultures of people in different and often exotic societies. They could relate stories about how people behave in other cultures, and implicit in such stories was how they themselves learned to adapt when they travelled to different parts of the world.

By the time I left school, I had developed a passionate interest in social life and people around the world. I satisfied this interest mostly by reading novels, but I was also a little acquainted with psychology books, and I knew I wanted to be either a psychologist or a writer. Of course, at that stage what I understood by *human* behaviour was not just the narrow band of topics explored with under-graduate students who serve as subjects in traditional psychological research.

UNIVERSITY DAYS IN ENGLAND

During my student days I used to live about eight months of the year in England and the rest of the time travelling in Iran, or in some other part of the world. This meant that each year I had an opportunity to reflect in very different non-Western contexts on the knowledge I had acquired during my academic studies. Inevitably, I experienced many situations where I had to re-evaluate what psychology offered me.

Even seemingly unimportant comments made by some psychologists led to curious bouts of re-evaluation, and underlined the cultural limitations of their psychological expertise, as well as their willingness or ability to comprehend another cultural perspective. For example, I well remember trying to explain my point of view on cognitive dissonance to a visiting professor, who responded by saying dismissively, 'Well, my grandmother could have told me that.' He undoubtedly meant to say that the comment I had made was not of value, but it was obvious he had not understood my point. Even his dismissive response showed us to be very far apart. You see, in the context of life back home in Iran, my grandmother was always someone of the highest status and wisdom. If my opinion was one that she could have expressed, then it could only have been deeply profound.

But there were instances when I felt that the central tenets of Western psychology were far more directly challenged by my experiences in Iran and some other cultures I had come to know. For example, the cognitive revolution was dominating social psychology by the 1970s, and central to this revolution were the ideas of Leon Festinger. His theory of cognitive dissonance inspired hundreds of studies and seemed to explain so much in a Western context. However, when I returned to Iran and thought about cognitive dissonance, it did not make much sense. The theory proposes that if a person holds two cognitions or a cognition and behaviour that contradict one another, then such an 'imbalance' will lead to negative experiences (e.g. anxiety), and the person will change a cognition or behaviour to make things balanced again.

Underlying the theory of cognitive dissonance is the Western ideal of rational beings whose lives are consistent, who do what they say and say what they think. I believe that when Festinger dreamt up this theory, he must have had an image of John Wayne shaking hands with his partner in Texas and saying: 'My word is my bond.'

Back in Iran, I noticed that the young were always being trained to cope with contradictions. Indeed, an inability to cope with contradictions is seen as a sign of immaturity. More generally, ideas such as 'speaking your mind', 'acting according to your beliefs', 'saying and doing' consistently in private and public, and the like, are simply not feasible in the political climate of places like Iran, before or after the Revolution.

But even in the West, I have always felt that the motivation to achieve 'balance', assumed to be central in cognitive psychology, does not reflect the realities of everyday life. People in the West do not strive to integrate and rationalise their ideas, as Festinger and others would have us believe. They are full of contradictions and unrelated and unintegrated ideas and actions. In fact, they often go out of their way to avoid integration of what is on their minds. I have now lived and researched over thirty years in various parts of Europe, Canada, and the United States, and my everyday experiences tell me that the lives of Western people are characterised by contradictions and paradoxes. Of course, they give importance to the ideal of a rationalising, consistent or balance-seeking being, and it is this ideal that monopolises cognitive psychology (Sampson, 1981).

THE REVOLUTION AND NEW WINDOWS OF OPPORTUNITY

I completed my PhD, doing traditional experimental social psychology laboratory research. Even though I have always believed that traditional social psychology is very limited and simply wrong in its basic assumptions, I felt it necessary to experience training in the traditional, so-called 'scientific' methodology (I say 'so-called' because the logico-positivistic philosophy of science underlying traditional psychology has been shown to have fundamental flaws. For an example of a study in this critical tradition, see Latour and Woolgar, 1979). My advice to students is always to get solid training in mainstream methods, because they will then be in a better position to assess such methods critically.

The revolution of 1979 in Iran seemed to present wonderful new opportunities for me to return and to contribute to the development of psychology in a Third World context. This was a thrilling period in the history of Persia: the over-throw of monarchy after 2,500 years, and the promise of a real democracy. Immediately after my return, I began teaching at Tehran University and at the National University, in an exciting atmosphere where everything good suddenly seemed possible. Hundreds of newspapers sprang up, theatre groups, poetry readings, countless political and social movements developing and expressing an amazing variety of exciting ideas . . . everything seemed to be changing. At the major universities, faculty and students looked critically at traditional disciplines, and the call went up for new directions in the social sciences, including psychology.

However, while at one level everything seemed to be changing, at other levels things seemed to be staying the same. Let me give three different examples of this contradiction, from the macro societal level to the micro interpersonal level. First, at the societal level, although the leadership had changed, in the sense that the Shah had been toppled and the monarchy ended, the style of leadership and the relationship between leaders and followers remained the same. Once again, all power was concentrated in the hands of one supremely powerful male leader, and voices of dissent were not tolerated. Second, although initially after the revolution the secret police was in a shambles, political prisoners were freed, and torture chambers were opened up to the public for inspection, the situation reverted to type after a relatively short period of time. By 1980, human rights were routinely trampled on, the secret police was as active as ever, and political prisoners were mistreated in overflowing prisons. Third, although lip service was paid to democracy, elections were far from free or open.

Within this tragic context, I looked critically at the kinds of concepts and theories offered by traditional psychology in the areas of, first, social change and, second, human rights. Once again, the cultural biases of traditional psychology became all too apparent. For example, the Harvard psychologist David McClelland (McClelland and Winter, 1969) has discussed motivation and national development, but to read McClelland is to listen to the preaching voice of America's brand of capitalism. Thus, it is to self-help, personal responsibility, and the motivation of *individuals* that McClelland looks to achieve social change and national development. If we get enough 'go-getters', in the American sense, then the economy will grow and society will change.

As regards human rights, well of course most Western psychologists do not see this as an issue in their own societies, so I could not find research of any significance directly on this topic. But the historic concern of traditional psychology with topics such as attitudes and behaviour, values, and moral development did seem to me to have a bearing on the psychology of human rights. From this traditional psychological research one could extract an ideal: the rational individual who acts according to universal principles, the thinker whose deeds follow his or her words. This was the same ideal underlying Festinger's cognitive dissonance theory. Years later, when I was working in Canada, I conducted research to demonstrate that in areas such as human rights, just as in all domains of moral thinking, behaviour is explained by ideological motives and not by so-called 'universal stages of moral development' as Kohlberg would have us believe (Moghaddam and Voksanovic, 1990).

Missing from traditional psychology was the essentially *social* nature of human life. By this I do not mean what traditional cognitive psychologists mean – I do not refer to supposed 'mechanisms' or 'cognitive processes' in the mind that are assumed to manifest themselves causally in social behaviour (as in Fiske and Taylor, 1991, and the like). It is not 'in the mind' that I look to explain social behaviour, but in the norms and rules that are embedded in social relationships and act as guides to correct behaviour for everyone who shares a culture.

Human-rights violations do not occur in Iran, or anywhere else, because people lack the 'right ideas' or attitudes or values, or any other abstract entity supposedly central to 'cognitive mechanisms'. We cannot end human-rights violations by changing isolated 'minds', any more than we can bring about social change and national development by getting individuals to 'think differently'. By studying the assumed 'cognitive processes' of individuals in isolation in laboratory contexts, traditional psychology has missed the essence of social life. To get to this essence, let me relate one small incident from life in post-revolution Iran.

During the first year of the post-revolution era, there was still some real rivalry between political factions, since no one political group had achieved a dominant position. This meant that during elections the voters enjoyed opportunities to choose between competing candidates. I went and observed what happened at more than a dozen voting stations. The scene that unfolded was remarkably similar at all the stations. Both the voters and the officials at the stations tended to break what might seem to be very simple rules required of fair and open elections. For example, either directly or indirectly, election officials tended to direct voters to cast their vote in favour of particular candidates. In some cases, they offered to fill out the voting form itself – and this happened particularly when the voter was female, or when the voter seemed to be illiterate. The voters themselves often offered each other ideas, or looked over to see how others were voting, or even bluntly told other people they had voted for the right or the wrong candidate.

Missing from this situation were the norms and rules that govern democratic elections, as well as the social skills required to recognise and follow an appropriate normative system. Voters could talk about democracy and the secret ballot in the abstract, but in practice the normative system to allow a secret ballot was not part of social relations in that context. After observing voter behaviour and then interviewing voters, I became convinced that if a traditional questionnaire method was used, then respondents would show strong support for all the usual democratic ideals (free speech, open elections, etc.), even though their actual behaviour and the behaviour of officials often contradicted such ideals.

LIFE IN THE GREAT WHITE NORTH

As we flew over Canada and approached Montreal in 1983, all I could see was expansive white surfaces. In the two years previous to this, I had been involved in United Nations projects in the Persian Gulf region, and I had been used to flying over large areas of white desert. Now, looking over the white Canadian landscape, I said to my wife that Canada must be covered with salt deserts. As soon as we stepped out from the plane in Montreal, the reality of snow and ice-covered Canada hit me. For the next six years I worked at McGill University, benefiting from the warm and highly stimulating companionship of Don Taylor and Wally Lambert.

The themes of social change and justice were still the main ones underlying my research. Canada is officially a multicultural and bilingual society. It is a land of immigrants, where people from all over the world arrive and either willingly or unwillingly experience change, in their languages, their values, their clothing, and in just about everything else. I conducted a series of empirical research studies on the integration strategies of immigrants to their new land. A major concern underlying all these studies has been the issue of how we can best manage culturally diverse societies. Should we attempt to achieve greater homogeneity by assimilating minorities, or should we encourage and support minorities to retain their heritage cultures and languages (Lambert, Moghaddam, Sorin, and Sorin, 1990; Moghaddam, 1992, 1993)?

Missing from the psychological literature on assimilation and multiculturalism are debates on the kinds of psychological characteristics citizens need to have in order to successfully achieve societies with different degrees of cultural diversity. For example, what kinds of citizens do we need in order to build and sustain a multicultural society? Such questions are seldom discussed, in part because we psychologists shy away from the issue of ideals. According to the criteria of 'science' adhered to in traditional psychology, we are supposed to be objective and 'neutral', and thus not allow ideals to 'bias' our research.

THE PhD OCTOPUS AND THE DIPLOMA DISEASE

About 2,500 years ago, a band of thinkers gathered around Plato to initiate the academic culture. This event took place in Greece, but the culture of the Academy in the most profound sense belongs to all humankind. It is the oldest democratic culture we know, and should be setting an example for all human societies.

However, the modern university has become very different from the ideal academy, where a democracy of ideas should be realised. My experiences of universities in different countries, both as a student and as a professor, bring to mind two phrases. The first is 'The diploma disease', after a book by Dore (1976), which sets out the scenario for diploma inflation. The story goes something like this: this year a high-school diploma is needed for job X, and 200 applicants show up. In order to save themselves the trouble of looking through so many applications, the employers decide to require a BA degree. After a few years, the number of applicants with BA degrees shoots up, so the employers decide to ask for an MA. Soon, hundreds of applicants with MA degrees come knocking on their doors, so they increase the requirements to a PhD. Within a matter of a few decades, a job that needed a high-school diploma now requires a PhD. The responsibilities of the job have not changed, but the requirements for the position have.

Some years ago, William James (1903) wrote about the terrifying 'PhD octopus' which is spreading its tentacles everywhere, even when it is not needed. Associated with this is increasing professionalism at universities. An outcome of these trends is that the university is no longer a democracy of ideas, because its primary focus is on narrow professional interests, rather than on broad but fundamental academic questions. I felt this shortcoming keenly during my student days in England, but finally got round to writing about it in *The specialized society* (Moghaddam, 1997) twenty years later.

The limitations of traditional academic psychology have to be assessed in the context of the failure of modern universities more generally. Modern universities are being managed more and more like businesses, using the same criteria as the business world. The two most important of such criteria are technical efficiency and profitability, both of which have a profound impact on traditional psychology. Traditional psychology is training technically efficient experts who are extremely successful at many types of measurement tasks, but most of the time they make invalid assumptions about what they are measuring. In other words, they have increased reliability in measurement, but lost sight of validity.

Traditional cross-cultural psychology is no better than traditional psychology proper. Instead of recognising that so-called 'cognitive processes' or 'mechanisms' are themselves the products of culture, traditional cross-cultural psychologists have bought into the assumptions of the cognitive revolution.

LOOKING TO THE FUTURE

Modern psychology, like most of modern academia, is to a large extent self-contained and self-regulating. Most psychologists do not have to get anything right according to any criteria of an external world in order to survive, they need only publish in their own journals. Just as societies support artists and writers, so they support psychologists. However, does this current support mean that the traditional psychology of today will be with us in a hundred years? I believe very little of it will survive – just as, for example, very little of nineteenth-century psychology has survived. This is because psychology is a normative science, and its findings are only 'lasting' and 'universal' in so far as norms are lasting and universal.

In one sense, then, I am very optimistic about a cultural psychology that focuses on human behaviour as it is patterned by normative systems. Some normative systems may be universal, in that they are common to many societies and across historical periods. However, normative systems are embedded in social relationships – not in isolated minds. Finally, I remain optimistic because I feel rooted in a Persian culture that spans thousands of years, and when thinking about progress in the future, the future for me is in terms of thousands of years.

And what of traditional psychology: can we be optimistic about its future? I believe we can in terms of the techniques it offers us, as long as we interpret our results within a normative rather than a causal model. As I have argued elsewhere (Moghaddam and Harré, 1992), the laboratory experiment can be very useful, particularly when considered as a piece of scripted drama, which has one or a few parts incomplete. Respondents step on to the stage and play their unscripted parts according to the cultural norms and rules they judge to be appropriate for the situation. Respondents can, and sometimes do, simply refuse to play their parts. Like all other researchers, I have conducted laboratory experiments where respondents simply walk out. But whether they stay to play the part or decide to exit from the play, their behaviour is intentional and patterned by normative systems – not 'caused by independent variables'. If we believe in human agency, then the causal model central to traditional psychology is contradictory.

And here I think we should turn back to the rationalising, ideal being, the ghost in the cognitive machine of traditional psychology. If one wanted to find definitive proof that Western societies are characterised by contradictions and paradoxes, we need only look to traditional psychology with its multitudes of contradictions and paradoxes. On the one hand, traditional psychology is the study of what Edward Sampson (1977) has referred to as 'self-contained individuals', the independent persons who occupy psychology laboratories. On the other hand, traditional psychology leaves no room for independence, since it assumes cause–effect (independent variable–dependent variable) relations. Thus, we are left with 'independence' without agency, and 'individualism' without choice.

If only cross-cultural researchers would not follow the same path (Moghaddam, 1998). Instead, my experience at the interface of many cultures leads me to propose the following. Students of human behaviour should, first, adopt a normative rather than causal model of human behaviour. The patterns we find in human behaviour are not indicative of 'causes', but indicative of normative systems that most people follow much of the time (see Robinson, 1996, ch. 6). Second, students should closely study social history, and in this way achieve a better understanding of the variations in social behaviour we humans have already experienced. A third objective should be to consider seriously the psychological characteristics citizens require in order to make workable different political systems. For example, what kinds of psychological characteristics are essential for citizens attempting to build and to *sustain* a democracy? By addressing this question, we shall inevitably enter the moral domain, and this gets me to my final suggestion: we must try to grow out of our current role as 'experts' (a more appropriate term might be *fachidiot*) to become academics in the tradition established so long ago by the Greeks (who, after all, learned so much from the Egyptians and, of course, from us Persians!).

REFERENCES

Dore, R. P. (1976). *The diploma disease: Education, qualifications, and development.* London: Allen & Unwin.

Fiske, S. T. and Taylor, S. E. (1991). *Social cognition* (2nd edn). New York: McGraw-Hill.

James, W. (1903). The PhD octopus. *Harvard Monthly, XXXVI,* 1–9.

Lambert, W. E., Moghaddam, F. M., Sorin, J. and Sorin, S. (1990). Assimilation versus multiculturalism: Views from a community in France. *Sociological Review, 5,* 387–411.

Latour, B. and Woolgar, S. (1979). *Laboratory life: A social construction of scientific facts.* Beverly Hills, CA: Sage.

McClelland, D. C. and Winter, D. G. (1969). *Motivating economic achievement.* Glencoe, IL: Free Press.

Moghaddam, F. M. (1987). Psychology in the Three Worlds: As reflected by the crisis in social psychology and the move toward indigenous Third World psychology. *American Psychologist, 42,* 912–920.

Moghaddam, F. M. (1990). Modulative and generative orientations in psychology: Implications for psychology in the Three Worlds. *Journal of Social Issues, 46,* 21–41.

Moghaddam, F. M. (1992). Assimilation et multiculturalisme: Le cas des minorites au Québec. *Revue québecoise de psychologie, 13,* 140–157.

Moghaddam, F. M. (1993). Managing cultural diversity: North American experiences and suggestions for the German unification process. *International Journal of Psychology, 28,* 727–741.

Moghaddam, F. M. (1997). *The specialized society: The plight of the individual in an age of individualism.* Westport, CT: Praeger.

Moghaddam, F. M. (1998). *Social psychology: Exploring universals across cultures.* New York: Freeman.

Moghaddam, F. M. and Harré, R. (1992). Rethinking the laboratory experiment. *American Behavioral Scientist, 36,* 22–38.

Moghaddam, F. M. and Harré, R. (1995). But is it science? *World Psychology, 1,* 47–78.

Moghaddam, F. M. and Studer, C. (in press). Cross-cultural psychology: The frustrated gadfly's promises, potentialities, and failures. In D. Fox and I. Prilleltensky (eds), *Critical psychology: An introduction.* Thousand Oaks, CA: Sage.

Moghaddam, F. M. and Voksanovic, V. (1990). Attitudes and behavior toward human rights across different contexts: The role of right-wing authoritarianism, political ideology, and religiosity. *International Journal of Psychology, 25,* 455–474.

Moghaddam, F. M., Stolkin, A. and Hutcheson, L. (in press). A generalized personal/group discrepancy. *Personality and Social Psychology Bulletin.*

Moghaddam, F. M., Taylor, D. M. and Wright, S. C. (1993). *Social psychology in cross-cultural perspective.* New York: Freeman.

Robinson, D. N. (1996). *Wild beasts and idle humours: The insanity defense from antiquity to the present*. Cambridge, MA: Harvard University Press.

Sampson, E. E. (1977). Psychology and the American ideal. *Journal of Personality and Social Psychology, 35*, 767–782.

Sampson, E. E. (1981). Cognitive psychology as ideology. *American Psychologist, 36*, 730–743.

17 An intercultural journey

The four seasons

Stella Ting-Toomey

INTRODUCTION

Summer in Iowa City is always languidly hot. I spent five years there. I can still remember the small airport in Cedar Rapids, Iowa. I can still remember the long ride to Iowa City in the summer of 1972 – thinking all the way I had been kidnapped into 'The Land of Corn'.

That was the beginning of my journey to a 'foreign land'. From Hong Kong to Iowa City, from Iowa City to Seattle, then on to New Brunswick, NJ, Tempe, AZ, and Fullerton, CA – I have now lived in the USA for almost twenty-five years. The USA is a beautiful land – from Bryce Canyon to the Shenandoah Range – it is a land of spectacular contrasts and textures. It is also a land full of promises, hopes, and disillusionments.

This chapter chronicles my intercultural journey on the US canvas. The chapter is organised along Vivaldi's *The Four Seasons*: (1) spring – the journey of searching; (2) summer – the journey of researching; (3) autumn – the journey of integrating; (4) winter – the journey of simplifying.

SPRING SEASON: THE JOURNEY OF SEARCHING

Overture to spring

Three American universities accepted my undergraduate applications in the spring of 1972 – one in Hawaii, one in Ohio, and one in Iowa. Since I had no clue as to how one university differed from another, I wrote down the names of the universities on three pieces of paper and asked my then nine-year-old brother, Victor, to pick one with his eyes closed. He picked Iowa. I decided then that fate called me to the University of Iowa. I packed. I came. I have lived in the 'Golden Mountain'[1] ever since.

I spent approximately five years in Iowa City, doing my undergraduate and master's work there. My undergraduate work was in broadcasting and TV production. My master's degree work was in mass communication theory. I was devoted to pursuing my degree. More importantly, I enjoyed my work. I had fun putting TV shows together – scripting, music, lights, camera angles, editing, etc. I relished the intensity of the work and the creative aspects of the process.

In 1972, Iowa City was an all-white, campus town. The University was huge – spread out and cut off by a river running through it. I was one of the first group of international students being admitted to the University from Asia. Life was composed of waves of culture shock in my first few months there. From overdressing (I quickly changed my daily skirts to jeans to avoid the question: 'Are you going to a wedding today?') to hyper-apprehension (e.g. the constant fear of being called upon to answer questions in the 'small power distance' classroom atmosphere). I experienced intense homesickness at times. The months flew by quickly.

I definitely felt 'different' in all of my years in Iowa City. There were not many Asians, let alone Chinese, in town. There was one small Chinese grocery store that opened 'sometimes'. There were not many other 'minorities' around either. 'Being different', however, had a carefree sense to it. It was a difference without calculation. I encountered constant questions such as: 'Where are you from?' 'Why did you pick U. of Iowa?' 'Where did you learn your British-accented English?' I answered each question amiably. The questions were innocent questions; my answers were innocent answers. My role was that of a Hong Kong international student.

After receiving my bachelor's degree in spring 1975, I went home. However, I soon returned to the Iowa campus for two reasons. I actually missed the learning part of a university setting, and I was 'in love'. I moved on to obtain my master's degree in mass communication theory in the winter of 1976. I was married on 15 January 1977 to Charles Toomey – an Irish American. After the wedding, we packed our car and drove north-west. I had sent out one doctoral application to the mass communication programme at the University of Washington. We were young. We were on an adventure. We thought our destiny awaited us in the Northwest.

The spring season

The trees at the University of Washington (UW) campus were blooming with pink buds. The two university libraries looked intimidating and inviting at the same time. The Red Square was crowded with students, but I was feeling immensely solitary. In my hand was a rejection letter from the UW School of Communication. The letter was a standard letter of regret because the selection process was competitive, etc., etc. I was crushed. I did not expect a rejection letter because of my reasonable GPA in the master programme and also the four glowing letters from my professors at the University of Iowa.

Later on, I did uncover the reasons for my admission rejection. The reasons were due partly to my low scores on the Miller Analogy Test (apparently, not knowing Waterford was analogous to crystal was a critical admission criterion) and partly because an international Asian student had not been able to complete his doctoral programme 'on time', therefore casting doubt on the whole of Asia. At that juncture, my pride and 'face' were wounded. I thought if they did not want me, I did not want them either. I was ready to quit school for good.

However, three precious people turned my fate around. They are: Dr Samuel Becker, Mae Bell, and my husband. It was Dr Samuel Becker from the University of Iowa who had offered me initial motivation and support to apply for the UW mass communication programme. He was the first one I turned to during my rejection shock. He wrote back a letter immediately. I still, to this day, remember his wise words: 'Stella, if this rejection is the worst thing that ever happened to your life, consider yourself having a very good life.' He also gave me advice to seek out his former advisee, Dr Mae Bell, in the UW Department of Speech Communication. He suggested that with my theoretical bent, the speech communication programme might be, after all, a better choice.

It was Mae's soothing Texan style and warmth that helped me through the first rainy spring in Seattle. Additionally, it was my husband who encouraged me not to accept failure and to 'take charge' of my fate (a relatively new cultural concept to me) that started me on the East–West trail. I submitted my application to the UW Department of Speech Communication in the spring of 1977. My application was reviewed and accepted. I was admitted to the doctoral programme in the autumn.

The doctoral programme was a roller-coaster time of learning. Just as you thought that you had almost 'got it', the roller coaster started again. It was also a transitional time for my identity – from that of an international student to that of a US 'permanent' resident. At school, I had to make up some courses in the 'interpersonal' and 'rhetorical' areas since my background was in mass communication. I was also learning how to teach.

The defining moment for me was walking as a teacher into class for the first time and feeling the silent stares of my forty American students. Being a highly introverted person, I remember wishing I could dissolve into the walls and become invisible for good. Thousands of questions rushed through my mind: Would my voice pop out from my scorched mouth? Would I be really able to teach the students something? Would they be willing to learn from me – an Asian graduate student in interpersonal communication?

During this period, besides taking classes and teaching, I also held several part-time jobs. I worked at various times for a community development programme, a communication consulting team, a job placement department, and a publishing office. In each job I learned something valuable – especially from the people I met along the way. While Dr Mae Bell served as my academic mentor and adviser, I met many of my informal mentors (via their ways of being) outside the academic setting. However, it was Mae who sustained me in the programme for the entire four years.

I remember one incident, in particular, in which Mae's support was critical in encouraging me to move on. The incident was an exchange between myself and a professor when he explained why I did not receive a full-year teaching assistantship like the rest of the TAs. The exchange went something like this: 'Stella, it's not that you're not good. It's just that life is like a horse race. Some horses get the first prize, and others are runner-ups . . . With your accent, it's just very difficult for you to make it to the first place . . . What I'm trying to say is . . .' My heart sank upon hearing those words. At that moment, I plunged into doubt about whether I belonged to this very Americanised 'speech' communication discipline. It was Mae's comforting words and academic faith in me that held me together in those days. It was also what my husband said to me that echoes still: 'Stella, you should go back and tell your professor, what happens in a real horse race is that most people bet on the wrong horse – they have chosen poorly.'

In searching my way through the doctoral programme, I was entranced by the learning process. I found the subject matters (e.g. interpersonal theory, rhetorical theory) perplexing and absorbing. Perplexing – because I could not relate to the many Western concepts (such as self-disclosure, constructive conflict, Aristotelian ethos) from an Asian point of reference. I studied and researched them from a distance. Absorbing – because I was learning a different way of thinking. It was a very Western, linear-logic mode of thinking that was in a constant clash with my Eastern, spiral-logic mode of experiencing.

I also did many independent study readings in the 'emerging' area of intercultural communication. Dr Gerry Philipsen's courses on ethnography of communication served as an inspiration for my budding interest. Additionally, Dr Robert Arundale's courses on language and communication paved the way for my first convention paper: 'Gossip as a communication construct' (as a counterpoint to the ideology of self-disclosure). By his concentrated immersion in scholarly ideas, he quietly sowed the motivational seed of my desire to be an academician.

Attending my first convention was a stimulating event that I can still vividly recall. Many professors wrote to me afterwards to request the 'gossip' paper along with some very encouraging comments on my first convention presentation. As a novice in the field, every kind word and every letter meant something to me. I treasured them appreciatively. During that time, a research paper I did on 'ethnic identity' (Ting-Toomey, 1981) was also accepted for publication in the *International Journal of Intercultural Relations*. I was slowly getting 'hooked' on the academic life. Walking down the aisles of the library and finding a fresh idea that inspired my dissertation was what I considered a 'fun' time on a Saturday afternoon.

While the paper work for my identity change process went quickly (i.e. from an international student to that of a US resident), the affective metamorphosis was incremental. Unlike Iowa City, the UW University District, in the late 1970s, did have a mix of white students, Asian students, and some black students. The interesting thing was that, despite this diversity, I encountered more racist remarks and episodes (especially directed at me or to my husband such as 'I heard you are married to a Chink' – and then demonstrating with a 'slant eye' gesture) than in my four years in Iowa City. I guess the concepts of 'majority' and 'minority' can only be formed, and intergroup consciousness can only be developed, when there is a critical mass of people in different niches. In such an intergroup environment, the awareness of scarce resources ascends steeply. During this stage, I was very conscious of my being 'different' – with a burden. I felt that my voice was consistently muffled when I tried to explain my 'place' in this adopted homeland.

No ethnic label – be it 'Chinese American' or 'American Chinese' – could accurately capture my sense of 'in-betweenness'. While my Chinese, collectivistic identity was strong, I had to learn to survive in an American, individualistic environment. The environment was competitive. The pressure to 'prove oneself' was intense. The dualistic tugs-and-pulls of values asserted tremendous strain on both my 'being' and my 'becoming'. The constant questioning of: 'Where did you come from?' 'Do you like being here?' 'Don't you miss your home?' accentuated my sense of being 'not at home'. It made me long for a 'home' to settle in and an address to claim as my own.

Under the patient guidance, expert advice, and unconditional support of Mae, I completed my PhD degree in August 1981 in the area of marital conflict negotiation. I received two job offers at that point. I decided to go for a diametrically opposite end of the USA – Rutgers University in New Brunswick, New Jersey. I had never lived on the East Coast, and I looked forward to the Atlantic Ocean experience.

SUMMER SEASON: THE JOURNEY OF RESEARCHING

Overture to summer

It was hot and humid when I entered the Rutgers campus in summer 1981. The department had hired several new assistant professors, such as Lea Stewart and Peter Ehrenhaus. Bill Gudykunst was already there. The atmosphere was 'fresh'. The work was competitive. Since Rutgers was a research institution, our mandate was clear: 'Publish or perish'. The fact that no one had received tenure prior to the ten years of our arrival instilled in us a strong sense of urgency and fear. It was work seven days a week – researching and then teaching. My typical day started from 6 a.m. and ended at 11 p.m. when my husband came and picked me up after his evening work.

The summer season

The Rutgers years went by quickly. I had a very supportive chair, Dr Brent Ruben. His only advice to me was a constant 'slow down and don't work so hard – or else you'll experience burnout too soon'. My colleagues were fun to be around. We were supportive of each other's work. We also realised that the 'tenure clock' ticked faster than we could run. Beyond our concerns for the 'sink or sail' idea of tenure, I believe that secretly we all held some passion or obsession for our own work.

During this East Coast sojourn, I continued to encounter racial epithets (such as 'Jap! Go back to your own country!' or 'Kungfu mama! Go back to Chinatown!') directed at me, especially on off-campus streets. While those remarks typically produced a humiliating shock and a numbing effect thereafter, the impact was shorter. The rebound was faster. I guess the years (by that time I had lived in the USA for ten years) of living the 'American Dream' made me realise that dreams also include nightmares and disillusionments. My ethnic identity was 'hardened' – you learned to grow a shell to protect yourself. More importantly, my 'professional identity' superseded any of my other identities.

Life was work, and work was life in the Rutgers years. I worked on pushing my dissertation publications out (Ting-Toomey, 1983a, 1983b) and revising other related articles (Ting-Toomey, 1984a, 1984b). I was also ready for a change of research direction. I started to reflect more deeply on the reasons why I could not relate to the volumes of interpersonal conflict literature that I had reviewed. My thinking became clearer when I went on a junior sabbatical leave to Fukui University in Japan.

There I was, alone again (my husband was working back home) in Fukui City on a Rutgers–Fukui faculty exchange mission for a semester. I did not speak Japanese and I did not know a soul at Fukui University. Flashbacks of my first Cedar Rapids, Iowa, experience came back to me instantly. Only this time, I was really very 'stuck' since I did not speak the language. Fortunately, since I could decode the written Kanji, I was able to semi-guess my way through a restaurant menu or have a halting, 'written' conversation with my Japanese colleagues. The understated atmosphere of a Japanese small town, the politeness rituals that surrounded me in everyday life made me realise how 'Western' I had become. At the same time, the experience also made me aware of how 'Eastern' I still remained. My core identity was 'in sync' with the rhythms that hummed gracefully around me.

In order to learn a little bit more about the Japanese culture in the short time available, I tried to participate in many of the Fukui cultural activities (such as paper-making, tea ceremony, etc.). While I had read many books about Japanese culture, I believe my true learning took place while I immersed myself in the artwork of the culture. Additionally, conversations with the locals, in this case especially with the help of good, seasonal *sake*, helped me tremendously in understanding the neighbourhood cultural scene. I also did some formal interviews with insiders and outsiders of the Japanese culture (Ting-Toomey, 1984c; Ting-Toomey, 1986a).

During my time in Japan, I did several guest lectures and also collected several data sets for a cross-cultural project on interpersonal relationships (Ting-Toomey, 1988a; Ting-Toomey and Gao, 1988). I was also receiving and reading many speech communication journals from the USA. At that point, my discontent at not being able to relate to the articles grew even stronger. I came to the conclusion that each of us can only write and experience through our own cultural lens. Both insiders and outsiders, however, can benefit from the others' vantage point by sharing their different sets of cultural vision. The sorcerer's key is that, as the writing gets more personal, the resonance becomes more universal. It was during this time that I wrote my piece on: 'Toward a theory of conflict and culture' (Ting-Toomey, 1985), which subsequently formed the basis of my next piece: 'Intercultural conflict styles: a face-negotiation theory' (Ting-Toomey, 1988b).

Both pieces appeared to appeal to a wide range of audiences from different cultures. The essays were cited in many subsequent textbooks and research articles. In both manuscripts, I drew from my own cultural and personal experiences in framing the core ideas of the chapters. In the quietness of my Fukui academic experience, I listened more closely to what my heart was saying concerning culture and facework issues rather than turning to external sources. I then framed the ideas in vocabularies that appeared to captivate some of the readers' imagination in different cultures. In both essays, I pushed for a more Eastern way of approaching interpersonal conflict. My own Chinese upbringing on 'face' (with my mother on 'social face' and my father on 'universal face') came to light through the two essays. I believe the immersion of my Fukui experience (albeit for a very short time) also brought out the more 'Eastern' side of me.

Ten years after the 'face theory' chapter (Ting-Toomey, 1988b), I still believe in the basic premise of the theory: people in all cultures have the concept of 'face', however, how they interpret the meaning of 'face' and how they enact facework are influenced by their cultural values and norms (Ting-Toomey, 1994a). The Western concepts of direct confrontation, assertiveness, and 'look people in the eye' conflict approaches may work well in Western cultures, but they may have disastrous effects in Eastern, Asian cultures.

Drawing from my own academic experience in faculty meetings, for example, I observed the great cultural chasm that exists between the East and the West. While logical persuasions and debates were common affairs in faculty meetings in the USA, the blunt 'no' and 'raising of voices' still took me some time to adjust to. Another fascinating aspect was the insistence of faculty to be viewed as the peers of their chair or dean. It appeared that while US culture tends to promote self-directed facework effectiveness, many of the Asian cultures tend to promote mutual-oriented facework appropriateness in accordance to the 'large power distance' dimension.

Furthermore, the 'small power distance' orientations of American students to their professors – from challenging their grading competence to filing grievances and complaints all the way to the higher-ups – were quite astounding and eye-opening to witness. Piecing the different parts of the American facework puzzles together, I learned that American 'face' is fairly 'I-oriented' in its 'face-saving' orientation. In contrast, as an Asian I had been conditioned early in my cultural life to 'save mutual face', to 'protect the other's face', and to 'give and honour face' in accordance to hierarchical status and role position (Ting-Toomey, 1988b). In my early childhood years, I learned the platinum rule of never embarrassing or insulting someone in public, to the degree that she or he has no room to '*hang* her or his face'. I believe my own traditional Chinese upbringing and my years of contrastive sojourning experience in America set the stage for my academic pursuit of intercultural facework.

On the universal level, 'face' is a metaphor for the net concept of 'identity respect'. *Face* is an intoxicating metaphor that connects identity, communication, and social life. People in all cultures can relate and resonate to the 'identity respect' phenomenon. People in all cultures experience blushing, embarrassment, pride, shame, dignity, honour, and dishonour. However, how we convey that sense of respect – from self-respect to other-respect issues via communication (e.g.

utilising different requests, conflicts, apologies, to diplomacy strategies, etc.) – differs from one culture to the next. While the 'I-identity' cultures would prefer the more direct facework approach in dealing with conflict, the 'we-identity' cultures would prefer the more indirect/smoothing facework approach in managing conflict (Cocroft and Ting-Toomey, 1995; Ting-Toomey, 1994a; Ting-Toomey, Gao, Trubisky, Yang, Kim, Lin and Nishida, 1991; Trubisky, Ting-Toomey and Lin, 1991).

Furthermore, culture is a paradoxical process. For example, the more collectivistic a culture, the more people may yearn for an alternative viewfinder such as a quiet space in a Japanese rock garden, a zen temple, etc. The more individualistic a culture, the more people may desire communal rituals such as a football game, or an intense relational connection (Ting-Toomey, 1994b). Culture is, in essence, logically paradoxical – intricately simple, and simply intricate. While it is easy for people to master the 'surface level' culture, the 'core level' culture takes the heart to experience.

It was difficult to say *sayonara* to my Fukui experience. I was distanced from my daily routines at Rutgers. I had a 'quiet space' with no clutter. The colleagues I met in Japan were gracious and courteous. But it was time to go 'home'. When I thought of 'home' at that point, I did look in a Western direction. I visited my parents in Hong Kong before I returned. I also realised that my birthplace, Hong Kong, would always tug at my heart with a twinkle.

In the autumn of 1985, I gave birth to our son Adrian Roland Toomey. He was born a feisty 9 lb 14 oz kid. He also has a Chinese name (Ting Yu Chuan – meaning 'abundant harvest') given by my father. I think it is only through the lens of being a mother that I could not see his skin colour, but I could see transparently into his heart. It is only through the lenses of my friends or strangers that I understand with each developmental stage whether my son now 'looks more Chinese' or 'looks more American'. It is interesting to note that what being an 'American' means to most 'multicultural' Americans still connotes 'whiteness'.

The summer season: an epilogue

Finally, in the summer of 1986, I put together my tenure file for 'promotion with tenure' from Assistant Professor to Associate Professor. We all had truckloads of files on 'research, teaching, and service.' We also joked with each other that we should all weigh our files and the person with the heaviest files should be declared the 'winner'. Many forests have disappeared because of xeroxed tenure packets in the USA.

In spring 1987, while I was awaiting news about my application for tenure, I also applied for a job at Arizona State University (ASU). After six years on the East Coast, and after one particular snowstorm, I decided it would be nice to move to the West for some warm weather. Arizona had an opening in intercultural communication, and my former colleague, Bill Gudykunst, was there developing a doctoral programme with a strong emphasis on intercultural communication. I thought I should give it a try. I interviewed and I got the ASU job offer.

I turned to the dean at Rutgers and asked for an early tenure decision before I made my final decision. He came back with the wonderful news that I would be promoted to Associate Professor with tenure at Rutgers. He also promised to 'plant palm trees' in my backyard if I decided to stay! ASU also offered me the position of Associate Professor with tenure. With two sets of good news, and after consulting my husband and my former adviser, Dr Mae Bell, the family decided to go West for a new adventure. My husband was ready to try out south-western cuisine (searching out the world's street cuisine is my husband's favourite hobby).

Getting ready for our south-west move, we packed everything in our car trunk and under the car seats. We abandoned or gave away most of the house junk and, with our toddler, we drove cross-country to Arizona. When we finally settled in Mesa, Arizona, it was autumn 1987. Just in time to celebrate Adrian's second birthday.

AUTUMN SEASON: THE JOURNEY OF INTEGRATING

Overture to autumn

There are no four seasons in the south-west. In Tempe, Arizona, the weather varies from hot, to very hot, to extremely hot. It was nice to be a colleague again with Bill Gudykunst. Bill has, over the years, served as a thoughtful reviewer of my intercultural work. He gives honest feedback efficiently and responsively. He cares deeply about the intercultural field. He also shares resources generously. We had overlapped as colleagues for one year at Rutgers. We were also working on an intercultural book together (Gudykunst and Ting-Toomey, 1988). The graduate students at ASU were a stimulation. They were inquisitive and they were supportive of each other.

The teaching load in the department was 2–2 (meaning two classes in the autumn, and two in the spring semester). The main mission of the university was research. Thus, again, teaching took a back seat. Graduate teaching, however, was deemed more important than undergraduate instruction. Graduate seminars were small and the graduate students appeared eager to learn. As an adviser to many of the thesis projects, my baseline expectation of my own advisees was that they felt 'passionate' about their thesis topic and that they *cared*!

The doctoral programme received initial approval during my second year at ASU. Several master's students stayed on and entered as the first cohorts in the newly developed communication PhD programme at ASU in the fall of 1988. The fact that the doctoral programme was in its developmental stage created both exciting momenta and tensions in the department. Different faculty members had different visions of what this ideal PhD programme should look like. Every bylaw or document relating to the PhD programme involved long faculty meetings, 'face-threatening' debates and votes, and 'behind the scenes' lobbying. I believe the tensions, in the end, took a heavy toll on both graduate students and faculty members. Somehow, the 'common ground' was filled with landmines and tremblers. The 115-degree 'heat' of the south-west finally got to me.

I went for an interview at California State University–Fullerton. The weather was cooler. The atmosphere was more vibrant. I could see multicoloured faces in the classrooms. I felt more at ease with palm trees there. Faculty actually mentioned the importance of 'teaching' and 'learning' beyond 'research'. I said goodbye with mixed emotions to many of the ASU graduate students whom I had befriended. In autumn 1989, I started my first semester at California State University–Fullerton. I have stayed on ever since.

The autumn season

It is at California State University–Fullerton (CSUF) that I learned to become a better teacher. The teaching load is heavy – it is a 4–4 teaching system (meaning four classes in autumn, and four in spring). Between teaching preps, grading, advising undergraduate and graduate students, plus professional service, time evaporates. Then there is always the research and writing at midnight and early mornings when the house is still. I enjoy writing, especially when I can find that block of time to write with no interruptions. Typically, an idea will first ferment or 'brew' in my mind for two to three months (or two to three years), I next visualise an outline, and then I sit down and write. When I write, I tend to block off everything else around me. Everything else becomes peripheral. I am not a fast writer. I am, however, an obsessive writer who values redrafting and rewriting.

Compared to my previous academic experience, the CSUF speech communication department gave me the opportunity to integrate both the research and teaching aspects of my profession. I have finally grasped the meaning of 'professing'. I have learned to really 'listen' to my students – to know where they are coming from. I have learned to 'listen' to myself and to know where I stand in relation to the students' enquiry process. I have also learned to set parameters, and at the same time encourage the students to bring out their own 'voices' in the learning process.

It takes time to learn to be a good teacher. It takes a supportive atmosphere to learn to teach well. In my previous two institutions, while teaching was recognised as important, no one actually discussed teaching. We all knew research reigned supreme over teaching. However, at CSUF, 'teaching' and 'learning' are part of everyday vocabularies, although I must quickly add that the rewards of good teaching continue to be intrinsic rather than extrinsic. Good teaching is difficult to 'measure' or 'quantify'; so is good research. However, higher education in the USA often uses the criterion of the number of publications to measure research output or productivity. An 'illusory correlation' principle is then applied to equate 'productivity' with 'quality'. If quality research is difficult to conceptualise, then quality teaching is that much harder to operationalise. I do, however, cherish students' feedback in my teaching evaluations and the many special notes and letters (especially from off-campus workshop participants) that have come my way throughout the years.

I have worked hard at my teaching. I enjoy experimenting with different teaching styles and methods. I can now teach a 125-student class without blushing, and without hoping that I will 'dissolve into the walls'. I actually thrive in the teaching–learning interactive environment. I derive joy as I witness the 'learning to learn' process being discovered by the students themselves. I marvel at how the process of education can transform lives (not many, but a few are a good start). I approach teaching with a playfully serious mindset. For the most part, I am able to teach what I enjoy teaching: intercultural communication, intercultural training, conflict management, and intercultural theory.

The fact that I have been invited to conduct more teacher training workshops on intercultural communication also propels me to hone my skills as a teacher. I feel that I should 'walk the walk' to become credible in front of other teachers. Additionally, given the changing demographics within my own classrooms (with 22 per cent Asian, 18 per cent Latino, 3 per cent African, 1 per cent Native American students, 44 per cent European American students, 4 per cent international students, and 8 per cent 'unknown'), I have constantly to modify teaching methods to address their diverse learning needs. CSUF is, indeed, an ideal ground for teaching and learning the concept of 'diversity.' Additionally, I have also been invited to do more corporate training in the area of intercultural workplace communication. Doing corporate training, walking into a roomful of adult learners, makes me realise that I have come a long way from my first year of teaching as a graduate student. I can now draw out the participants' viewpoints with ease – be it a roomful of managers or of administrators. I can bring in theories and mix them with practical applications. I feel very 'at home' in a classroom setting.

In terms of my research and writing I have closely merged my two areas of research interest: ethnic identity and interpersonal conflict. I continue my 'obsession' with intercultural facework as it relates to either the identity issue (Ting-Toomey, 1986b, 1989a, 1989b, 1993, 1996; Ting-Toomey and Chung, 1996; Ting-Toomey and Korzenny, 1989, 1991) or the conflict issue (Ting-Toomey, 1994b, 1994c, 1997) or both (Ting-Toomey, 1986c; Ting-Toomey and Cole, 1990; Ting-Toomey *et al.*, 1991, 1994). As a full Professor (I was promoted to full Professorship in the autumn of 1992), I have experienced more 'freedom' now to write, to research, and to 'profess'. I can pick and choose my projects. I especially enjoy conducting research projects with graduate students, then letting them 'shine' in front of the audience, while I can sit back and relax at a conference. The autumn season is, indeed, for me, a journey of coming together – an integration of the different aspects of my professional self.

In terms of my ethnic identity transformation process, it is still not very easy for me to answer the question, 'Where are you from?' I am uncertain whether I should answer California, Arizona, New Jersey, Washington, Iowa, Hong Kong, or finally, China. Lately, I catch myself muttering the word, 'California'. To be a 'Californian' is still a long way to naming myself as an 'American'. However, to be able to reach this 're-inventing' stage of one's identity is, I suppose, another form of creative play in the journey of one's life.

WINTER SEASON: THE JOURNEY OF SIMPLIFYING

The winter season

As I see my professional journey passaging between the autumn and the winter seasons, I would like to use the winter season as a reflective period. I would like to answer briefly the three most common questions that people ask me in many of my off-campus workshops. These three questions, especially coming from 'fresh' Assistant Professors or graduate students, are: Is it worth 'it'? How do you find time to write, teach, and do everything else? What do you want to work on next?

To the 'is it worth it?' question, my answer is an affirmative 'yes' – especially if you enjoy 'freedom' of movement (i.e. you can go into your office at 10 a.m. and exit at 11.30 p.m. with no supervisory interference), you value solitude, you like to 'play' with ideas, you like to write, and you like to 'perform'. Academic life is, basically, a very solitary life. In the end, when you write your journal article or chapter, it is you and the computer, alone with your 'playful' ideas.

My added advice is, as you 'play', you need to assert tremendous self-discipline to 'bracket' the ideas and bring them to fruition. Imagination and discipline are both keys to a creative, composed life. You also need to 'love' to write. Writing constitutes a major part of the academic life. You have to learn to write and write well. You also need to learn to 'perform'. It takes more energy for an introvert to 'perform' in a classroom than for an extrovert. I believe, however, that I have learned to perform and, at the same time, stayed true to my own personality. My simple advice for many entry graduate students is: Do it for the love of it. Do not do it for any other reasons. The reward is intrinsic; the process is a long-term, spiralling journey.

In answering the second question, 'How do you find time to write, teach, and do everything else?', my answer is: 'With great difficulty and not a lot of sleep.' I am still searching for balance in how to *simplify* my life. My family and my work are both central to me. But time is a limited resource and something has to give. I am fortunate enough to have a supportive husband who takes care of many household needs. Additionally, I am blessed with a wonderful son who seems to be 'born happy', a content kid with harmonious East–West attributes. He even takes comments like, 'You don't look like a "banana" [meaning yellow *outside*, white *inside*] – you look like an "egg"!' (meaning white *outside*, yellow *within*) in his stride, while I cringe. Beyond family, teaching, and researching, I do not engage in many extra activities. I live simply – walking between home and work, and home. Once or twice a year, the entire family travels somewhere – to a new place we have not visited before. We also travel simply.

As for the question, 'What do you want to work on next?', I am interested in applying creative (or 'alternative') methods of teaching and training in intercultural communication. I am especially intrigued about using artwork and other methods in invoking the affective process of intercultural learning. I am also trying to develop more training materials on intercultural facework negotiation. Finally,

I would like to devote more time to researching identity change and the process of intercultural learning.

The winter season: finale

As I close this section on the winter season and as I re-read the chapter, I realise how much I owe my 'career' to the many individuals who have helped me along the way. Without them, I would not have been invited to write such a chapter and to reflect upon my 'journey'. To each of you, and especially to my doctoral adviser, Dr Mae Bell, I dedicate this chapter. I hope I have carried your light, laughter, and wisdom a little bit further. I treasure your lights in my heart – with profound gratitude.

NOTE

1 'Golden Mountain' is the name given by early Chinese immigrants to the USA – the land of fabled riches where they would become wealthy.

REFERENCES

Cocroft, B. and Ting-Toomey, S. (1995). Facework in Japan and the United States. *International Journal of Intercultural Relations, 18,* 469–506.

Gudykunst, W. and Ting-Toomey, S., with Chua, E. (1988). *Culture and interpersonal communication.* Newbury Park, CA: Sage.

Ting-Toomey, S. (1981). Ethnic identity and close friendship in Chinese-American college students. *International Journal of Intercultural Relations, 5,* 383–406.

Ting-Toomey, S. (1983a). An analysis of verbal communication patterns in high and low marital adjustment groups. *Human Communication Research, 9,* 306–319.

Ting-Toomey, S. (1983b). Coding conversation between intimates: A validation study of the Intimate Negotiation Coding System (INCS). *Communication Quarterly, 31,* 69–77.

Ting-Toomey, S. (1984a). Perceived decision-making power and marital adjustment. *Communication Research Reports, 1,* 15–20.

Ting-Toomey, S. (1984b). Communication of love and decision-making power in dating relationships. *Communication, 31,* 17–30.

Ting-Toomey, S. (1984c). Qualitative research: An overview. In W. Gudykunst and Y.Y. Kim (eds), *Methods for intercultural communication research* (pp. 169–184). Beverly Hills, CA: Sage.

Ting-Toomey, S. (1985). Toward a theory of conflict and culture. In W. Gudykunst, L. Stewart and S. Ting-Toomey (eds), *Communication, culture, and organizational processes* (pp. 71–86). Beverly Hills, CA: Sage.

Ting-Toomey, S. (1986a). Japanese communication patterns: Insider versus the outsider perspective. *World Communication, 15,* 113–126.

Ting-Toomey, S. (1986b). Interpersonal ties in intergroup communication. In W. Gudykunst (ed.), *Intergroup communication* (pp. 114–126). London: Edward Arnold.

Ting-Toomey, S. (1986c). Conflict communication styles in black and white subjective cultures. In Y. Y. Kim (ed.), *Interethnic communication: Current research* (pp. 75–88). Newbury Park, CA: Sage.

Ting-Toomey, S. (1988a). Rhetorical sensitivity style in three cultures: France, Japan and the United States. *Central States Speech Communication Journal, 38,* 28–36.

Ting-Toomey, S. (1988b). Intercultural conflicts: A face-negotiation theory. In Y. Kim and W. Gudykunst (eds), *Theories in intercultural communication* (pp. 213–235). Newbury Park, CA: Sage.

Ting-Toomey, S. (1989a). Identity and interpersonal bonding. In M. Asante and W. Gudykunst (eds), *Handbook of international and intercultural communication* (pp. 351–373). Newbury Park, CA: Sage.

Ting-Toomey, S. (1989b). Culture and interpersonal relationship development: Some conceptual issues. In J. Anderson (ed.), *Communication yearbook 12* (pp. 371–382). Newbury Park, CA: Sage.

Ting-Toomey, S. (1991). Intimacy expressions in three cultures: France, Japan, and the United States. *International Journal of Intercultural Relations*, *15*, 29–46.

Ting-Toomey, S. (1993). Communication resourcefulness: An identity-negotiation perspective. In R. Wiseman and J. Koester (eds), *Intercultural communication competence* (pp. 72–111). Newbury Park, CA: Sage.

Ting-Toomey, S. (ed.).(1994a). *The challenge of facework: Cross-cultural and interpersonal issues.* Albany, NY: State University of New York-Albany Press.

Ting-Toomey, S. (1994b). Managing conflict in intimate intercultural relationships. In D. Cahn (ed.), *Intimate conflict in personal relationships* (pp. 47–77). Hillsdale, NJ: Lawrence Erlbaum.

Ting-Toomey, S. (1994c). Managing intercultural conflicts effectively. In L. Samovar and R. Porter (eds), *Intercultural communication: A Reader*, 7th edn (pp. 360–372). Belmont, CA: Wadsworth.

Ting-Toomey, S. (1996). *Managing ethnic identity: An identity–dialectics framework.* Paper presented at the Speech Communication Association convention, San Diego, CA, November.

Ting-Toomey, S. (1997). Intercultural conflict competence. In W. Cupach and D. Canary (eds), *Competence in interpersonal conflict* (pp. 120–147). New York: McGraw-Hill.

Ting-Toomey, S. and Chung, L. (1996). Cross-cultural interpersonal communication: Theoretical trends and research directions. In W. Gudykunst, S. Ting-Toomey and T. Nishida (eds), *Communication in personal relationships across cultures* (pp. 237–261). Thousand Oaks, CA: Sage.

Ting-Toomey, S. and Cole, M. (1990). Intergroup diplomatic communication: A face-negotiation perspective. In F. Korzenny and S. Ting-Toomey (eds), *Communicating for peace: Diplomacy and negotiation across cultures* (pp. 77–95). Newbury Park, CA: Sage.

Ting-Toomey, S. and Gao, G. (1988). Intercultural adaptation process in Japan: Perceived similarity, self-consciousness, and language competence. *World Communication*, *17*, 193–206.

Ting-Toomey, S. and Korzenny, F. (eds) (1989). *Language, communication, and culture: Current directions.* Newbury Park, CA: Sage.

Ting-Toomey, S. and Korzenny, F. (eds). (1991). *Cross-cultural interpersonal communication.* Newbury Park, CA: Sage.

Ting-Toomey, S., Gao, G., Trubisky, P., Yang, Z., Kim, H.S., Lin, S. L. and Nishida, T. (1991). Culture, face maintenance, and styles of handling interpersonal conflict: A study in five cultures. *International Journal of Conflict Management*, *2*, 275–296.

Ting-Toomey, S., Yee-Jung, K., Shapiro, R., Garcia, W., and Wright, T. (1994). *Ethnic identity salience and conflict styles in four groups: African Americans, Asian Americans, European Americans, and Latino Americans.* Paper presented at the Speech Communication Association convention, New Orleans, LA, November.

Trubisky, P., Ting-Toomey, S. and Lin, S. L. (1991). The influence of individualism–collectivism and self-monitoring on conflict styles. *International Journal of Intercultural Relations*, *15*, 65–84.

Index